SOURCES AND DOCUMENTS OF THE PENNSYLVANIA GERMANS: X

Records of Purchases at the King George Hotel, Schaefferstown, Lebanon County, Pennsylvania, 1762-1773

Transcribed and translated by

Frederick S. Weiser and Larry M. Neff

Birdsboro, Pennsylvania

The Pennsylvania German Society

1987

The Pennsylvania German Society is an organization of over sixteen hundred persons and institutions devoted to scholarly study of America's first wave of settlers from Germanic lands. In addition to *Sources and Documents of the Pennsylvania Germans*, the Society publishes a journal, Der Reggeboge, and an annual volume on one or more phases of its subject's heritage.

The Society's mail address is

The Pennsylvania German Society
Box 397
Birdsboro, PA 19508

On the front cover: The Franklin House, formerly King George Hotel, Schaefferstown

On the back cover: Entry 230 in the accounts. Henry Schaeffer, the adolescent recordkeeper, records his displeasure with the schoolmaster. He "is a rag. This is most certainly true."

First edition, all rights reserved
Printed in the United States of America

Library of Congress Card Number: 87-062007

International Standard Book Number: 0-911122-53-2

Foreword

The study of the Pennsylvania Germans -- largest cultural minority in colonial and early national America -- has often been marred by self-congratulatory eulogies produced by well-meaning, but only partly informed heirs of the cultural group who were overreacting to the label "dumb Dutch" often applied to them. On a more serious level, scholarship has been hampered by the absence of source materials or by their existence only in obscure places, in a type of German that often defies reading, and containing references not readily interpreted. Some of the most significant materials relating to the Pennsylvania Germans continue to be in private hands, frequently among descendants of those who prepared the documents.

To remedy this situation, The Pennsylvania German Society (established in 1891) has published many monographs and other source materials in the one hundred volumes it has produced. However, the need for a specific outlet for source materials about the Pennsylvania Germans continues to press because of the rich variety of unpublished materials at hand. To expedite the satisfaction of this need, the Society inaugurated a new series, *Sources and Documents of the Pennsylvania Germans*, in 1975, in which it proposes to publish from a revolving fund adequate translations and editions of documentary materials which will illuminate life in Germanic Pennsylvania.

Among contributions anticipated for this series are the account books of a variety of handscraftsmen and small businesses -- seamstresses, hotels, cabinetmakers, farmers -- records of early and significantly located churches -- diaries, letters, and even legal records which fulfill the intention of the series: to make available to students of American life precise evidence from the men who made history in Pennsylvania themselves.

Each contribution will include sufficient annotation to clarify the document, introductory materials to place it in its time and setting, maps and photographs, and bibliographical notes to assist students to use the materials even more intelligently. But the document will speak for itself.

The various issues will appear as sales restore the working fund initially created for the series.

Suggestions for materials to include in the series are wholeheartedly welcomed. Nor will financial contributions to sustain it be discouraged!

Pastor Frederick S. Weiser, Editor

The revolving fund enabling this series
of publications has been created by

Robert C. Bucher
The Dietrich Foundations
Anthony and Beatrice Garvan
Alan G. Keyser
Larry M. Neff
George Olinger
Charles Price
Donald A. Schuder
Glenn P. Schwalm, M. D.
W. W. and Dorothy Weiser Seale
Carl D. Snyder
Frederick S. Weiser
The John Conrad Weiser Family Association

Sources and Documents of the Pennsylvania Germans

1. The Account Book of the Clemens Family of Lower Salford Township, Montgomery County, Pennsylvania, 1749-1857.

2. Records of Pastoral Acts at Trinity Evangelical Luthern Church, New Holland, Lancaster County, Pennsylvania, 1730-1799.

3. The Accounts of Two Pennsylvania German Furniture Makers -- Abraham Overholt, Bucks County, 1790-1833, and Peter Ranck, Lebanon County, 1794-1817.

4. Friedrich Heinrich Gelwicks, Shoemaker and Distiller -- Accounts, 1760-1783, Manheim Township, York County, Pennsylvania.

5. Records of Pastoral Acts at the Lutheran and Reformed Congregations of the Muddy Creek Church, East Cocalico Township, Lancaster County, Pennsylvania, 1730-1790.

6. Conrad Weiser's Account Book, 1746-1760.

7. Tulpehocken Church Records, 1730-1800. Christ (Little Tulpehocken) Church and Altalaha Church, Rehrersburg.

8. Records of Pastoral Acts At Emanuel Lutheran Church, Brickerville, 1745-1799.

9. Journals of Anna Weber, Lancaster County seamstress, 1826-1876.

10. Records of Purchases at the King George Hotel, Schaefferstown, Lebanon County, Pennsylvania, 1762-1773.

11. Records of Pastoral Acts at Zion Lutheran Church, Harrisburg, Dauphin County, Pennsylvania, 1795-1827.

Introduction

1. Alexander Schaeffer

Alexander Schaeffer was born on 8 January 1712 at Schriessheim on the Bergstrasse, a few miles north of Heidelberg, the capital city of the Palatinate at the time. Hans Henrich Schaeffer, Alexander's father, was baptized there 17 September 1673, son of Hans Schaeffer, a cooper's apprentice from "Marten in Alsace," and Anna Margaretha, daughter of Hans Michael Karg. Hans Henrich married 21 November 1702 Anna Margaretha Mayer, daughter of Hans Veltin Mayer, deceased, of Hohensachsen. Their children:

1. Maria Magdalena, sponsor in 1728, married 14 January 1731 Johan Ludwig Lentz.
2. Anna Maria, baptized 9 February 1707, confirmed 1719, married 9 November 1737 Hieronymus Trautmann.
3. Hans Jacob, baptized 14 October 1709.
4. Alexander, baptized 8 January 1712, confirmed 1725.
5. Sophia Philippina, baptized 24 June 1714, married 20 October 1737 Philipp Böckle.
6. Hans Philip, baptized 9 October 1716, married 3 July 1740 Anna Maria, widow of Wilhelm ---.
7. Anna Catharina, baptized 22 October 1719, died 14 October 1769.
8. Maria Catharina, baptized 16 November 1721
9. Anna Barbara, baptized 12 March 1728.

Joh. Henrich Schaeffer died 13 March 1746, was buried 16 March, and is called a citizen of Schriessheim. Anna Margaretha Schaeffer died at Schriessheim on August 23, 1761. She was born July 12, 1681 in Hohensachsen, a short distance north of Schriessheim.[1]

Long after Alexander Schaeffer and the two siblings who emigrated had left Schriessheim, there was an inheritance matter which involved them and came before the local courts. A document preserved in the public archives in Karlsruhe (Badisches Generallandesarchiv) reports in 1789 that the siblings Anna Maria, Anna Barbara, and Alexander Schäfer were summoned in vain on account of an inheritance matter; the province of Pennsylvania was to find them. But by then Alexander, and perhaps his sisters, were dead and very likely nothing came of the matter.[2]

Schriessheim is situated at the base of the Odenwald a few miles east of the Rhine. Its recorded history begins more than twelve centuries ago. As is true of many towns in its neighborhood, Schriessheim contributed heavily to American emigration in the eighteenth century. Its most famous emigrant, Alexander Mack (1679-1735) left for Schwarzenau, where he was the pioneer of the Church of the Brethren, and moved from Schwarzenau to America. But Werner Hacker lists over thirty persons who applied for manumission and/or permission to emigrate to the New World between 1726 and the 1750s, not to mention others who went to Denmark, Prussia, Austria, Hungary and Galicia (in Poland). In the period before Alexander Schaeffer's emigration, Johann Martin and Stefan Brecht (1726), Joh. Alexander Diebendörffer (1717), and Gabriel Fischer (1731) may be named. Schaeffer's brother-in-law Hieronymus Trautmann and his brother Johannes, Bernhard Dübinger, and perhaps Georg Hofstaetter all applied for manumission in 1743; Hieronymus Trautmann and Bernhard Dübinger are on the ship lists and Johannes Trautmann may be found in Pennsylvania records. Conceivably, one of the many emigrants named by Hacker for the period 1749-1753 might have been married to Anna Barbara

---

[1]Genealogical information provided by Annette K. Burgert obtained by reading the microfilm of the Schriessheim Reformed church records. See also "A Translation of the Letter of Pastor Knoepfel Recommending Alexander Schaeffer, " and "Family History of Alexander Schaffer". *Historic Schaefferstown Record* 7(1973), 17-21. See also Alexander Schaeffer's tombstone in the Reformed cemetery, Schaefferstown.

[2]Werner Hacker, *Kurpfälzische Auswanderer vom Unteren Neckar* (Stuttgart und Aalen, 1983), p. 166. See also Friedrich Krebs, "Palatine Emigration Materials from the Neckar Valley, 1726-1766, " *Pennsylvania Folklife* XXIV (1975), 4, p. 30.

Hacker for the period 1749-1753 might have been married to Anna Barbara Schaeffer, but the names of none of the men listed turn up in the records below which Alexander Schaeffer kept. On the other hand, the Trautmanns are to be found there, and, as will be seen below, one of Alexander's daughters married a Brecht.

Schaeffer arrived in Philadelphia on the Robert and Alice on September 11, 1738.[3] Johann Gottfried Roehrer, the founder of Rehrersburg, a few miles from Schaefferstown, was also on this vessel. No ages of the passengers are given on the various lists from this passage. Nor are women or children listed. Alexander Schaeffer made a mark. He never learned to write.

There is no record of Alexander Schaeffer's marriage in Schriessheim, nor are any children to him named in the baptismal records there. No records pertaining to his marriage or children's baptisms have been found in America. His wife's name was Anna Engel, maiden name unknown. Her tombstone in the Reformed cemetery is authority for a birthdate of 1708, and a death date of November 22, 1772. They had six children who survived into adulthood, about whom there is considerable information in the Brendle history of Schaefferstown.[4] Their names were:

1. John Schaeffer married Barbara Miller. There are two children listed in the Schaefferstown Reformed records (1764 and 1766) to this couple. They moved away from the area.
2. Sabina married Machael Haak or Hack. One son was baptized for this couple at Schaefferstown in 1764.
3. Anna Maria married Christopher Myer or Moyer. One daughter was baptized for this couple in 1766.
4. Catharina married John Myer or Moyer.
5. Margaret married Johannes Brecht. Three of their children were baptized at Schaefferstown in 1760, 1762 and 1764.
6. Johan Heinrich Schaeffer, known as Henry, born June 5, 1749, died October 12, 1803. Married first Anna Eva Schweitzer (April 27, 1753-January 2, 1790) and second Margaret Hoffman (December 11, 1764-April 30, 1851). Henry and his descendants remained at Schaefferstown. All but the last of his children were born to his first wife:

   a. Catharina, November 27, 1774, married John Bomberger
   b. Elisabetha, October 29, 1776, married Abraham Rex
   c. Anna Maria, July 9, 1778, married Frederick Oberlin
   d. Johannes, June 15, 1782, married Esther Weiss
   e. Susanna, October 21, 1785, married Dietrich Goschert
   f. Anna Eva, October 5, 1787- April 21, 1790
   g. Henry, who lived in Schaefferstown.

Only Alexander Schaeffer's son Henry played an important role in the life of his father's town.

The biography of Alexander Schaeffer in Brendle's history of Schaefferstown relates a number of stories about land purchases and moves of Schaeffer which cannot be verified. He warranted several tracts of land in the course of time. It is however his purchases in 1758 which concern us here. On June 20, 1758 Schaeffer bought about a third of the tract which had been patented in 1736 to John Miley, sold by him to Durs Thomas, inherited from him by his children Durs, Martin and Anna, who sold it to Philip Weiser. Weiser immediately sold the entire tract back to Martin Thomas. In 1755 Thomas sold 224 acres of this property to George Schwengel. Meanwhile he had warranted more land, north of the first tract, in 1737. He patented this land in 1758 and sold it, a tract of 100 acres, to Schaeffer on June 2, 1758. In each deed Schaeffer is designated by the alias of "Sander Shaffer," which indicated that he went by the shortened German form of his given name. The first tract Schaeffer used as a farm and home: the house on it still stands and is owned with some of the acreage by Historic Schaefferstown, Inc. The second tract of 100

---

[3] Strassburger-Hinke, I, 212-216

[4] A. S. Brendle, *A Brief History of Schaefferstown* (Schaefferstown, 1979), reprint ed., 216-227, and other places.

exclusive use. In this town Schaeffer eventually lived, for when he died on April 10, 1786, he was "of Schaefferstown." He also owned and operated the King George Hotel there, which he apparently erected. It is one of the records of customer purchases at his hotel which is translated in this volume.

Alexander Schaeffer died a rich man. He was owed nearly 2500 pounds, much of it by his children and sons-in-law. He had a house full of furniture and owned considerable farm equipment. There were luxuries, including a wire bird cage listed among the beds and bedding. He owned a chair (a means of conveyance which older well-to-do men had), as well as saddles and horses. While there were enough chairs, tables, and beds to outfit a tavern in his possession, he had none of the store merchandise and none of the beverages which the account book lists. No doubt the operation of his tavern had passed into the hands of others. Alexander Schaeffer, an illiterate peasant from a lower class family in Europe, exercised the prerogative of the American dream and became a success.

2. Schaefferstown

Since Alexander Schaeffer acquired the land on which he laid out Heidelbergtown in 1758 as an intact tract, no one legally could have occupied it other than its owners prior to that date. There is some evidence, however, that there were people living there prior to 1758, as local historians have long maintained. On North Market street a log house has recently been studied extensively, on one of whose corners there is a remarkable Germanic carved post with the date 1757 carved in a heart. The surviving tax lists are not helpful, since they list only the amount of tax and not the amount of land owned until the list for 1771. Nor do the deed records of Lancaster county shed much light on the picture, since there are virtually no deeds recorded of Schaeffer's lot sales before Dauphin county was erected in 1787, out of which in 1813 Lebanon was created. There is a deed for August 22, 1758, for a lot sale, so that we may conclude that the formal establishment of the town took place in that year.

Creating a town in the eighteenth century Pennsylvania countryside was fundamentally an entrepreneurial action. Schaeffer's was no exception. Income was realized from the project in two ways: first, the lots were sold, initially in the case of Schaefferstown for 5 shillings each (with stipulation that the new owners must build on the lot within a certain number of years and incorporating the right of the proprietor of the town to repurchase the lot). But in the second place, the town's proprietor required in all deeds for his lots an annual ground rent to be paid to him and to his heirs forever. This amounted to 3 3/4 or 3 shillings a year in the case of Schaefferstown. This share of the investment could be inherited or sold. Henry Schaeffer received the rights to the ground rents on his father's death and they passed into other hands before the various lot owners paid a flat sum to acquire clear title to their lots. In Schaefferstown this happened in the third quarter of the nineteenth century. In some towns it had happened earlier. In Middletown, since the ground rents were willed to an institution, they still exist.

Town proprietors were eager to attract craftsmen and merchants to their towns. They also knew that churches and schools would attract settlers. Schaeffer was no exception. He was a member of the Reformed church. On August 31, 1763, he deeded John Wolfersberger and John Lauser, in trust for the "Dutch Reformed and Dutch Lutheran" congregations in common lot number 225 to be used as a burying ground. The cost was 5 shillings and an annual ground rent of one penny (which he undoubtedly did not expect to be paid). On September 6, 1765, Schaeffer deeded lot 42 to John Wolfersberger and Durst Thomas in trust for the Reformed church on the same terms. On March 8, 1765, the Lutherans and the Reformed entered an agreement by which the Reformed purchased the Lutherans' share in a church and schoolhouse which both had erected there. The Lutheran share was 80 pounds. The Lutherans then purchased on March 29 part of lot 16 from Peter Rihm, Jr. A cornerstone was laid July 8, 1765. The agreement between the two congregations permitted the Lutherans to continue to worship in the Reformed building until October 1, 1766. The Reformed congregation has built a new church in the course of its history, but the Lutherans enlarged and remodeled their building in the nineteenth century and continue to use it. Henry Melchior Muhlenberg characterized the church the Lutherans built as "one of the best in this land," an indication of the promise Schaefferstown held for its residents in the years between the French and Indian War and the War for American Independence.

Residents of Schaefferstown agreed with one another on February 13, 1759, to maintain a "fountain" on Market street into which water flowed from a spring located in the southern portion of the town. Wooden pipes for this purpose were laid under the surface of the earth. A second outlet for the water was located on south Market street. On July 16, 1763, Schaeffer and his wife deeded the lot on which the spring was located to George Ulrich and Frederick Albright, in trust, for a purchase price and an annual ground rent. It cannot be called a gift, therefore. But this arrangement (which survives as a local water company) also made the town more attractive to lotholders.

As had nearly every town laid out in Pennsylvania in this period, Schaefferstown had a series of outlots. These served as pasture for the town's residents, most of whom had gardens in their yards, and for production of grains. Sale of these lots constituted another source of income for the proprietor. Not every inhabitant of the town purchased an outlot, of course.

3. The King Georg Hotel

Alexander Schaeffer retained lot 15 for himself. It was at the northwest corner of the square, a high and commanding location in the town. Here he built and operated the King George Hotel. Although Brendle's history of Schaefferstown gives two divergent dates for its erection, 1746 and 1752, and implies a third, 1758, we do not know exactly when the inn was erected. 1758 seems reasonable, for Schaeffer did not own the land until then, but what kind of lease, whether written or verbal, he might have had with Durs Thomas before 1758 is unknown.

The King George Hotel still stands, much remodeled in 1884, but probably retaining its original room distribution on the first floor. To the left is the barroom, overlooking the square, with benches still running around the outer wall. To the right are two rooms, one of which must have been the shop in which Schaeffer had wares for sale. It is from this hotel that we have what is the second volume of a record of the purchases of customers. Because of that fact we may assume that some customers' accounts began in the first book, even as some of them were continued into another. If the first book could be found, it would probably give the date of the hotel opened.

A hotel was a lively place in the eighteenth century as the records below suggest. Windows and glasses were broken, people sometimes drank heavily as they tried to conclude a deal, one customer is almost anonymously identified as the "Irishman who urinated on the floor," an unpoplar schoolmaster is dubbed in boyish handwriting a "Lumbe" (which is about equivalent in sense to an old bag), and many folks dropped in to purchase something in the store and had a glass of cider or beer or something stronger. Events in the little town's history are transparent in the record: a church is built, Henry William Stiegel's workmen are building his tower and eating and drinking his capital, all the while fathers buy catechisms and ABC books for their children, trinkets for their daughters or wives, fruit tree saplings for their orchards and a pipe or some gun powder for themselves. One cannot help but be amazed at the wide variety of "shopgoods" which Schaeffer carried, nor can one control his wish to have been a mouse and seen it all.

Alexander Schaeffer could not write, so that the records of purchases in his tavern-store had to be made by someone else. They begin in 1762, when his son Heinrich, or Henry, was thirteen years old. The handwriting in the accounts seems to be his, with some exceptions. Individuals made purchases and charged them, coming in periodically with some cash to pay on the bill or to settle it completely. Once in a while some good or service was traded and appropriately credited. A few customers are identified by indefinite names which must have been clear to the Schaeffers but are elusive to us.

The procedure of this transcription is as follows: the entire document has been transcribed into modern typed copy from the German script original. The German transcription follows. The many objects and potions mentioned are listed in an appendix in their German form (and spelling as used in the accounts) with a brief statement of the object's nature. Thus someone interested in what an individual purchased may make his own translation handily. Portions of the text which are not reference to an object are translated in square brackets in the course of the text.

In order to help users of this document understand the nature of the customers more, the 1771 tax list of Heidelberg township has been transcribed and is included as a second appendix. The original list is owned by the Lancaster County Historical Society. A brief statement of explanation will make that document more useful to readers.

Schaefferstown is graced today by a large number of architecturally important eighteenth century buildings. Its historical agency, Historic Schaefferstown, Incorporated, maintains the Schaeffer farm, the Brendle library, and sponsors a variety of activities. Robert C. Bucher, who owns the original of the record below, has spent much of his time and other resources in preserving the heritage of the town. This transcription is a step towards greater understanding of this particular little village and of the whole phenomenon of towns in Pennsylvania German culture.

I should like to thank Larry M. Neff for his faithful assistance in the long and tedious task of transcribing the record, Alan G. Keyser for assistance in identifying the objects named here, and Robert C. Bucher for his enthusiasm and encouragement.

Frederick S. Weiser

Parrehof
Peter-Paul, 1987

[i]

My ancestor a/c book
Alex Shaeffer's founder of
Shaeffers Town (1745) John F. Young
Philada 1873

1766 Die Frau ins Schencken [The woman in Schencken]
July 30 1 lb Zucker 0 - 0 - 10

1768

[Various devices and doodling]

[ii]

Allexander Shafer
Allexander Schäfer No 80000
Allexan Shaefer - Shafer

---

hanss adams annamarÿ [Annamary, wife of Hans Adam]

1/2 lb alspeis 1/2 lb imber 0 - 1 - 9

Schultzen Christina [Christina Schultz]

1/2 b. wein vor Bendel 0 - 1 - 4
2 1/2 yd: Borschet 0 - 8 - 4
Vor Blauen Neths 0 -
1 q : Thron 0 - 1 - 0
Bezahlt [Paid] 0 - 9 - 4 1/2
1. yd: Band 3/4 yd: foret 0 - 1 - 0
1. bol: senckery 0 - 1 - 6
1. q: Rom 0 - 1 - 0
1. q: 1/2. b: Rom 0 - 1 - 5
1. b: Rom 1. lb: Zucker 0 - 1 - 4

Michael Mauri sein frau [Michael Mauri's wife]

1. sichel 0 - 2 - ?
[Illegible (crossed out)]

betz wingerin ihr schwester [Betz Winger's sister}

Namen Buch 0 - 0 - 9

[Pages iii - xxxiv are the index to the customers]

[iii]

[iv]

Jacob Brecht No 33 179 No: 237 No; 261
Michel Bolinger No 40
Mardien Brodtbeck No. 47
Friedrich Bersing No 56
Bär Adam 195
Brubacher Christian 183
Broch nickel No: 130
Bäcker Jacob No: 109 No: 276
Bolman Adam No: 152
Betesen sein fuhr Leit No: 238 No: 285 [Betesen's drivers]
Beltz der Zimmerman 119 [Beltz the carpenter]
filbina Beustlerin No: 70
Beyer Anderas Kieffer No: 281 [Andreas Beyer, cooper]
Besch Henrich No: 258
Betz der Jung 120 [Betz, Jr.]
Besch Andereas No: 278
Brennel William 316
Bauermann Georg No: 206
Becker Hannes Bey Hamer No: 43 [Hannes Becker at the Forge]

[v]

Lisabeda Bunschen No. 48
Christian Bollinger No. 57
Jacob Bamberger No: 60
Breght John 81 No 252
Bäustlerin Regina 88
Bollinger Authy 90
Barget Sebastian 94
Bolender Adam 95 No: 245
Bollman Nicklos 84
butschers Magd 10 [The butcher's maid]
Beusch Johannes 130
Brunnen Compagnÿ 121 [Fountain company]
Bollmann Abraham 110
Berger Jacob 62
Bollmann Adam 152
Borckhart Jehu 156
Becker Johann 20
Billing Johann 146
Breitin Bach Phillip 43
Brill Henrich 14
Phillip Bohler 15 [crossed out]
Bickel Tobias 180
Bach Adam 69
Bäyer Martin No: 307
Beuler Jacob No: 195

[vi]

Conrad Georg Magnus 75 110
Clerck John 68 No: 269
Daniel
Clerck Etwart 19
Conrad Danil No: 101
Conrad Jacob No: 1
Conrad George 63 No: 234 No: 269
Claus No: 208 No: 238 No: 283 312

Clerck Naday 19
Clerck John No: 68 No 90

[vii]

[A] ndon Derder No 38
Dock William No 56

[viii]

Drucken Müller Peter 102 228
Dürr Abrah 123
Dinjus Johan 69
Duÿ Jacob 9
Dinjus William 139
Johann Dengler No: 16
Dinjus Valedin 206
Dinjus Conrad 88
Dinjus Hannickel No: 56
Derr Ludwig No: 119
Derter Baltzer No: 267
Druck Georg No: 142
Dell Jacob No 184
Ditrich Georg No 257

[ix]

Johannes Endres no 61 202
Eckert Frantz 98
Ewig Wilem 97
Ewÿ Georg 97
Endres Johannes ju: 122
Erisch der Holtz hacker
Von der fornis 142 [The Irish woodchopper from the Furnace. Irish here may mean only non-German.]
Ewig Adam No: 99
Ewig Christian No: 98
Abraham Ern No: 263
Michael Egold No: 271

[x]

Johannes Fischer pg No 14
Casper Fieding No 41
Josep Frenck No 46
Johannes Feck No 12
Johannes Flicker No 69
Fertig Johannes 94
Fischer schneiters sohn 58 [Fischer, the taylor's son]
Fried Adam 146
Fotler Jacob 99
Fehler Jacob 219
Fiel William No: 161
Fuchs auf der fornes No: 51 [Fuchs at the Furnace]
Frantz Johannes sen 101
Fratzos No: 263 [sic: the Frenchman]
Fiel John No: 161
Folck George No: 1

[xi]

Jacob Geib No 133
Glatz No: 228

[xii]

Georg Gallen Meÿer No. 21
Paull Gemberling No 24 No: 25
Andress Gadiner No 42
Peder Gudman No 68
Gass Jacob 93 No: 279
Gerdraut die Nähern 110 [Gerdraut, the seamstress]
Gerber der Versoffne 162 [Gerber, the drunk; or the drunken tanner]
Gibby 179
Gotten Stiegels heffengiesser 198 No: 258 No 303 [Gotten, Stiegel's pot pourer]
Gabriel George 156
Gossweiller John No: 166
Geiger Johannes No 164
Gehonn No: 278
Gay Samuel No: 277
Gemberling Jacob No: 89
Georg Gärtner Doctor No: 228

[xiii]

Nicklos Husecker No 3
Hofius Johann No: 229 No: 230 No: 244 No: 247 No 270
Heise Jurg No 142
Heid Abraham No: 117
Heil Martin No: 156
Heiry auf der fornes 53 [Heiry at the furnace]
Billy Hay 273

[xiv]

Michel Holstein 26
Johannes Hack No 57
Hag Michael 82 No: 266
Heffelfinger Martin 87
Hetzel Jacob 92
Hiltebeitel Adam 107
Harnisch Sammel 113
Hoffer Johannes 120
Hetzler Georg 93
Hoffmann Adam 134 No 302
Heeffer Andreas 148
Hauer Sebastian 175
Hack Michel 171
Haman Jacob 7
Hensching Henrich 207
Hack Georg 1
Hofmann Jacob 36
Herlÿ Jacob 99
Hack Tobias 107
Hummerum Johannes No: 211
Adam auf dem Hammer No: 257 [Adam at the forge]
Jacob Helder auf der Fornes No: 257 [Jacob Helder at the furnace]

Heberling Georg No: 56
Huber John No: 38
Haushalter George No: 84

[xv]

Pernd Jacob pg No 12 147 226 251 291
Stefen Jacÿ No 15
Iba Casper No 74 76 313
Jung von der Fornis 113 [Jung from the Furnace]
Jacobÿ Matheis 58
Ilg Faladin No: 130
Jury von steitzen Weg No: 258 [Jury on the road to Lebanon = Steitzen]

[xvi]

Koll Fridrich No 30
Krinter Jacob 165
Kerschner Conrad No: 249 No: 299
John Kohrr No: 278
Keÿser in Redin No 138 [Keyser in Reading]
Kern sein fuhrmann No: 3 [Kern's drivers]
Krebs Henrich No: 299
Kister Peter No: 21
Kegler Peter No: 221

[xvii]

Henrich Koch 1
Lorentz Keller 4 8 80 141 149 171
Henrich Keÿler No 22 79 155 177 181 201 223 221
Andreas Kapler No 47
Philleb Kiesecker No 70 No: 259
Kartiger Andreas 41
Klein Andreas 88
Kohl Ludwig 89
Kapp Friedrich 101
Kreiter Christian 126
Kratzinger Conrad 76
Kring Henrich 124
Kreiter Jacob 140
Küfey Melcher 117
Kob Georg 140
Kintzel, Michel 123
Knauer Andreas 162 121
Kapp Christoph 163
Kister Christoph 21
Kurtz Leonhart 206
Kiffer 108
Kapler 108
Keller Bastian No: 263
Knauer John No: 282
Kapp John No: 288
Klein Philipp No: 296
Kotolisch Doctor No: 89 [Catholic doctor]

[xviii]

Leinewewer Peter No: 211
Lautermilch Adam 133
Lautermilch John No: 235 No: 274
Lepo Paul No: 69
Leb Casper No: 255 No: 309
Anengel Löb No: 255
Lang Benedictem No: 276

[xix]

Henrich Lejneweber No 66 No: 217 225 240
Leckes Michael No 75
Leible Simon 34 118 163 169
Lautermilch Melcher 86
Lautermilch Godfried 91
Lauser john 102 209 No: 236
Levÿ Jacob 111
Losser Der Junge [Young Losser]
Lautermilch Jacob 91 No: 227
Lautenschleger George 194
Lautermilch George 96
Leidig Michael No: 169
Lautermilch Wendel No. 144
Doctor Land No: 263
Lechner Georg No: 140
Lutz Schuhmacher ins Steitzen No. 121 [Lutz, shoemaker in Lebanon = Steitzen]

[xx]

Georg
Michel Meÿer Stofel Meÿer Adam Bolender 35
des Mausen Mad 195 [Mause's maid]
Meyer Michael Gatshal Brenner No: 205 [Michael Meyer, distiller of Gatshal]
Minnig Henrich No: 139
Maiser Henrich No: 260
Mercker John 182
Maurer Hanickel No: 275
Miller John No: 280
Mohr Andereas No 69
Meÿly Martin jung [Jr] No: 15
der Mann ins dreirs Hauss No: 175 [The man in Dreier's house]
Meyer Jacob No: 11
Michael Miller sein Miller No: 170 [Michael Miller's miller]

[xxi]

Michel Miller No 2 No: 233
Georg Mauerer No 40
Anderes Miller No 44 No: 250
Stofel Meÿer No 54 184 316
Michel Meyer No 54 No: 235
Michel Meÿser No 62 No: 256
Georg Meder No 70
Meisser Georg No 72
Müller Friedrich Pr 78 No: 284
Miller Friedrich ju 78 168 284

Meisser Adam 71
Mohr Johan 100 No: 241
Miller auff der alten Fornes 96 [Miller at the old furnace]
Müller Friedrich 131
Mauss Lutwig 144
Miller Jacob 158 213
Mercker Dieder 182
Meisser Johann 183
Henrich Meÿer 86
Mettler Jacob 142
Müller Andreas blos: 4 [abbreviation for bellows maker]
Meÿer Johanes Juge [sic] [Jr.] No: 4 No: 317
Meÿer Johanes alte [Sr.] 4 No: 286
Henrich Müller 3
Miller Dewald 199
Moths Henrich 20
Meÿle Henrich 15
Muckenfus Carl 145 No: 220 308

[xxii]

Johannes Neÿb No 43
Nathan Benjamin 108
Neeff Michael ju 53
Neaff Michael alt 198
Numan John No: 74
Neff John 43
Neff Jacob jung [Jr.] No: 277

[xxiii]

Johannes Offenmann No 50
Ohrendorff Peter 178
Oberman Casper No: 90

[xxiv]

Adam Paffenberger No 53
Jacob Philepe No 60
Person Friedrich 88
Christina Peffern 3
Panne Schmitt 211 286
Peffer Henrich alte [Sr.] No: 254 No 289 [see also Beffer]
Peffer Phillip No: 297
Ploferber No: 171 [Bluedyer]
Philipÿ Conrad No: 42

[xxv]

Aberham Ruedie No 17
Andress Ricker No 31 104 143 192 232 275
Marden Riess 36 41
Ried Peter 29
Reyer Michel 109 112 114 127 151 174 190 221 No: 305
Risser Uhlÿ 115 No: 301
Rust Henrich 100

Ruland Abraham 83
Riem Petter 35 No: 270
Reicher Henrich 60
Riel Johann und Andreas 205 No: 273
Renner Nicolaus No: 206
Gottfried Rohrer un Nicolaus Kintzer un Henrich Leineweber 241
Jacob Ried No: 120
Rieser John No: 292
dem Restuner No: 292 [the man from Raystown]

[xxvi]

Henrich Stigel No 28 103 129 135 137 150 193 315
Jacob Schenck No 34 132 210
Michael Schwengel No: 16
Cadrina Steinern No 48
Andres Scholl No 12
Georg Schmidt beim [at] Dorst Thomas No 55
Henrich Schwertzler No 55
Stiegels Moler 136 138 172 187 164 [Stiegel's painter]
Stiegels Maure 138 [Stiegel's mason]
Steinern Marilisbetth 48
Schregle Michael No: 113
Schwertzler Jost No 46
Schreiner Wilhelm No: 89
Stiegels Gartner 203 [Stiegel's gardener]
Jacob Spangler 100
Schreiter Johannes 15
Spengler No: 207
Schumacher Johannes 65
Simon Henrich No: 67 No: 270
Jacob Seltzer Vor die Kirch No: 222 [Jacob Seltzer for the church]
der Alt Shwitzer 144 [Old Mr. Shwitzer]
Schutÿ Martin No: 156 No: 234
Speck Hanss No: 165
Stoner Henry No: 107
Schäffer John No: 243
Schel Butscher No: 144 [Schel, the butcher]
Georg Strely No: 46
Speck Adam No: 253
Stigels Fuhrleit No: 295 [Stiegel's drivers]

[xxvii]

Casper Schweitzer No 6 106 170 190 216 231 290
Nicklos Schwengel No 16
Frantz Schmidt No 29 No: 264
Ernst Schwertzler No: 165
Carel Seÿbolt No 32 110
Jacob Schaub No 45 154 186 197 212 224 239 248 No: 265
der Simen auf Hamer No 58 [Simen at the forge]
Jacob Seltzer No 64 No: 300
Stumpff Abraham No 73 No: 304
Schanck Dewald No 76
Schwanger Jacob 83
Stiegel Atony 85 191
Stroh Georg 96
Schwob der Grosse 76 [The tall Swabian]

Strasborger Schneiterin 71
Schneiter Abraham 125
Scheurer Jacob 72
Stiegels Schreiner 108 [Stiegel's joiner]
Schwengel Georg 25
Speck Martin 42
Schramm Henrich 157 No: 310
Schneÿter Johannes 120
Strack Henrich 176
Schadt Balser 195
Strohm Georg 36 75
Schneider Michael 1
Schmit Georg 175
Jacob Scheiner No 122
Adam Scheiner No 122
Ludwig Schelman No 222
Friedrich Stumb No: 208
Hannes Schub No 12

[xxviii]

Traut Mann Georg 128
Tascher Petter 160 173
Thorst Thomas 98
Friedrich Taxis No: 7 No: 306
Tribschuh Christoph No: 211
Thomas Thorst 203
Tempel Sem No: 140
Jacob Thomas No: 203
Jacob Thomas No: 199
Tollmeyer Peter auf dem Hammer No 257 [Peter Tollmeyer at the forge]
Johann Michael Trautmann No: 163
Tollmeÿer Serwes Tochtermann No: 258 [Tollmeÿer, Serwe[Zerbe]'s son-in-law]
Trautner Gorge No: 288

[xxix]

Ungar John No: 282

[xxx]

Philleb Wolffersperger pg No 13 204
Adem Wiest No 18 19
Christian Willÿ No 25
Peder Wolfersperger No 49 No: 272
Philleb Wagner No 51
Johannes Wolffersperger No 52 214
Fridrich Wolffersperger No 59 No: 108
Friedrich Walser No 63
Johannes Weber No 68
Weissin Magdalena 117
Weick Gerhart No 124
Weÿand Adam 125 200
Wagner Conrad 36 No: 287
Weber Martin 133
Wagner Jacob 115
Walter Henrih 145

Witman Lutwig 38
Wummelsdorff John 146
Winter Michael 159
Wissler Nicklos 161 111
Weitzell Schuhmacher in Lan: 194 [Weitzell, shoemaker in Lancaster]
Wohlwein Phillip 200 280
Thomas Weller 208
Lisabetha Wolferspergerin 84
Weber Bernhard 87 No: 257
Wolf Jacob 75
Welfersperger Michael No 298

[xxxi]

[W] olford No
[Jacob] Widmer No 71 No: 178
[die] alt Wolferspergern No 53 [Old Mrs. Wolfersperger]
Wittemeÿer Adreas 35
Walter Johannes beÿ [at] Hersch 168
die alt Hanss Webern No 51 [Old Mrs. Hanss Weber]
[Wiss] ner Jacob No: 161
Würtz Friedrich No: 140
Catharina Wolferspergern No: 84
Friedrich Weitenthal No: 9
Weber Michael No: 166
Wisnand Philip No 271
Wolfersperger Friedrich No: 298
[Frie]drich Weiser George Becker No: 300
[Ban]del Wicker Maurer [mason] No: 295

[xxxii]

Georg Ullrich 110 No: 268
Urich Felden No: 72

[xxxiii]

Zimmerman Jacob 119
Zartmann Jacob 63
Ziabach Badel No: 3
Nicolaus Zehrfass No: 47
Zöller David No: 318
Zufall No: 316

[xxxiv]

Xander Jacob No: 162

[xxxv]

No 1

Georg Folck

1768		
Aprill 16:	1 Kummet	0 - 5 -

1

Henrich Koch Docder

1762		
8 Nov	4 beint Wein	0 - 4 - 8
10 Nov	1 beint Wein	0 - 1 - 2
16 Nov	1 beint Maderÿ Wein	0 - 2 - 0
23 Nov	2 Tschill Rom	0 - 0 - 8
4 Dec	gehlehnt an Gelt [Lent in money]	1 - 0 - 0
4 Dec	1 hut un 1 Seiden Halls Duch	2 - 2 - 6

Michael Schneiter

1764		
Novem 24	1 Bole Mimm	0 - 1 - 0
1765		
July 9	1 w: Schling	0 - 0 - 9

Jacob Conrad

1764		
July 6	1 sichel un 1 q: Rom 1 bottel un Zucker	0 -10- 0
	1 band	0 - 0 - 3

Georg Hack

1765		
January 10	1 strang seiten	0 - 0 - 10
Febru: 4	1 hut	0 - 7 - 0
Sebt 30	1 q: seiter	0 - 0 - 4
1766		
October 10	2 yd: schalun	0 - 6 - 0
		0 -14- 2

2

1762

Michel Miller

8 Nov	vor nodlen	0 - 1 - 0
8 Nov	2 lb Seifen	0 - 1 - 8
14 Julis	1 q un 1 1/2 beint rom un	
	2 lb. weisen Zuger	0 - 5 - 0
22 Nov	vor Knep un Zuger	0 - 5 - 0
10 Dec	4 lb Zuger un 2 moskedetnoss	0 - 3 - 7
16 Dec	1 lb beffer un 1 lb Alspeiss	0 - 5 - 0
30 Dec	1 jert flenel	0 - 3 - 6
30 Dec	2 beint maderÿ wein	0 - 4 - 0
1763		
3 Januarÿ	1 strang Camelgarn 1 strang seiden un 5 d netz	0 - 1 - 9
7 Jan	1 dutzen Kreb camel garn	0 - 1 - 2
15 Jan	4 lb Zuger	0 - 3 - 0
2 Febr:	1 1/2 b: matherÿ wein	0 - 3 - 0
3	5 lb Rothen Zucker a o/9 und 2 lb hut Zucker	0 - 6 - 9

Mertz 15	1 q: ma: wein	0 - 4 - 0
30 May	1 1/2 q: m: wein und vor safferan	0 - 7 - 0
Juni 6	2 1/2 q Rom	0 - 4 - 2
24	6 1/2 lb unschlit 3 lb Zucker	0 - 8 - 10
30	1 1/2 y Kelsch	0 - 7 - 6
1764	d: 24 August 1763 gerechnet mit Michel Müller bleibt nichts [Settled with Michael Müller. No remainder]	
July 16	3 sicheln	0 -10- 0
Sep: 15	1 lb Peffer	0 - 3 - 4
October	7 1/2 lb Unschlit	0 - 4 - 0
Novem 4	1 Hut das sein Knecht geholt [1 hat which his servant got]	0 - 7 - 0
26	2 hüt	0 -15- 0
30	2 messer	0 - 1 - 2
Decem: 28	1 strang seiten 6 streng neths 1/4 yd Leinetuch	0 - 2 - 3
1765 Mertz 27	8 1/4 lb: Unschlicht	0 - 4 - 10
Aprill 19	1 hut un 1 Enge Kam	0 - 9 - 6
May 19	7 lb: Zucker un 1 hut un seitenen Knöp	0 -18- 11
Sebt 16	5 gallen rom und 2 lb: hut Zucker	1 - 3 - 0

3

1762

Nicklos Husecker

10 Nov	1 beind maderÿ wein	0 - 2 - 0
1763 Mertz 5	gelend [lent]	0 - 3 - 0
1767		
April 28	2 b: m: wein	0 - 4 - 0

Bardel Zebach

Febrary		
1766		
1	1 bottel	0 - 0 - 9

1764 **Henrich Müller**

May 26	1 sattel	2 -15- 0
	vor trincken	0 - 0 - 9
	Bezahlt an Geld [Paid in money]	1 - 0 - 0
	Bezahlt an Geld [Paid in money]	1 - 5 - 0

1764 **Christina Peffern**

Juny 14	1/2 yd: Band	0 - 0 - 8
	vor Corallen	0 - 4 - 0

1767 **Kern sein Fuhrmann bei Reden**
[Kern's driver near Reading]

Sebtember 12	5 geil bey Hoi 10 q: Haber 2 mal Essen 1 gill rom [5 horses at hay 10 q: oats 2 meals, 1 gill rum]	0 - 7 - 6

4

1762 **Lorentz Keller**

11 Novem	Auf abregnung wegen sein schwer an Gelt [On settlement for his father-in-law in money]	15 - 17 - 5

1762	wider vor Margreda Eskuchen [again for Margreda Eskuchen]	
11 Novem	wegen sein Schwer [for his father-in-law]	7 - 11 - 8
		23 - 9 - 1
1762	hab ich Alexander Shafer von Lorentz Keller empfangen Ein Berl bier [I Alexander Shafer received a barrel of beer from Lorentz Keller]	1 - 10 - 0
1763		
4 Janÿ	ein Berl bier	1 - 10 - 0
29 Jan	ein Berl bier	1 - 10 - 0
1764	**Andreas Müller** Blas balck Macher [bellows maker]	
Mertz 6	vor trinken	0 - 1 - 9
1768	**Jacob Meÿer**	
Augst 29	1 q: Rom	0 - 1 - 0
1764	**Johanes Meÿer** Junge [Jr.]	
Mertz 19	1 wein schling	0 - 0 - 9
1765		
Jany 12	1 m: w: schling	0 - 1 - 2
1764	**Johannes Meÿer** alt [Sr.]	
May 21	1 q: bir	0 - 0 - 6
1765		
Febr: 29	1/2 b: M: wein 2 weck	0 - 1 - 2
1766		
Juni 16	1 sattel Beck	0 - 15 - 0

5	**Willem Besch**	
1762		
11 Nov	3 rom schlinck 1/2 tschill tram 1 q seider 1/2 beint maderÿ wein	0 - 3 - 0
13 Nov	1 fisch	0 - 0 - 3
13 Nov	13 gallen brandenwein gebrent [for distilling 13 gallons brandy]	0 - 16 - 3
13 Nov	8 Jert bedzeig die jert 6 S 6 d	2 - 12 - 0
16 Nov	1 q seider un 1 beint maderÿ wein	0 - 2 - 0
17 Nov	1 q seider	0 - 0 - 4
18 Nov	1 q darr	0 - 0 - 5
19 Nov	1 q seider	0 - 0 - 4
6 Dec	1 beint seider öill	0 - 0 - 4
13 Dec	1 q fisch tron un 1 q seider öill tram	0 - 8 - 2
	gelent wegen des Beistels dochder [lent for Beistel's daughter]	0 - 3 - 8
21 Dez	2 q seider un 1/2 tschill tram	0 - 0 - 10
29 Dec	2 q seider	0 - 0 - 8
	1 tschill rom	0 - 0 - 4
	1 beint seider	0 - 0 - 2
	1 q. seider	0 - 0 - 4
30 Dec	1 q seider	0 - 0 - 4
29 Dec	1 q seider	0 - 0 - 4
5 Jeny	2 beint wein	0 - 2 - 4
1763		
5 Febru:	3 b: seiter eol 1 q: seiter	0 - 1 - 4
8	1 q: seiter	0 - 0 - 4

12	1 b: seiter eol	0 - 0 - 4
18	3 q: seiter	0 - 1 - 0
19	2 q: seiter	0 - 0 - 8
24	3 b: seiter eol	0 - 1 - 0
25	1 b: Ditto	0 - 0 - 4
26	3 b: Ditto	0 - 1 - 0
5 Mertz	1 b: seiter eol	0 - 0 - 4
7	3 b: Ditto	0 - 1 - 0
	1 q: seiter eol	0 - 0 - 8
12	1 q: seiter	0 - 0 - 4
1 April	2 1/2 q: seiter eol 2 weck	0 - 1 - 10
3	Vor trincken	0 - 0 - 5
Mertz 12	2 b: seiter eol	0 - 0 - 8
21	1 1/2 seiter 1 b: s. eol	0 - 0 - 10
	Credit wegen einer Noth [credit on account of a note]	0 - 6 - 0

No 6

1762	**Casper Schweitzer**	
13 Nov	3 q seider	0 - 1 - 0
14 Nov	1 q seider	0 - 0 - 4
16 Nov	1 q seider	0 - 0 - 4
20 Nov	3 beint maderÿ wein un 2 q seider un 1 wein schlinck	0 - 7 - 10
22 Nov	2 beint maderÿ wein un 2 q seider	0 - 4 -8
23 Nov	2 q seider 1 wein schlinck un 1 beint wein maderÿ	0 - 3 - 9
27 Nov	2 q bier	0 - 1 - 0
16 Dec	2 q bier	0 - 1 - 0
19 Dez	1 bottel bamöll	0 - 3 - 4
25 Dec	2 beint maderÿ wein	0 - 4 - 0
27 Dec	2 q seider 1/2 beint maderÿ wein	0 - 1 - 8
1763	**Casper Schweÿtzer**	
3 January	bleibt schultig in der abregnung [remains owing at the accounting]	3 - 4 - 4
9 Jeny	1 q seider öill	0 - 0 - 8
24 Jan	2 q seider	0 - 0 - 8
26 Jan	1 beint maderÿ wein	0 - 2 - 0
7 Febru:	Vor saffran	0 - 1 - 0
18	2 q: seiter	0 - 0 - 8
19	1/2 gill schimber	0 - 0 - 3
	1/2 Ditto	0 - 0 - 3
25	1 gill schimber	0 - 0 - 6
4 Mertz	4 b: seiter eol	0 - 1 - 4
	gelend an Geld [lent in money]	1 - 10 - 0
5 Mertz	1 b: m: wein	0 - 2 - 0
21 Mertz	1 1/2 b: Ditto	0 - 3 - 0
21	3 b: seiter eol 1/2 gill schimber	0 - 1 - 3
22	3 b : Ditto	0 - 1 - 0
25	3 b: M: wein 1 q: seiter	0 - 6 - 4
1 April	Vor weitzen	0 - 4 - 6
	3 1/2 q: seiter eol	0 - 2 - 4
13	1 q seitereol	0 - 0 - 8
18	3 b: seitereol	0 - 1 - 0

No 7

1764	**Friedrich Taxis** schneiter [taylor]	
April	and it came	
13	1 beck saltz	0 - 1 - 6
May 7	1 strengel seiten	0 - 0 - 9
May 12	Vor land auff brechen [for breaking land]	0 - 10 - 0
1765	**Fridrik Taxis**	
Juny 8	2 q: bir 1 q: seiter	0 - 1 - 4
July 13	1 q: seiter	0 - 0 - 4
Nov: 20	1 fass	0 - 2 - 6
Decem: 23	8 q: syter	0 - 2 - 0
	6 lotten zucker	0 - 6 - 0
	3 gallen seiter	0 - 3 - 0
	Abgerechnet mit friedrich Taxis d: 21 ten Febrary 1766 bleibt nichts [Settled with Friedrich Taxis February 21, 1766. No remainder.]	
Decem: 15	1 beck saltz	0 - 1 - 0
	Jacob Hamman	
	1 lb: pech 1 b: thron	0 - 0 - 10
	1 b: thron	0 - 0 - 6
1765		
January	**Jacob Wolf**	
14	1 1/2 yd: flenel	0 - 5 - 3
	1/2 lb: zucker	0 - 0 - 5
1765	**Jacob Hamman** junor	
Decem: 23	1 yd: Barget un 4 yd: floret un 1 b: seiteröl	0 - 4 - 4

No 8

1762	**Lorentz Keller**	
13 Nov	1 q seider	0 - 0 - 4
14 Nov	1/2 beint maderÿ wein	0 - 1 - 0
14 Nov	vor fuer lohn nach Lencesder [for driving costs to Lancaster]	1 - 0 - 0
16 Nov	2 beint maderÿ wein	0 - 4 - 0
16 Nov	4 geill beim heÿ un Esen [4 horses at hay and eating]	0 - 3 - 8
18 Nov	1 tschill tram	0 - 0 - 3
20 Nov	1 beint maderÿ wein un 1 wein schlinck un Esen	0 - 3 - 10
22 Nov	3 beint maderÿ wein	0 - 6 - 0
23 Nov	1 beint maderÿ wein	0 - 2 - 0
3 Dec	1 q fisch tron	0 - 1 - 2
		1 - 2 - 3
1762	**Lorentz Keller**	
4 Dec	bleibt schultig in der abregnung [remains owing at the accounting]	1 - 7 - 0
6 Dec	glehnt an gelt [lent in money]	2 - 0 - 0
12 Dec	2 beint maderÿ wein	0 - 4 - 0
14 Dec	2 q bier	0 - 1 - 0
15 Dec	2 rom schlinck	0 - 1 - 0
16 Dec	1 beint un 1 halb beint maderÿ wein	0 - 3 - 0
17	1 rom schlinck	0 - 0 - 6
21 Dez	2 q bier	0 - 1 - 0
21 Dez	vor maltz zu holen in Längäster [for bringing malt from Lancaster]	1 - 0 - 0

26 Dec	1 beint maderÿ wein un 1 rom schlinck	0 - 3 - 0
29 Dec	1 beint maderÿ wein	0 - 2 - 0
1763		
15 Jan	1 beint and 1/2 beint maderÿ wein	0 - 3 - 0
17 Jan	2 beint seider öill	0 - 0 - 8
18 Jan	1 q bier	0 - 0 - 6
22 Jan	1 rom schlinck	0 - 0 - 6
7 Febr:	1 schling	0 - 0 - 6
4 Febr:	1/2 b: m: wein	0 - 1 - 0
10	sein gaul bei heu gehabt 1 nacht und 1/2 tag [his horse at hay 1 night and 1/2 day]	0 - 1- 6
	3 q: haber	0 - 0 - 6
		5 - 10 - 8

No 9

1764	**Jacob Duÿ**	
febru 17	1 zinnerne schissel	0 -11 - 1
April 20	1 w: schling	0 - 0 - 9
Sept 3	1 hut	0 - 4 - 0
1765 March 27	1 gill Rom	0 - 0 - 4
	1 w: schling	0 - 0 - 9
1765 Juny 8	1 hut	0 - 7 - 0
July 9	1 q: bir	0 - 0 - 6
	Bezahlt [paid]	0 - 8 - 2
1766		
Jan: 20	1 Calender	0 - 0 - 8
febrary 5	1/4 lb: Peffer 1/4 lb alspeis 1/4 lb: Imber	0 - 2 - 2
July 13	Bleibt schultig vor 1 hut [owes for 1 hat]	0 - 3 - 0
	abgerechnet mit Jacob Duÿ d: 11 ten Janray 1768 Bleibt nichts [Settled with Jacob Duy 11 January 1768. No remainder]	
Mertz 26	2 q: seiter	0 - 0 - 8
May 20	verzehrt von weiss [eaten by Weiss]	0 - 6 - 1
July 7	1 sichel	0 - 3 - 4
1769		
feb 6	1 q: seiter	0 - 0 - 4
1770		
May 12	1 q: seiter	0 - 0 - 4

1764	**die schräcken [Mrs. Schrack]**	
Octo 15	1 b: thron	0 - 0 - 6

1766	**friedrich Weitenthal** Holtz Hacker [wood chopper]	
May 20	2 b: wein 3 q: Bir 1 gill Rom	0 - 4 - 2

No 10

1762	**tschiem Dieueÿ [? Jim]**	
8 Meÿ	vor schap gut	1 - 11 - 4
6 Junÿ	vor camlot	0 - 1 - 4
	vor barget	0 - 7 - 0
17 Junÿ	2 q un 1 beint rom	0 - 3 - 0
27 Junÿ	Ein hut	0 - 3 - 0

27 Junÿ	2 1/2 jert bendel	0 - 0 - 5
12 Julÿ	un 1/4 lb beffer	0 - 15 - 0
23 Nov	Ein par strimb un 1 Kap un 1/2 lb bech	
	1 q seiter	0 - 10 - 0
		3 - 1 - 1

Butschers Magd [Butcher's maid]

1764		
febuary	1 yd flored	0 - 0 - 4
20	1 yd. un viertel Tuch	0 - 5 - 0
	1 nestel un spellen	0 - 0 - 7

1763	**Tschim Die ju**	
Sep 19	3/4 yd Cattun	
	1 yd. 1/2 Viertel Camlot	
	1/2 b: wein	0 - 8 - 8
	bezal an der schult [paid on the debt]	0 - 6 - 0
1764		
April 13	2 yd: floret	0 - 0 - 8
	1/2 yd: Barget 2 strengel Hauben garn	0 - 1 - 10
	1 schnub Tuch	0 - 3 - 0
Sep: 6	1 yd. Barget 2 streng seiten	0 - 4 - 6
	2 Namen Bücher	0 - 1 - 4
	Abgerechnet mit Tschim dieju d: 12 Seb: 1765	
	[Settled with Tschim dieju Sep 12, 1765]	
	Bleibt er schultig [He still owes]	0 - 13 - 2
	Bezalt [Paid]	0 - 11 - 0
1766		
Novem: 15	1/2 b: Br: wein	0 - 0 - ?

No 11		
1762	**Henrich Beffer** D. Junge [Jr.]	
9 Ocdo	bezalt vor Digens [Paid for Digens]	
	vor Licack Lodery [for Leacock Lottery]	4 - 5 - 6
15 Nov	1 beint maderÿ wein	0 - 2 - 0
	Henrich Pfeffer	
	gelent 1/2 beck lein samen [lent 1/2 peck linseed]	
1763		
No: 5	**Henrich Peffer**	
	1 B: wein	0 - 1 - 2
De: 24	1 b: m: wein	0 - 2 - 0
	1 wein schling	0 - 0 - 9
	sein schwester [his sister]	
24	Vor Corallen	0 - 4 - 0
De: 24	**Henrich Beffer**	
	sein schwester [his sister] vor Corallen	0 - 4 - 0
1764		
April	**Henrich Peffer**	
30	1 Par schnallen	0 - 0 - 6
July 1	1 q; seiter	0 - 0 - 4
Aug: 10	1 b: wein	0 - 1 - 2
16	1 yd. drugget und Neths	0 - 4 - 0
25	1 bottel 1 q: Rom	0 - 2 - 0
Sep: 3	1 bol L: bunsch	0 - 1 - 6
6	1 q: Rom	0 - 1 - 0
10	1 b: wein	0 - 1 - 2

Oct 8	1 q: thron	0 - 1 - 0
9	8 buschel äpffel	0 - 5 - 0
	1 b: seiter	0 - 0 - 2
19	gelent [lent]	0 - 2 - 6

No 12		
1762	**Pernd Jacob**	
29 Dec	1 beint maderÿ wein and 1 q: seider	0 - 2 - 4
29	1 tschill rom	0 - 0 - 4
2 Janÿ	1 beint maderÿ wein 1 beif	0 - 2 - 1
3 Janÿ	1 wein schlinck	0 - 1 - 2
1763	**Bernd Jacob**	
Febru:	Extra	
7	1 gill Rom	0 - 0 - 4
May 23	2 lb zucker	0 - 1 - 6
Juny 20	Vor trincken beÿ handel zwischen Casper Schweitzer [For drinking while dealing with Casper Schweitzer]	1 - 11 - 4
22	1/2 gill schinwer	0 - 0 - 3
Sep: 5	2 q: seiter	0 - 0 - 8
	1/2 b: gatsel 1 gill gatsel	0 - 0 - 11
6	2 M: wein schling	0 - 2 - 4
	1 Par schnallen 3 Peifen	0 - 1 - 8
1762	**Johannes Feck**	
29 Dec	1 beint maderÿ wein	0 - 2 - 0
1768	**John Schub**	
July 20	2 Sichlen	0 - 5 - 6
	Bezahlt [paid]	0 - 4 - 0
1762	**Andres Scholl**	
29 Dec	1 beint maderÿ wein	0 - 2 - 0

No 13		
1762	**Philleb Wolffersperger**	
1 Nov	1 wein schlinck	0 - 0 - 9
	Philleb Wolffersperger un **Domes Basler**	
1763		
Januarÿ	3 wein schlinck un 1 q seider	0 - 2 - 7
15	bezalt Basler [Basler paid]	0 - 1 - 3
Mertz	**Phillip Wolffersberger**	
25	1 wein schling	0 - 0 - 9
July 25	2 wein schling	0 - 1 - 6
Sep 12	1 feil 1/2 yd kelsch	0 - 4 - 2
	Phillip Wolffersberger	
	noch schuldig von schuttin Mätsch [still owing from the shooting match]	0 - 5 - 0
1764	**Philip Wolfersberger**	
Mertz 19	1 q: bir	0 - 0 - 6
	1 w: schling 2 weck	0 - 0 -11
	1 gill Terbetinöl	0 - 0 - 6
May 12	1 wein schling	0 - 0 - 9

26	1 lb Pulwer	0 - 4 - 0
	1 lb Bley	0 - 0 - 6
	1 w: schling	0 - 0 - 9
	2 q: haber	0 - 0 - 3
	1/2 b: Rom	0 - 0 - 6
Junÿ 10	4 w: schling 2 weck	0 - 3 - 2
	1 q: bir 1 weck	0 - 0 - 7
	1 q: bir	0 - 0 - 6
July 2	3 Sickeln un 1 feil	0 - 13 - 3
12	2 lb: zucker	0 - 1 - 8
12	1 q: seiter	0 - 0 - 4
August	1 1/2 bol. senckery 5 weck	0 - 2 - 8
9	1 wein schling	0 - 0 - 9
	6 bogen bappier	0 - 0 - 6

No 14

1763	**Johannes Fischer**	
12 Aug	1 1/2 beint maderÿ wein	0 - 3 - 0
23 Aug	1 beint maderÿ wein	0 - 2 - 0
1767		
July 3	**Anen stein**	
	1 Wetz stein	0 - 2 - 0
1764		
October	**Henrich Brill**	
11	2 Catechismus	0 - 3 - 0
1765	**John Numan**	
July 2	1 hut	0 - 7 - 0

No 15

1762	**Stephen Jacÿ**	
2 Aug	1 beint maderÿ wein	0 - 2 - 0
1764	**Philip Bohlwein**	
November 6	2 Seuger	0 - 3 - 0
1765	**Johannes Schneiter** schumacher [shoemaker]	
Febru 20	1 hut 2 Peiffen	0 - 7 - 8
	Henrich Meÿle	
	2 q: tar 1 schling	0 - 1 - 6
1767	**Martin Meÿly** Jung [Jr.]	
July 25	1 1/2 q: Bir 1/2 gill Rom	0 - 11- 0

No 16

1762	**Nicklos Schwengel**	
16 Meÿ	vor strimpf un barget	0 - 13 - 0 bezahlt
	Nicklos Schwengel	
1763	schultig [owes]	0 - 8 - 0
6 Jan	bezalt [paid]	0 - 5 - 5
1763	**Nicklos Schwengel Jung** [Jr.]	
De: 26	1 1/2 vir: yd. schallun	
	2 strengel Neths	0 - 1 - 6
1765	**Johann Dengler** Zeugmacher [toolmaker]	
January 10	1 gill Rom 1 b: Bir	0 - 0 - 7
1766	**Michael Schwengel**	
July 11	2 gallen Br: wein	0 - 6 - 8
Augst 2	1 q: Br: wein un 1 stober	0 - 0 -11
1769	**Michael Schwengel**	
Febru: 9	1 gesang Buch	0 - 8 - 6
18	1 R: schling 1/2 gill tram un 2 Messer	0 - 2 - 4

No 17

1762	**Aberham Ruedie**	
17 Nov	1 q rom un 1 q mallasis	0 - 2 - 3
22 Dez	1 q rom un 1 q mallasis un 1 q fisch Tron	0 - 3 - 5
1763		
Febr 17	1 q: thron un 1 licht	0 - 3 - 8
April 13	2 q: Brandwein	0 - 2 - 0
1763	**Abraham Rudÿ**	
De: 19	2 q thron	0 - 2 - 0
1764		
Jan: 7	1 q fisch thron	0 - 1 - 0
July 6	1 sichel	0 - 3 - 5
1765		
January 10	4 q: thron 1 B: m: wein	0 - 6 - 0
Merz 18	1 1/2 b: m: wein	0 - 3 - 0
1765	**Abraham Ruthÿ**	
Sebt 13	1 q thron	0 - 1 - 0
1767	**Abraham Ruthy**	
January 8	bezahlt an Geld [paid in money]	1 - 2 - 6
	Vor deed zu Knaletschen	0 - 6 - 0
	[For acknowledging a deed]	
	Abgerechnet mit Abraham Ruhty d: 16tn January 1767	
	Bleibt er schultig	0 - 2 - 0
	[Settled with Abraham Ruhty January 16, 1767. He still owes]	

No 18	**Adem Wiest** schmidt [smith]	
15 Dez	1 q brandewein	0 - 1 - 0
18 Dez	1 Calender	0 - 0 - 8
	5 q seider un 1 q seider oill	0 - 2 - 4

27 Dec	2 q seider un 1/2 beint wein	0 - 1 - 3
	d 3 Jenarÿ 1763 hab ich mit Adem Wiest zu samen gerechnet bleibt keiner den andern nichts mehr schultig von dado an [I settled together with Adam Wiest. Neither owes the other anything from this date on.]	
1763	**Adem Wiest**	
17 Jan	1 tschill tram un 1 q seider un 6 Jert flored	0 - 2 - 2
18 Jan	2 q Maderÿ wein	0 - 8 - 0
	Bleibt rest [The remainder owed]	0 - 1 - 4
	1 b: seiter	0 - 0 - 2
April	**Adam Wüst** Extra [additional]	
12	1 b: seiteroel	0 - 0 - 4
23	2 b: wein	0 - 2 - 4
27	1 1/2 quart seitereol 1/2 b: wein	0 - 1 - 7
28	1 q: wein 1 q: seitereol	0 - 3 - 0
May 2	1 b: seiter	0 - 0 - 2
3	1 q: Rom 1 b: seitereol 4 lb: Kalb fleisch	0 - 2 - 8
	1 q: seiter	0 - 0 - 4
4	1 gill Rom 1 q seitereol	0 - 1 - 0
	gelent [lent]	0 - 14 - 0
7	4 saffran und Peffer u 2 Galle Brandwein	0 - 9 - 3
10	2 q: seiter	0 - 0 - 8
		1 - 15 - 4
Ad: Wüst	bleibt schultig in der Abrechnung [still owes at the accounting]	0 - 11 - 5

No 19	**Adem Wiest** schmidt [smith]	
1764		
January	**Etwart Clerck**	
27	Noch schuldig von schuttin Mätsch [Still owes from the shooting match]	0 - 2 - 0
1765		
May	**Naday Clarck**	
27	1 q: bir	0 - 0 - 6
1764	**Adam Wist**	
May 4	1 q: bir	0 - 0 - 6
	1/2 gill Rom	0 - 0 - 2

No 20		
1764	**Johannes Becker**	
Mertz 7	1 q: bir	0 - 0 - 6
May 26	1 q: bir	0 - 0 - 6
July 13	1 b: m: wein	0 - 2 - 0
1769	**John Becker**	
Juny 11	1/2 lb alspeis	0 - 1 - 3

	Henrich Meths	
	1 b: tram 1 b: seiter	0 - 0 - 8

No 21		
1762	**Georg Gallenmeÿer**	
17 Nov	verzert	0 - 3 - 10
1768	**Peter Kister**	
febru 5	1/2 b: m: wein 2 q: haber	0 - 1 - 4
1764	**Christopher Kister**	
febr: 21	3 b: m: wein 2 bänd	0 - 6 - 4

No 22		
1762	**Henrich Keÿller**	
16 Nov	1 beint maderÿ wein	0 - 2 - 0
16 Nov	bezalt an seiner schult [paid on his debt]	0 - 5 - 0
22 Nov	1 q seider 1 wein schlinck	0 - 1 - 10
26 Nov	1 q un 1 beint bier un 2 q seider	0 - 1 - 5
5 Dec	1/2 beint maderÿ wein	0 - 1 - 0
6 Dec	1 beint maderÿ wein	0 - 2 - 0
13 Dec	2 q seider	0 - 0 - 8
20 Dez	1 scher	0 - 1 - 0
29 Dec	1 q seider un 1 q seider öill un 1 beint seideröill	0 - 1 - 4
30 Dec	2 q rom un 1 q seideröill	0 - 3 - 2
	Auss Zug 1 q rom	0 - 1 - 3
1763		
8 Jany	2 streng camel garn	0 - 0 - 8
15 Jany	1/2 tschill tram un 1 beint seideröill	0 - 0 - 6
16 Jan	1 bar ledner hose	0 - 15 - 0
16 Jan	1 beint un 1 q tram un 2 q seider	0 - 2 - 2
18 Jan	1 lb Zuger un bsalder	0 - 3 - 0
24 Jan	3 q seider	0 - 1 - 0
	den 9th February 1763 gerechnet mit Henrich Keiler	
	bleibt schuldig	6 - 12 - 4
	[February 9 1763, settled with Henrich Keiler, still owes]	
Febru:		
9	2 b: wein	0 - 2 - 4
10	3 q: seiter 1 gill bitters 1 gil gadel	0 - 2 - 0
12	1 gill Rom	0 - 0 - 4
12	1 schling	0 - 0 - 6
15	1 lb Zucker	0 - 0 - 9
19	1 1/2 gill Rom 1/2 beint Rom 1 q seiter	0 - 1 - 3
21	1 q: seiter	0 - 0 - 4
24	3 b: seitereol	0 - 1 - 0
25	3 b Ditto	0 - 1 - 0
4 Mertz	1 b: seitereol	0 - 0 - 4
5	3 b seitereol 1 lb Zucker 1 fisch	0 - 2 - 0
5	1 q: seitereol	0 - 0 - 8
7	1 q: Ditto	0 - 0 - 8
		7 - 5 - 0

[23, 24 are missing]

No 25

1762	**Christian Willÿ** spengler [tinsmith]	
19 Nov	2 jert un 3 ferdel hasenbrick un 1/8 lb deh	0 - 5 - 4
1766	**Paul Gemberling**	
Aprill 18	Vor kelsch	0 - 4 - 4
October 3	1 b: m: wein	0 - 2 - 0
1769		
Octbr 2	1/2 b: wein	0 - 0 - 7
Novem: 14	1 b: m: wein	0 - 2 - 0
Decen 6	1 q: Br: wein	0 - 0 - 10
11	1 q: Br: wein	0 - 0 - 10
16	1 q: Br: wein	0 - 0 - 10
16	2 q: seiter	0 - 0 - 8
1770		
January 8	1 q: Br: wein	0 - 0 - 10
Juny 20	2 q: seiter	0 - 0 - 8
		0 - 7 - 3
1763	**Georg Schwengel**	
Sept. 24	2 q: thron	0 - 2 - 0
1764		
Sept. 22	1 b: oehl	0- 0 - 8
Decem: 17	1 lb: Peffer 1 lb: alspeis 1/2 4 yd: Schechter un 1 1/2 Dutzend Krosse Knöp [large buttons]	0 - 8 - 1?
19	1 lb: Bleÿ	0 - 0 - 7
1765		
Febr 13	4 q: Bir	0 - 2 - 0
May 27	4 q: bir	0 - 2 - 0
July 10	2 q bir	0 - 1 - 0
1765		
28 Dec	mit Georg Schwengel Liquidiert und bleib demselben schuldig [Settled with Georg Schwengel and still owe to him]	0 - 1 - 9
Sep: 23	3 q tron	0 - 1 - 0
1766		
Jan: 1	1/4 lb: Peffer un 1/4 lb: alspeis	0 - 1 - 6
1768	**Georg Schwengel**	
Maertz 14	1 w: schling	0 - 0 - 9

No 26

1762	**Michel Hollstein**	
3 Nov	Ein par hosen schnallen	0 - 0 - 9
1762	**Michel Hollstein**	
3 Dec	2 jert halb dick 6 jert bendel un camel garn	0 - 8 - 8
1763		
19 Jan	Ein par schuh bezalt beim Henrich Rung [one pair of shoes paid for Henrich Rung]	0 - 8 - 0
2 Febr:	3/4 yd Rattin	0 - 7 - 0
8	Bar Geld	1 - 12 - 0
12	1 wein schling	0 - 0 - 9

19 Mertz	1 Pahr strumpf bänder	0 - 0 - 9
25	1 wein schling	0 - 0 - 9
26	Bar geld vor Ein hut [cash for a hat]	1 - 15 - 0
29	Bar geld welches Hannes Schaffer vor in zahlt in Lebanon [cash which Hannes Schaffer paid for him in Lebanon]	0 - 2 - 0
April 13	vor schreiben und 1 b: m: wein	0 - 3 - 0
	vor sattel und zaum	2 - 15 - 0
May 7	Bar geld bezalt an Henrich Pfeffer [cash paid to Henrich Pfeffer] vor tisch Schublat [for a table drawer] 1 yd 1 bloss rohr	0 - 6 - 0
	1 wipp vor in Bezalt Bey Johannes Huber [1 whip for him paid by Johannes Huber]	0 - 6 - 0
	aus alten Buch fol: 251 [from the old book, p. 251]	3 - 16 - 1
		12 - 1 - 6

1764

Georg Michael Holstein

	Vor in Zalt beÿ Christoph Kapp [Paid for him by Christoph Kapp]	0 - 7 - 8

No 27

1762

Christian Bernhart

26 Nov	1 q tram	0 - 1 - 0
26 Nov	1 q tram	0 - 1 - 0
28 Nov	1 q tram	0 - 1 - 0
12 Dec	1 q tram	0 - 1 - 0
13 Dec	2 q seider	0 - 0 - 8
16 Dec	1 q tram	0 - 1 - 0
18 Dez	1 q tram	0 - 1 - 0
18 Dez	1 q seider	0 - 0 - 4
21 Dez	1 q tram	0 - 1 - 0
23 Dez	1 q tram	0 - 1 - 0
23 Dez	gelehnt an Geld [lent in money]	0 - 1 - 5
	auss Zug 1 q seider un 1 q rom un 2 lb reiss	0 - 2 - 1
1762		
13 July	auss Zug 4 q seiter 1/4 lb Imber un 1/4 lb Alspeiss	0 - 2 - 3
14 July	auss Zug 1 q rom	0 - 1 - 3
24 Dec	1 q tram	0 - 1 - 0
15 July	auss Zug 1 q rom	0 - 1 - 3
24 Dec	1 q tram	0 - 1 - 0
27 Dec	5 q seider un 1 beint fisch dron	0 - 2 - 1
29 Dec	2 q seider	0 - 0 - 8
30 Dec	1 q un 1 beint seider un 1 beint tram	0 - 1 - 0
1 Jany	1 q fisch tron	0 - 1 - 2
1 Jany	gelent vor Alt eisen [lent for used iron]	0 - 12 - 4
2 Janÿ	1 q tram	0 - 1 - 0
3 Janÿ	1 q tram	0 - 1 - 0
8 Jany	1 beint rom	0 - 0 - 9
	1/2 beint wein	0 - 0 - 7
9 Jany	1 beint rom	0 - 0 - 9
	2 beint seideröill un 1 q seider	0 - 1 - 0
10 Jany	1 q tram	0 - 1 - 0
12 Jany	1 q rom	0 - 1 - 3
14 Jany	1 q tram	0 - 1 - 0
15 Jany	1 q tram dieses ist alles [this is all	0 - 1 - 0
16 Jany	1 q tram verrechnet settled]	0 - 1 - 0
18 Jan	beint fisch tron	0 - 0 - 7

No 28

1762	**Henrich Stigel**	
26 Nov	3 bole bunsch	0 - 3 - 0
30 Nov	verzert vor Esen un tringen [consumed by eating and drinking]	1 - 13 - 2
30 Nov	4 seiden hals diger	1 - 8 - 0
	17 gallen un 2 q seider am auf blocken [at raising the log building]	0 - 17 - 6
	vor Kost vor auf schlagen [at the raising]	3 - 13 - 6
	vor kost Geld von die zimer Leid [carpenters]	17 - 10 - 0
21 Mertz	4 q tram von Erst wegen Zimer man [carpenter]	0 - 4 - 0
	1 q maderÿ wein der Zimer man [carpenter]	0 - 4 - 0
30 Nov	1 buschel haber un heÿ un Kleser	0 - 10 - 0
1 Dec	vor 2 man 3 dag kost gelt	0 - 6 - 0
	wider 80 buschel kalck	2 - 13 - 4
	6 fuer stein gefahr un sand un waser gefahr un auf die fornes gefahr [6 loads of stone carted, and sand and water carted and carted to the furnace]	1 - 5 - 0
	das holtz zum hauss gefahr [wood carted to the house]	0 - 12 - 0
	wider holtz von des henlies blatz gefahr [again, wood carted from Henly's place]	1 - 1 - 0
29 Dec	1 seiden halss duch un 4 jertbant	0 - 12 - 0
29	1 beint maderÿ und 1 q rom un 1 glass	0 - 4 - 3
30 Dec	6 bole bunsche	0 - 6 - 0
1763		
3 Jenarÿ	2 bole bunsch	0 - 2 - 0
	vor Deett iber 1 lodt [deed for 1 lot]	0 - 15 - 0
4 Jenarÿ	34 laden gelent jeder 18 fuss lang [34 lathes borrowed each 18 feet long]	
5 April	1 fuhr latten geholt auff Michel Millers Mühl [1 load of lathes brought from Michael Miller's mill]	0 - 7 - 0
Mertz 7	vor Trincken	0 - 10 - 0
22	1 bol mimm	0 - 1 - 0
29	2 bol mimm	0 - 2 - 0
April 9	2 b: m: wein 3 bol 1 Mimm	0 - 7 - 0
21	1 q: Rom	0 - 1 - 8
	1 bol Mimm	0 - 1 - 0

No 29

1762	**Franz Schmÿdt** sadler	
30 Nov.	1 q bier	0 - 0 - 6
31 Nov. [sic]	1/2 beint rom	0 - 0 - 5
4 Dec.	1/2 beint maderÿ wein	0 - 1 - 0
1763	**Frantz Schmit**	
Juny 12	1 lb Zucker und vor saffran	0 - 1 - 3
Dec. 10	1 q: m: wein	0 - 4 - 0
13	1 q: seiter	0 - 0 - 4
1764	**Frantz Schmitt**	
July 12	1 q: seiter	0 - 0 - 4
16	2 q: seiter	0 - 0 - 8
Aug. 9	1 schling	0 - 0 - 6
Oct. 24	1 lb Nägel	0 - 1 - 0
Decem 20	1 b: m: wein	0 - 2 - 0
1766		
Febrary 16	1/2 lb: Pulver un 1 lb: schrot un 1 gill Rom	0 - 1 - 9
Aprill 5	2 Äpfel bäum	0 - 0 - 10
10	1 Lott gezackert [1 lot plowed]	0 - 4 - 0
	1 beck flags Samen	0 - 2 - 0

Augst 2	1 gill annis	0 - 0 - 5
1763	**Peter Ried**	
Febr: 9	1 q: fisch thron	0 - 1 - 0
Aug 15	Vor Ehl 1/2 gill tram	0 - 0 - 4
Jan: 15	1 q: thron	0 - 1 - 0
16	1 q: thron	0 - 1 - 0
21	1 q: Bir	0 - 0 - 6
25	1 q thron	0 - 1 - 0
	1 q: br: wein	0 - 1 - 0
1764	**Peter Ried**	
Octo 24	1 1/2 yd Rattin 1 strängel Camelgarn	
	1/2 gill Rom	0 -14- 0
November 15	1 b: seiter	0 - 0 - 2

No 30		
1762	**Koll Fridrich** beim Dorst tomes	
3 Dec	1/2 lb deh un 3 q haber	0 - 6 - 0
2 May	Vor Tram und seiter	0 - 3 - 6
Juny 27	Vor Trincken	0 - 9 - 4
	1 hut	1 - 5 - 0
	1 hals tuch 2 nestel 1 q Rom	0 - 8 - 5
	Bezahlt an Geld [Paid in money]	0 -15- 0
Aug 24	1 q: m: wein das Beidele melhell geholt	
	[1 quart madera wine which Beidele melhell fetched]	0 - 4 - 0
Sept: 17	Vor wein Rom und Essen 2 yd Halb Leinen	0 -13- 4
24	1 q: wein 3 b: Rom 2 q: Br: wein	0 - 6 - 7
24	3 b: wein	0 - 3 - 6
30	4 q: Rom 1/2 b: wein das John Boget geholt	
	[which John Boget fetched]	0 - 6 - 8
Nov: 5	3 b: Rom	0 - 2 - 3
21	1 yd Camlot 1/2 lb thee	0 - 8 - 0
17 Dec	Ein sadel un Thee un schnub tuch un Zugar un netz	2 - 7 - 10
1764		
January 9	3 lb Zucker	0 - 2 - 6
	1 q: Rom	0 - 1 - 4
	1/2 buch Bappir 3 q: haber	0 - 1 - 2
	3 1/2 q: Rom	0 - 3 - 6
	1 1/2 q: Rom vor Nadeln u: 6: Peiffen	0 - 2 - 4
October 31	2 q: fisch thron 1 1/2 q: Rom 2 lb Zucker	0 - 6 - 2
	6 lb. Zucker	0 - 5 - 0
November 19	1/4 lb: Thee	0 - 3 - 0
		8 - 9 - 5

No 31		
1762	**Andres Ricker**	
3 Dec	vor beffer	0 - 0 - 3
5 Dec	1 q seider	0 - 0 - 4
24 Dec	1 q seider	0 - 0 - 4
29 Dec	2 beint maderÿ wein	0 - 3 - 11
5 Jenÿ	2 q seider	0 - 0 - 8
5 Jenÿ	wider 1 q seider un 1 q seideröill	0 - 1 - 0

9 Jenÿ	1 beint wein	0 - 1 - 2
15 Jenÿ	5 q seider 1 calender 1 beint seideröill	0 - 3 - 2
	wider 1 beint seider	
17 Jan	2 beint seideröill	0 - 0 - 8
18 Jan	gelent [lent] un nestel un tram	0 - 3 - 4
19 Jan	3 beint seideröill	0 - 1 - 0
29 Jan	1 tschill rom	0 - 0 - 4
6 Feb:	wegen Carl Seÿbold [on Carl Seÿbold's account]	0 - 6 - 0
	übertrag vom alten Buch folio 187	1 - 4 - 11
	[brought over from the old book, page 187]	
	Mehr von folio 200 [more from page 200]	0 - 6 - 10
Februa: 5	5 b: seiter eol	0 - 1 - 8
12	1 Messer und 2 b: seitereol	0 - 1 - 6
7 Mertz	2 q: seitereol 1 weck	0 - 1 - 5
12	vor weck	0 - 0 - 6
12	1 b: seiter 1/2 gill Rom 1 b: seitereol	0 - 0 - 8
15	1 q: seitereol	0 - 0 - 8
19	1 b: seitereol	0 - 0 - 4
	1/2 gill bitters	0 - 0 - 3
25	1 q: seitereol	0 - 0 - 8
31	3 1/2 q: seitereol 2 weck	0 - 2 - 6
1 April	1 1/2 q: seitereol	0 - 1 - 0
3	1 b: seitereol	0 - 0 - 4
Mertz	3 q: seitereol 1 weck 2 yd zeig	
7	2 1/2 yd Bandel	0 - 7 - 10
26	1 q: seitereol	0 - 0 - 8
25	3 1/2 q: seitereol 1/2 lb Zucker 4 weck	0 - 3 - 1
April	Credit wegen Philip Wagner	0 - 5 - 6
	[credit on Philip Wagner's account]	
13	verzehrt	0 - 1 - 0
18	1 b: seitereol	0 - 0 - 4
19	1 b: seitereol	0 - 0 - 4
20	1 q seiter	0 - 0 - 4

No 32

1762	**Carel Seÿbalt**	
3 Dec	1 beint maderÿ wein un 1 tschill rom	0 - 2 - 4
9 Dec	2 beint seider un 5 halb schill tram	0 - 1 - 2
12 Dec	2 beint seider	0 - 0 - 4
	1/2 tschill tram	0 - 0 - 2
20	5 halb tschill tram und 1/2 beint tram	0 - 1 - 2
25	1 bar strimb	0 - 5 - 6
	1 tschill tram	0 - 0 - 3
29 Dec	3 halb tschill rom	0 - 0 - 6
1763		
9 Janÿ	4 halb tschill rom	0 - 0 - 8
15 Jan	vor wein	0 - 0 - 6
17 Jan	1 q seider und tram	0 - 0 - 10
18 Jan	1 tschill tram 1 beint seider	0 - 0 - 6
29 Jan	vor tram	0 - 0 - 6
4 Feb	bezalt an Gelt [paid in money]	0 - 7 - 6
	Credit wegen Andreas Ricker	0 - 6 - 0
	[credit on Andreas Rickers account]	
8	1 b: seitereol 1 gi tram un 1/2 gill Rom	0 - 0 - 9
10	1 gill tram	0 - 0 - 3
11	1/2 gill Rom	0 - 0 - 2

Mertz 21	1 1/2 gill Rom	0 - 0 - 6
22	1 b: seitereol	0 - 0 - 4
	2 gill Rom	0 - 0 - 8
26	Credit	0 -10- 0
29	1/2 b: seitereol	0 - 0 - 2
3 April	vor Trincken	0 - 1 - 2
7	1 1/2 gill Rom	0 - 0 - 6
Febr: 12	1 gill tram	0 - 0 - 3
April 7	1 1/2 gill Rom	0 - 0 - 6
9	1 b: seidereol	0 - 0 - 4
	vor Trincken	0 - 0 - 5
12	1 b: seidereol	0 - 0 - 4
13	vor Trincken	0 - 1 - 5
21	Credit	0 - 5 - 0

No 33

1762	**Jacob Brecht**	
16 Dec	1 stang tubac	0 - 0 - 6
	sein Jung 2 jert Hasenbrick 1/2 dutzen	
	Kneb 1/4 jert schechder [his son:]	0 - 4 - 6
	1/2 beint rom 1/2 beint rom	0 - 1 - 3
23 Dec	Ein hutt	0 - 7 - 6
23	2 schnub dicher	0 - 5 - 6
	bezalt oder ein kalbs haut bracht [paid: or, a calf's hide brought]	0 - 3 - 2
30 Dec	1 q seider	0 - 0 - 4
1763		
4 Dec	1 bar schnallen	0 - 1 - 0
14 Jenÿ	1 bsalder un 1 cadisem	0 - 3 - 3
14 July	1 calender	0 - 0 - 8
	gelend an gelt [lent in money]	1 -10- 0
	bezalt oder ein haut bracht [paid, or one hide brought]	0 - 7 - 9

1763	**Jacob Brecht**	
14 Feb	bleibt schultig in der abregnung [still owes in the settlement]	2 - 0 - 0
31 Mertz	1 b: Rom 1 b: wein	0 - 2 - 0
1 April	vor saffran	0 - 0 - 6
7	vor Kirschbäum un trinken	0 - 2 - 0
	1/4 yd seiten Camelot	0 - 0 - 11
9	1 b: m: wein	0 - 2 - 0
May 2	1 b: Rom	0 - 0 - 10
7	1 b: Ditto	0 - 0 - 10
	gerechnet mit Jacob Brecht den 22t junÿ 1763 bleibt er schuldig [settled with Jacob Brecht the 22nd June 1763. He still owes]	0 -11- 0
4 Julÿ	gelend an gelt [lent in money]	2 - 0 - 0
Juny 22	1/2 y Cattun	0 - 8 - 3
July 25	1 q seiter	0 - 0 - 4
Aug 3	2 lb Pulver Zum brunen [to the fountain]	0 - 8 - 6
20	1 b: seitereol	0 - 0 - 4
	Bezahlt an seiner Schuld [paid on his debt]	1 -10- 0
	bezahlt [paid]	0 -15- 0

No 34

	Jacob Schenck	
1762		
14 Dec	1 q seider	0 - 0 - 4
1763		
15 Jenÿ	vor schap gut un tringen un Calender	1 - 4 - 8
Febru: 7	2 q: seiter	0 - 0 - 8
15	1 b: Ditto	0 - 0 - 2
24	1 1/2 seiter	0 - 0 - 6
19 Mertz	1 b: seitereol	0 - 0 - 4
April 25	1 q tram	0 - 1 - 0
May 20	1 hut	0 - 7 - 6
23	1 q: seiter	0 - 0 - 4
24	2 q: seiter	0 - 0 - 8
Juny 14	1 q: seiter	0 - 0 - 4
20	1 q: seiter 1 b: seitereol	0 - 0 - 8
20	1 q: tram und Neths	0 - 1 - 2
22	1 1/2 yd cartun	0 - 8 - 3
	1 gallen Br wein	0 - 4 - 0
24	1 lb Doback 2 q: Br: wein	0 - 2 - 5
		2 - 4 - 3

	Simon Leible	
1763		
7 febru:	1 gill Rom	0 - 0 - 4
8	1 q: Brand wein	0 - 1 - 0
	aus Zug vom alten buch folio 197 [extract from the old book page 197]	3 - 4 - 11
10	1 gill bitters	0 - 0 - 6
18	1 q: seiter	0 - 0 - 4
4 Mertz	2 q seiter	0 - 0 - 8
12	1 q Ditto	0 - 0 - 4
22	2 q Ditto	0 - 0 - 8
24	vor trinken	0 - 0 - 1
April 23	2 q: Bier	0 - 1 - 0
25	2 q: tram	0 - 2 - 0
27	2 gallen tram	0 - 8 - 0
30	1 gallen Brandwein	0 - 4 - 0
May 10	2 galle Ditto 1 b: seitereol	0 - 8 - 4
	1 q seitereol	0 - 0 - 8
19	1 gill Rom	0 - 0 - 4
20	1 q: thron	0 - 1 - 0
23	1 q: bir	0 - 0 - 6
Juny 2	3 q: seiter 1 weck	0 - 1 - 1

No 35

	Michel meÿer Stofel Meÿer un **Adem Bolender**	
1762		
	3 beint wein	0 - 3 - 6
	vor kost gelt [for food money]	0 - 6 - 0
	1 beind maderÿ wein	0 - 2 - 0
29 Dec	vor kost gelt an des stickels hauss [for food money at Stiegel's house]	0 -15- 0
		26- 6
1763		
6 Dec	Adem Bolender sein bard dar anbezalt von obigen [Adam Bolender paid his part of the above]	

	Henrich Leineweber	
	auss Zug vom alten Buch folio 129	1 - 5 - 5
	[extract from the old book, page 129]	
	Michel und **Stoffel Meÿer** und **Adem Bolender**	
Mertz 7	vor trinken in Comp:	0 -10- 0
Mertz 7	2 q: s. eol	0 - 1 - 4
April 21	Mehr 3 q: bier	0 - 1 - 6
1763	**Petter Riem** junior	
Juny 24	1 hut	0 - 3 - 0
1763	**Peder Rem**	
31 Ocdo	Belleibt schultig in der obregnun	0 - 0 - 8
	[still owes in the settlement]	
1765	**Andreas Wittemeier**	
Mertz	1 q: thron 1/2 lb: alspeis	0 - 2 - 0
May 27	1 q: bir 1 lb zucker	0 - 1 - 4
1766	**Andres Widenmeiÿer**	
30 Junÿ	bezalt in foll von dado an 5/4	
	[paid in full on this date 5/4]	
1768	**Andereas Widemeÿer**	
Decem: 12	Bezahlt in voll von dato an 2/0 [paid in full on this date 2/0]	

No 36		
1762	**Marden Riess**	
15 Dec	bezalt vor hauss zientz [paid for house rent]	0 -15- 0
20 Dec	1 beint maderÿ wein	0 - 2 - 0
	1 lb bulfer wegen Meiser [1 lb powder on Meiser's account]	0 - 4 - 6
1763		
14 Jeny	1 calender	0 - 0 - 8
	vor wein	0 - 0 - 6
1763	**Marden Riess**	
14 Mertz	bleibt schultig in der abrechnung	0 - 8 - 2
	[still owes in the settlement]	
1763	**Conrad Wagner**	
July 3	1 q: bir 2 1/4 lb Doback	0 - 1 - 5
1765	Conrad Wagner	
May 27	1 b: Rom	0 - 0 - 6
1765	**Georg Strom**	
Sebt 16	2 1/2 q: Rom un 1 q: thron	0 - 3 - 6
1764	**Georg Strom**	
August 25	1 yd Muslin	0 - 5 - 0
1765	**Jacob Hofmann** in Reden [in Reading]	
Febr: 1	3 1/2 b: m: wein	0 - 7 - 0

No 37

	Gottlieb Engelland	
	vor safferon	0 - 1 - 0
1763 July	**Theophill Engelland**	
July 14	2 b: m: wein	0 - 4 - 0
16	3 q: Rom	0 - 5 - 0
18	2 q: rom	0 - 3 - 4
24	1 q: Rom	0 - 1 - 8
Aug. 3	1 q: Br: wein	0 - 1 - 2
22	1 hut	1 - 8 - 0
29	1 q: Br: wein	0 - 1 - 2
30	2 q: Br: wein	0 - 2 - 4
Sep: 24	1 b: m: wein	0 - 2 - 0
Octo 18	1 q: Tarr	0 - 0 - 5
28	gelent [lent]	4 - 0 - 0
28	ist schuldig blieben [still owes]	0 - 1 - 1
28	1 b: m: wein	0 - 2 - 0
Mertz	1 q: m: wein	0 - 4 - 0
26	Bezahlt an geld [paid in money]	5 - 0 - 0
	2 Pahr schnallen	0 - 1 - 8
May 7	vor wein	0 - 1 - 2
		1 -19- 0
1765	**Engeland**	
Juny 1	1 q: Br: wein	0 - 1 - 0
1766		
July 25	1 q: seiteröl	0 - 0 - 8
1767		
Mertz 23	1 q: thron	0 - 1 - 2
Sebtem 19	1 q: W: Rom	0 - 1 - 6
21	2 b: m: wein	0 - 4 - 0
30	1 b: W: Rom	0 - 0 -10
1768	**Theophilo England** bleibt	
Sebtem: 28	schultig in der Rechnung [**Theophilo England** still owes in the settlement]	1 -12- 7

No 38

1762	**Andon Derder** Kiefer [cooper]	
20 Dec	1 seiden halss duch 1 bar strumbendel	0 - 8 - 3
20	wider an gelt [again, in money]	0 - 0 - 5
1763	**Antony Därter**	
July 25	2 1/2 q: seitereol 1 Peiff	0 - 1 - 9
1765	**Antony Derter**	
Novem 8	1/2 4 lb Peffer un 1 Muschcattenus	0 - 0 - 10
1767	**John Huber**	
Sebtem: 19	2 griene Peiffen	0 - 0 - 4
1763	**Ludwig Wittmann**	
Sep 15	3 wein schling 1 q: seiter 2 gill tram 1 Peiff	0 - 3 - 4
1764		
May 21	1 R: schling	0 - 0 - 6
May 28	2 q: bir 1 q: seiter	0 - 1 - 4
1768		
Augst 29	2 q: seiter 1 gill Br: wein	0 - 0 - 11
Sebt 12	1 gill Br: wein	0 - 0 - 4

1766		
Aprill 16	1 q: seiter 1 gill Rom	0 - 0 - 8
1767		
July 9	1 1/2 q: seiter 1/2 gill Rom	0 - 0 - 8
Augst 15	1 q: seiter	0 - 0 - 4
25	2 q: seiter	0 - 0 - 8
29	2 q: seiter	0 - 0 - 8
Octo: 29	1 R: schling	0 - 0 - 6
Augst 6	2 q: seiter	0 - 0 - 8
		10 - 7

No 39		
1762	**Friedrich Albrecht**	
24 Dec	1 q rom un 1 beint wein	0 - 2 - 5
26 Dec	1 beint wein un 2 weck	0 - 1 - 4
29 Dec	1 q rom	0 - 1 - 3
		0 - 5 - 0
1763	**Fritrich Albrecht**	
	Von Bernhardts Vendu 2 pr strümpff [From Bernhardt's sale, 2 pairs of stockings]	0 -12- 9
Febru 26	1 q Rom	0 - 1 - 8
Febru 26	2 quart seitereol	0 - 2 - 0
Febru 26	1/2 lb Imber	0 - 0 - 5
Febru 26	1 quart Rom	0 - 1 - 8
28	1 quart Rom	0 - 1 - 8
7 Mertz	1 quart Rom	0 - 1 - 8
12	1 b: wein	0 - 1 - 2
15	1 quart Rom	0 - 1 - 8
31	1 q: Rom	0 - 1 - 8
1764	**Friedrich Albrecht**	
Juny 14	2 w: schling	0 - 1 - 6
	1/2 lb alspeis	0 - 1 - 0
1765	1/4 lb Peffer 1/4 lb alspeis	0 - 1 - 5
Janury 21	1 gill gatshel	0 - 0 - 6
Mertz 4	1 q: Thron	0 - 4 - 0
Aprill 13	1/2 lb: Negel	0 - 0 - 6

No 40		
1762	**Michel Bolinger** Michael	
27 Dec	1 jert Cardon	0 - 5 - 0
1763		
July 30	1 b: wein	0 - 1 - 2
Aug 24	1 bol. senckery	0 - 1 - 6
1763	**Michel Bollinger**	
De: 24	1 w: schling	0 - 0 - 9
Jan 29	1 Bol. senckerih	0 - 1 - 6
Aprill 13	1 schnub tuch un 1 seiten nestel	0 - 4 - 0
20	1 w: schling	0 - 0 - 9
July 23	1 Nestel	0 - 1 - 0
1768	**Georg Maurer**	
October 15	1 q: Thron	0 - 1 - 0

Novem 21	3 q: Mallassis	0 - 2 - 6
Decem 1	4 q: Mallassis	0 - 3 - 4
7	1 lb Pulver	0 - 3 - 0
1769		
Janury 2	1 Par strümb	0 - 5 - 0
1762	**Georg Mauerer**	
26 Dec	1/4 1/8 jert schechder un 1 oely Netz	0 - 1 - 2
1763		
5 Mertz	2 yd. Tuch a 3/6	0 - 7 - 0
21 Ap:	1/2 yd Tuch	0 - 1 - 9
1764	**Georg Maurer**	
May 7	1 hut	1 - 3 - 2
	1 w: schling	
1766	**Georg Maure**	
Juny 16	1 sentz	0 - 4 - 0
	1 messer	0 - 1 - 0
Augst 11	1/4 lb Pulver	0 - 0 - 11
Sebtm: 25	1/4 lb Pulver	0 - 0 - 11
1767		
February 28	ist schultig vor schisen un spilen	0 -11- 7
	[owes for shooting and gambling]	
	1 q: Thron	

No 41		
1762	**Casper Fieding**	
26 Dec	2 Kapen	0 - 6 - 0
	Casper Fieting	
Mertz 22	1 q: seiter	0 - 0 - 4
Ap: 7	1 q seiter 1 q: Tarr	0 - 0 - 9
1763		
9 Aug	3 1/2 jert celsch	0 -17- 6
9 Aug	ein hudt	1 - 7 - 0
Junÿ 21	1 Stroh hut 1 yd. flored	0 - 3 - 4
	Bezahlt [paid]	1 - 0 - 0
1768	**Martin Riss**	
Octo 15	1 Neb senckery	0 - 0 - 9
1769		
May 1	1 q: seiter	0 - 0 - 4
Juny 9	1 b: seitöl	0 - 0 - 4
176	**Andreas Kartiger**	
Febr. 11	1 gill Bitters	0 - 0 - 6
1765	**Johannes Haise**	
Febrary 29	13 lb Negel	0 -13- 0
	1 lb Negel	0 - 1 - 0

No 42		
1762	**Andres Gadiener**	
27 Dec	1 1/2 jert Cardon un 1/2 beint maderÿ wein	0 -10- 0

Date	Entry	Amount
1764	**Andreas Gadiener**	
	bleibt schuldig [still owes]	0 - 0 - 10
1764		
May 4	Vor haber Trinken un Vor dem Gaul [for oats, drinking, and for the horse]	0 - 2 - 11
Aug: 23	1 q: bir 1/2 gill tram und Essen [eating]	0 - 1 - 0
1766	Andereas Gadinger	
July 30	2 q: haber 3 b: Bir un Essen [eating]	0 - 1 - 7
1763	**Martin Speck**	
Meÿ 29	1 q: seitereol	0 - 0 - 8
Octo 3	1 gill Rom 1 weck	0 - 0 - 5
1764	**Martin Speck**	
Mertz 7	3 b: seitereol	0 - 1 - 0
1767	**Conrad Philibÿ**	
October 29	1 q: Br: wein	0 - 0 - 10
1770		
January 15	1 b: wein	0 - 1 - 2
Febr: 12	1 1/2 jd schalun	0 - 4 - 6
Mertz 1	Credit Vor 1 Par strümb anzustricken [credit for knitting the feet into a pair of stockings]	0 - 1 - 0
Juny 12	1 q: Mallassis	0 - 0 - 10
1771		
Ap: 30	1 q: Mallassis	0 - 0 - 10
Juny 17	1 b: Rom	0 - 0 - 6
24	1 b: Rom	0 - 0 - 6
1772		
January 13	Gerechnet mit Conrad Philpÿ seiner Frau bleibt nichts [Settled with Conrad Philipy's wife. Owe nothing.]	

Date	Entry	Amount
No 43		
1762	**Johannes Neÿb**	
Dec 25	1 hut	0 - 4 - 0
4 Mertz	Vor Musslin	0 - 1 - 2
1765	**John Neff jugr**	
Sebtem: 2	1 wein schling	0 - 0 - 9
1766		
Febru 25	1/2 b: m: wein un 1 b: Bir	0 - 1 - 3
1771	**Becker Hannes** Bey Hamer [at the forge]	
Juny 17	1 b: wein 1 q: seiter	0 - 1 - 8
	Phillip Breiten Bach	
	15 lb schintel Nägel 2 lb Clapport Nägel	0 -17- 0
	Bezahlt an geld [paid in money]	0 -12- 0
1767	**Philipp Breitenbach**	
October 20	1/2 b: m: wein	0 - 1 - 0

No 44

1762	**Andres Miller**	
30 Dec	5 jert hasenbrick 0 - 7 - 6	
30	noch ein jert hasenbrick	0 - 1 - 6
	1/4 lb Beffer	0 - 0 - 9
1763		
5 Janarÿ	4 Jert hasenbrick	0 - 6 - 0
11 Janÿ	1/4 Jert radien	0 - 2 - 6
April 1	1 q: Rom 1/2 lb hut zucker	0 - 2 - 5
	Andreas Müller	
Meÿ 25	1 sattel	1 -15- 0
	1 1/2 viertheil stroh	
	d: 5t November 1763 gerechnet mit' Andreas Müller	
	bleibt schuldig	0 -16- 0
	[5 November 1763 settled with Andreas Müller. Still owes]	
1763		
5 Dec	wider vor schapp gut [again, for shopwares]	8 -12- 6
Nov: 14	1 q: thron	0 - 1 - 0
	2 Par schnallen	0 - 2 - 11
21	1 Namen Buch 2 bogen Babir	0 - 0 - 10
Jan: 13	1 q: thron	0 - 1 - 0
April 13	4 - 3/4 yd werckentuch 1 1/2 yd calmick 1/2 yd. schalun	0 -14- 5
May 4	3 q: Tar	0 - 1 - 6
31	1 beck saltz	0 - 1 - 6
July 2	1 q: Rom	0 - 1 - 2
7	1 q: seiteröl	0 - 0 - 8
Decem. 14	10 yd. Wercken Tuch	0 -16- 8
May 31 1765	bleibt schuldig vor Bend	0 -18- 0
	[still owes for bonds]	
1765		
Decem: 23	1 hut un 3 Par schnallen un 1 lb Zucker	0 -10- 10
1766		
January 15	4 lb: zucker	0 - 3 - 4
20	1 q: wine	0 - 2 - 4
26	2 lb: zucker	0 - 1 - 8
30	1 q: thron	0 - 1 - 0
Febiary 3	1 lb zucker	0 - 0 - 10
Mertz 10	1 lb schrot	0 - 0 - 7
Aprill 2	1 beck flags samen	0 - 2 - 0

No 45

1763	**Jacob Schaub**	
4 Januarÿ	bleibt schultig in der abregnung	4 -16- 2
	[still owes in the settlement]	
4 Janurÿ	noch vor Hosen[again, for pants]	0 - 7 - 6
27 Jan	1 beint seider öill	0 - 0 - 4
19 Febr:	gelent an geld seiner frau [lent in money to his wife]	0 - 5 - 0
9 April	verzehrt	0 - 1 - 10
Juny 22	4 q seiter und Essen	0 - 1 - 10
30	14 1/2 lb Letter	1 - 6 - 4
July 6	1 q: bir	0 - 0 - 6
11	1 stroh hut 1 yd. floret	0 - 3 - 4
	1 gill Rom	0 - 0 - 4
18	1/2 Beck Haber 1/2 gill Rom	0 - 0 - 10
Aug: 1	1 q: seiter	0 - 0 - 4
3	2 q: seiter	0 - 0 - 8

6	3 q: seiter 1 bol. mimm	0 - 2 - 0
8	1/2 b: m: wine 1 b: seiter	0 - 1 - 2
	gelent 1 schnäbel gebiss [lent one snout bit]	
24	1 q: 1/2 b: sitereol	0 - 0 - 10
	1 gill Rom	0 - 0 - 4
27	2 B: seitereol 1 weck	0 - 0 - 9
29	Essen 1 b: seitereol	0 - 0 - 8
30	1 b: seitereol	0 - 0 - 4
Sep: 5	1 lb unschlit	0 - 0 - 8
10	1 b: seiter	0 - 0 - 2
21	1 gill tram	0 - 0 - 3
24	1 q: seiter	0 - 0 - 4
27	1 q: Ditto	0 - 0 - 4
Octo 8	1 gill Rom	0 - 0 - 4
17	1 q: seiter	0 - 0 - 4
19	1 q: seiter	0 - 0 - 4
No 5	1 b: seiter und vor fleisch	0 - 0 - 4
7	1 Bett lad 1 p: schu	0 - 4 - 6
	1 gill tram	0 - 0 - 3
10	1 1/2 b: m: wein	0 - 3 - 0
14	1 q: seiter	0 - 0 - 4

No 46

1762	**Josep Fenck**	
29 Ap	1 schnub duch un 1/4 lb Bulfer	0 - 4 - 0
1763		
4 Jany	1 beint seider öill	0 - 0 - 4
10 Febr:	1/2 b: Rom 1/2 b: malassis	0 - 0 - 10
May 2	1 hut 1 par strümpff	1 - 9 - 6
1767		
January 25	1 q: Bir 1 gill Rom	0 - 0 - 10
31	2 q: seiter	0 - 0 - 8

1764	**Jost Schwertzler**	
Mertz 14	1/2 lb: Pulver	0 - 2 - 0
	1 q: seiter	0 - 0 - 4

1766	**George Sprely**	
29 Mertz	3 q: Br: wine un 1 q: Rom 2 lb Zucker	
	un 1 b: Bir Vor Essen un den Gaul bei Heu	0 - 7 - 9
	[For eating and the horse at hay]	

No 47

1763	**Andres Kapler**	
1 Jeny	ein bar hosen	0 -15- 0
1 Jeny	wider ein bar alden hosen	0 - 6 - 0

1766	**Nicolaus Zehrfass**	
October 18	Bezahlt auf den Weitzen	3 - 0 - 0
	3 b: M: wine 4 q: haber un 1 q: seiter	0 - 6 - 10

1767		
July 4	Bezahlt an Bolmans geld [paid on Bolman's money]	0 -18- 9
1763	**Mardin Brodtbeck**	
4 Junÿ	vor hosen	0 - 1 - 0
1764		
Jan 4	1 q: tron	0 - 1 - 0
1765	**Henrich Peffer**	
Febr: 1	2 buschel Haber gelehnt [lent two bushels vats]	
Mertz 20	1/2 b: wine 1 weck	0 - 0 - 9
1769	**Henrich Feffer**	
Octo: 25	1 b: M: wine	0 - 2 - 0
Nov 10	2 jd: kelch	0 - 4 - 0
12	1 q: seiter un 1 bogen Babir	0 - 0 - 5
	1 bol: mim	0 - 1 - 0
18	1 q: seiter	0 - 0 - 4
Decem: 7	1/4 lb: Peffer un 1/2 lb: alspeis un 1 q: seiter	0 - 2 - 2
23	1 buch Babir	0 - 1 - 6
1766		
Janary 8	gelehnt an geld [lent in money]	1 - 0 - 0
24	1 q: bir	0 - 0 - 6

No 48		
1762	**Lisabeda Bunschen**	
10 Julÿ	Vor Celsch	0 - 3 - 0
3 Feb	1 Jert un 1/4 Jert Camelot un netz	0 - 4 - 9
	vor 4 hasenbrick	0 - 2 - 0
1763	**Katharina Steinern**	
Nov: 7	1 yd Cattun	0 - 5 - 6
	Vor schwartz band	0 - 1 - 6
1765		
Decem: 25	Vor schab gut	0 - 6 - 3
1766		
Mertz 27	3 yd: Band	0 - 3 - 1
July 11	1/2 yd: weiss tuch	0 - 2 - 0
Sebtem: 16	1/2 yd: grin tuch un 1/2 yd hasen Brick	0 - 7 - 10
1768		
January 23	1 strang neths	0 - 0 - 2
		1 - 6 - 4
1762	**Cadarina Steinern**	
	vor schap gut	0 - 1 - 4
Febr: 15	1 schnup tuch	0 - 2 - 6
April 18	vor schap gut	0 - 7 - 10
1763	**Marilisabeth Steinern**	
July 25	1 1/4 yd tuch und neths	0 - 5 - 0
Aug: 8	1 q: thron	0 - 1 - 0
April 1776	**Philbena Beustlerin**	
7	1 stück weisen schnur	0 - 0 - 10
	2 yd Bendel	0 - 0 - 4

No 49

1762	**Hanss Peder Wolffersperger**	
	1 gallen Mallasis	0 - 4 - 0
	3 q rom	0 - 3 - 9
6 Nov	1 bodel bamel	0 - 4 - 6
17 Nov	1 q rom	0 - 1 - 3
29 Dec	1 q rom un calender	0 - 2 - 2
1763	**Petter Wolffersberger**	
June 22	2 sicheln	0 - 7 - 0
July 5	1 q: Rom	0 - 1 - 8
1763	**Petter Wolffersberger**	
Nov: 14	3 1/2 yd shallun	
	3/4 yd schäter 2 1/2 Doz Knöff 1 strengel seiten	0 -16- 0
Dec: 30	1/4 yd Cartun 3 yd floret	0 - 2 - 1
1764	**Petter Wolfersperger**	
Dcem: 6	1/4 lb: Pulver 1 lb: schrot	0 - 1 - 6
1765		
Mertz 4	1 q: Rom 1 b: wein	0 - 2 - 2
17	sein sohn [his son] 1 gill Rom 3 weck	0 - 0 - 7
Aprill 6	1 q: Rom	0 - 1 - 0
1765	**Peter Wolfersperger**	
May 19	1 q: wein	0 - 2 - 4
Juny 13	6 lb: Reiss	0 - 1 - 9
	35 lb: Nägel	1 -15- 0
1766		
January 8	2 hüt	0 - 8 - 0
	Abgerechnet mit Peter Wolfersperger d: 19tn May 1766 Bleibt nichts [Settled with Peter Wolfersperger, 19 May 1766. Owes nothing.]	
Juny 30	vor Endego	0 - 1 - 0
July 30	1/2 gallen Rom un vor segetgarn	0 - 3 - 0
Sebtm: 5	2 q: Rom	0 - 2 - 0
6	1 q: wein 1 lb: Zucker	0 - 5 - 2
16	2 q: bir un 1 q: Rom	0 - 2 - 0

No 50

1762	**Jacob Geib**	
	Auss zug 1 q mallasis	0 - 1 - 0
12 Aug	1 beint maderÿ wine	0 - 2 - 0
18 Aug	1 q fisch tron	0 - 1 - 0
1763		
febr: 17	1 q: seiter	0 - 0 - 4
	1 babirir doss	0 - 3 - 6
May 30	1 gill Tram	0 - 0 - 3
Sep 15	1 bottel	0 - 0 - 8
Octo 17	1 q: thron	0 - 1 - 0
April 20	1/4 catun	0 - 1 - 4
	1 sentz	0 - 5 - 0
Juny 30	1 q: thron	0 - 1 - 0
	d: 23 July 1764 gerechnet mit Jacob Geib bleibt Er schuldig [23 July 1764 settled with Jacob Geib. He still owes]	0 - 7 - 2
August 10	1 par strümpff	0 - 5 - 6
	1 Catechismus	0 - 1 - 0
January 4	1 Kap	0 - 3 - 0
Mertz 6	1 q: seiter	0 - 0 - 4
July 10	1 b: wine	0 - 1 - 2

1766		
Aprill 14	gelehnt an geld [lent in money]	0 -17- 0
1766		
1 November	Jacob Geib bleibt schultig der abrechnun [Jacob Geib still owes at settlement]	0 -14- 0

Johannes Ochsenman

1763		
6 Junÿ	1 Kap	0 - 3 - 3
	aus alten Buch fol: 11 [from the old book, page 11]	0 -19- 8
1764		
Nov: 26	4 lb: Negel	0 - 4 - 0
1765		
Aprill 13	4 lb: Negel	0 - 4 - 0
	abgerechnet mit Johannes Oxenman d: 19 ten May 1766 Bleibt er schultig auf alle abrechnung [Settled with Johannes Oxenman 19 May 1766. He still owes on all accounts]	6 - 0 - 1
October 18	1 q: seiter	0 - 0 - 4
	Credit	0 -15- 0
	abterechnet mit Johannes Oxenman d: 4 December 1769 Bleibt schultig [Settled with Johannes Oxenman 4 December 1769. Still owes]	7 - 0 - 4
1770		
Mertz 1	1 b: wein 1/4 lb: Imber	0 - 1 - 7

No 51

Philleb Wagner Nagelschmidt [nailsmith]

1762		
2 Julÿ	Auss zug 2 lb reiss	0 - 0 - 6
23 July	2 q rom	0 - 2 - 6
4 Octo	2 q seider öill	0 - 1 - 4
14 Nov	3 beint seideröill	0 - 1 - 0
17 Nov	vor wein	0 - 1 - 9
18 Nov	1 q seider	0 - 0 - 4
18 Nov	2 jert hasenbrick	0 - 3 - 0
1763		
29 Jan	gelent an gelt [lent in money]	1 - 2 - 6
Feb: 24	3 b: seitereol	0 - 1 - 0
25	2 q: seitereol 2 weck 1 yd Cattun	0 - 7 - 6
April 13	1 q: seitereol	0 - 0 - 8
April 18	3 b: seitereol 1 weck	0 - 1 - 1
21	verzehrt	0 - 3 - 0
	Bezahlt an geld	0 - 2 - 6
July 16	1 g: seitereol	0 - 0 - 8
30	1 q: seitereol	0 - 0 - 8
Sep 5	2 q: seitereol 1 weck	0 - 1 - 5
27	1/2 gill Rom	0 - 0 - 2
Nov: 7	3 q: seiter	0 - 1 - 0
Dec 6	2 q: seiter	0 - 0 - 8
22	2 q: seiter	0 - 0 - 8
12	1 q: thron	0 - 1 - 0

Die alt **Hans Weberin** [Old Mrs Hans Weber]

July 26	3 q: w: Rom un 2 q: bir	0 -13- 0

Fuchs auf der fornes [Fuchs at the furnace]

1766		
Aprill 5	1 q: seiter	0 - 0 - 4

No 52

1762	**Johannes Wolffersperger**	
4 Octo	1 buch bappier	0 - 1 - 2
20 Octo	1 1/4 jert krien duch un camel garn un vor rom	0 -18- 4
	vor die kirch geholt 1 q rom 2 q seider	
	[fetched. . . . for the church]	0 - 1 - 11
26 Dec	1/2 beint maderÿ wine	0 - 1 - 0
29 Dec	1 beint wine 1 weck un 1 q bier	0 - 1 - 9
1763		
29 Jan	1 q bier	0 - 0 - 6
Febr: 17	1/2 yd wüllen Tuch	0 - 7 - 0
April 1	1 b: seitereol	0 - 0 - 4
Mertz 7	1 b: m: wein	0 - 2 - 0
3	1: bol senckerÿ	0 - 1 - 6
May 2	1 q seiter 1 b: seiteroel	0 - 0 - 8
18	1 Catecismus	0 - 1 - 6
19	1 q: Rom	0 - 1 - 8
20	1 b: M: wein 1 bol. mim 2 weck	0 - 3 - 2
30	1 q bir	0 - 0 - 6
Juny 12	Credit	0 - 1 - 4
9 aug	6 jert flored	0 - 1 - 6
July 28	2 q: Brand wein	0 - 2 - 4
30	1 neb senckery 1 wein schling 4 weck	0 - 1 - 10
Aug 8	vor m: wein 1/2 gill rom 2 weck	0 - 1 - 8
Nov: 10	1 lb. Pech	0 - 0 - 4
14	1 b: wine	0 - 1 - 2
28	1 q: seiter	0 - 0 - 4
	von der schuttin matsch noch schuldig	0 - 8 - 0
	[still owes from the shooting match]	
1763		
Jan: 4	1/2 yd schallun 2 streng Camel garn	0 - 2 - 0
April 12	1 lb: Pulver	0 - 4 - 0
May 26	2 lb: Zucker	0 - 1 - 8
Oct 31	5 lb Nägel 300 schuhnägel	0 - 6 - 5
November 21	1 lb: Pulver 1 Par strümp 6 lb Nagel 1/2 b: warm wein	0 -12- 3
26	2 lb: Nägel	0 - 2 - 0
1765		
January 4	2 w: schling 3 weck	0 - 1 - 9
14	1/2 lb: alspeis	0 - 1 - 2
February 13	gelehnt an geld [lent in money]	3 - 0 - 0

No 53

1762	**Conrad Wolfahrd**	
29 Dec	Ein licht	0 - 2 - 6
29	1 q: seider	0 - 0 - 4
1763	**Michel Neaff** ju:	
July 16	1 bol senckerÿ 2 weck	0 - 1 - 8
1768	**Heÿry** auf der fornes	
July 24	1 bol Mim	0 - 1 - 0
1762	**Adem Paffenberger**	
	bleibt schultig vor tringen [owes for drinking]	0 - 3 - 6
	1 q seideröill	0 - 0 - 8
1 Nov	vor schlinck	0 - 0 - 6

1764	die **alt wolferspergern** [old Mrs. Wolfersperger]	
April 6	1 q: wein	0 - 2 - 4
	Bezahlt [paid]	0 - 1 - 0

No 54		
1762	**Stofel Meÿer**	
28 Dec	1 beint maderÿ wein	0 - 2 - 0
1763	**Stofel Meÿer**	
7 Janÿ	hat noch zu fodern an Alesender shafer vor arbeit [has coming form Alexander Schaeffer for labor]	2 -17- 6
May 23	1/2 b: m: wein	0 - 1 - 0
June 6	1 q: s. eol	0 - 0 - 8
July 16	1 bol senckerÿ 3 weck	0 - 1 - 9
25	1 bol senckerÿ	0 - 1 - 6
Aug	1 messer	0 - 0 - 8
	1 Neb: senckerÿ 3 weck	0 - 1 - 0
29	1 b: m: wein seiffen	0 - 2 - 3
Octo 24	1 q: seiter	0 - 0 - 4
Dec: 12	vor wein	0 - 0 - 6
	1 q: Rom 1/2 lb hut zucker	0 - 2 - 3

1763	**Michel Meÿer**	
7 Jany	hat noch zu fodern Alexander Shafer vor arbeid [has coming from Alexander Schaeffer for labor]	1 -15- 8
July 16	1 Bol senckery 3 weck	0 - 1 - 9
Aug 8	1 wein schling	0 - 0 - 9
Sep 5	1 sentz	0 - 5 - 6
Nov: 14	1 b: m: wein	0 - 2 - 0
1764		
Febru 19	1 b: seitereol 1 weck	0 - 0 - 5
Mertz 19	1 w: schling	0 - 0 - 9
April 26	vor Bunsch	0 - 0 - 8
28	1 w schling	0 - 0 - 9
	abgerechnet mit Michel Meÿer d: 17 September 1764. Bleibt no rest [settled with Michel Meÿer. No balance remains.]	
1764		
Sept 15	1/2 b: m: wein	0 - 1 - 0
19	1 b: wein	0 - 1 - 2
Oct 15	1 b: wein	0 - 1 - 2
November 21	1 b: seiteröl	0 - 0 - 4
1765		
	1/2 lb. Bulver	0 - 1 - 9
Febr: 2	1 gill Rom	0 - 0 - 4
Mertz 8	1 bole Mim 2 w: schling	0 - 2 - 6

No 55		
1762	**Georg Schmiedt**-beim Dorsttomes [at Dorst Thoma's]	
1 Dec	1 licht	0 - 2 - 9
1763	**Georg Schmitt** auff Stiegels Blatz [at Stiegel's place]	
Mertz 16	5 q: rom	0 - 8 - 4
21	1 b: seitereol	0 - 0 - 4

April 7	1 q: Rom	0 - 1 - 6
Juny 7	1 q: m: wein 1 q: seitereol	0 - 4 - 8
July 16	vor Rom bir und weck	0 - 3 - 0
Octo 20	1 q seiter	0 - 0 - 4

1762	**Henrich Schwertzler**	
Nov	bleibt schultig	0 - 3 - 3
1763		
22 Jan	1 dutzen beifen	0 - 0 - 8

1765	**George Schmitt** auf stigels Blatz	
Juny 13	1 sentz un 1 wetzstein un 1 hut	0 -12- 6
July 8	1 seichel	0 - 3 - 6
August 15	1 hut	0 - 4 - 0
Sebt 16	1 q: Thron	0 - 1 - 0
1766		
Mertz 3	1 b: wein	0 - 1 - 2
1768	**George Schmitt** auf stigels Blatz	
May 5	1 q: mallasis	0 - 0 -10
July 7	1 q: seiter	0 - 0 - 4
1769		
Seb 25	2 hüt	0 -15- 0
1770		
Oct 11	Vor Endengo	0 - 1 - 0

No 56		
1762	**Friedrich Bersing**	
21 Octo	Bleibt schultig in der abrechnung [Still owes in the settlement]	1 -19- 0
21 Octo	1 wein schlinck	0 - 0 - 9
25 Dec	1 beint bier	0 - 0 - 3
		2 - 0 - 0

1767	**Georg Heberling**	
July 6	1 sichel	0 - 2 - 6

1764	**William Dock**	
Mertz 19	1 1/2 q: seiter 1 weck	0 - 0 - 7

1766	**Hannickel Dinjes**	
Mertz 29	1 w: schling	0 - 0 - 9
1767		
July 4	2 1/4 yd: kelsch	0 - 7 - 11
Sebt 19	1 lb: schrot	0 - 0 - 6
30	1 b: wein 1/2 b: m: wein	0 - 2 - 2
		0 -11- 4

No 57		
1763	**Christian Bollender**	
8 Janÿ	1 buch	0 - 6 - 0
1764	**Christian Bollinger**	
Mertz 19	1 q: tarr	0 - 0 - 6

1763	**Johaness Hack**	
8 Juny	2 jert hasenbrick	0 - 3 - 0
	1 1/4 jert wullenduch	0 - 4 - 4
1764	**Johannes Hack**	
Febr: 18	1 q: s. eol 2 weck	0 - 0 - 10
	1 boll mim	0 - 1 - 0
1764	**Johannes Hack**	
Dember 1	1 q: seiteröl 1 weck	0 - 0 - 9
1765		
Febr 20	1 lb: Bleÿ 1 q: bir	0 - 1 - 1
Juny 1	gelehnt an geld [lent in money]	0 -18- 0

No 58		
1763	der **Simen** auf dem Hamer [Simen at the forge]	
8 Janÿ	Ein hut	0 - 7 - 6
	1 bol. senckery 1 seiten nestel	0 - 2 - 6
1767		
January 29	1 q seiteröl	0 - 0 - 8
31	1 q seiteröl	0 - 0 - 8
Febrary 2	1 b: seiteröl	0 - 0 - 4
5	1 gill gatschal	0 - 0 - 5
1769	Der **Simen** auf dem Hamer	
June 9	2 messer	0 - 1 - 8
1770		
Febru: 18	1 q: seiter 1 gill rom	0 - 0 - 8
1765	**Matheis Jacobÿ**	
Merz 8	2 Psalter	0 - 4 - 0
May 17	Bleibt schultig vor Kelsch [still owes for Kelsch]	0 - 3 - 0
1768		
April 26	Credit	0 - 2 - 6
1764	**Fischer Schneiter** sein Sohn [his son]	
Mertz 3	1 lb Bleÿ	0 - 0 - 7
1765	**David Glas Brenner**	
May 19	1 b: Rom 1 b: seiteröl	0 - 0 - 10

No 59		
1763	**Friedrich Wolffersperger**	
8 Jenÿ	1 beint seideröill	0 - 0 - 4
Febru: 18	Von Bernhards Vendu 2 p: strümpff	0 - 4 - 7
	[From Bernhard's sale 2 pairs of stockings]	
	1 1/2 yd Rattin a 9/0	0 -13- 6
1763	**Friedrich Wolffersberger**	
Juny 6	1 q: bir	0 - 0 - 6
9	1 q: bir	0 - 0 - 6
9 Aug	Ein hudt	0 - 7 - 6
9 Aug	vor wein	0 - 1 - 4
1763	**Frietrich Wolffersberger**	
De: 16	1 1/2 yd tuch	0 - 5 - 3

1764		
February 14	1 q: bir	0 - 0 - 6
Mertz 5	1 b: Wein	0 - 1 - 2
1764	**Friederich Wolfersperger**	
Mertz 12	8 q: Bir	0 - 3 - 4
14	1 q: Wein	0 - 2 - 4
19	2 gill Terpetinöl	0 - 1 - 0
	1 q: m: wein	0 - 4 - 0
	4 q: Bir	0 - 1 - 8
30	1 q: m: wein	0 - 4 - 0
Aprill 6	1 q: m: wein	0 - 4 - 0
9	vor saffran	0 - 1 - 0
	1 strang seiten un 1 strang Camel garn	0 - 1 - 2
12	1 q: M: wein	0 - 4 - 0
13	1 q: m: wein	0 - 4 - 0
May 7	1 q: Br: wein das Ewig geholt [1 quart brandy which Ewig fetched]	0 - 1 - 0
	1 q: bir	0 - 0 - 6
	1 q: m: wein	0 - 4 - 0
	1 q: m: wein	0 - 4 - 0
	1 b: wein essig	0 - 1 - 0
	1 yd Rattin	0 - 9 - 6
	vor schiessen von Reyers schuten metsch [for shooting at Reyer's shooting match]	0 -15- 0
July 28 1765	sein tochter [his daughter] 1/2 buch Babier	0 - 0 - 9
		3 - 5 - 3

No 60		
1762	**Jacob Philepe**	
1 Dec	1 schlosch	0 - 3 - 6
1763		
Juny 20	1 sichel	0 - 3 - 6
1764	**Jacob Phillipe**	
Octo 15	1/2 lb. Pulver	0 - 1 - 9
1766	**Jacob Phillipy**	
Jani 26	7 q: thron	0 - 7 - 0
1764	**Henrich Reiher**	
February 17	1 q: tarr	0 - 0 - 4
1765	**Jacob Bamberger**	
Juny 18	1 sentz	0 - 5 - 0

No 61		
1763	**Johannes Endres**	
9 Jenÿ	1 tschill tram	0 - 0 - 3
April 23	1 gill tram	0 - 0 - 3
Juny 12	1 1/2 Rom junior [= his son]	0 - 2 - 6
Juny 23	Vor Indigo und 2 lb Reis	0 - 3 - 1
July 6	1 yd Cattun	0 - 5 - 0

Sep 21	1 gallen thron	0 - 4 - 0
	d. 1st November 1763 abgerechnet mit Johannes Endres bleibt nichts [1 November 1763 settled with Johannes Endres. Owes nothing.]	
1763		
Dec: 16	4 q: fisch thron	0 - 4 - 0
	1 1/2 vierthel Cattun 2 p: strumpff Bendel 5 yd. floret	0 - 4 - 9
	aus alten buch vom 1760 jahr stehet noch das nicht verrechnet [from the old book from 1760 stands still unsettled]	0 - 9 - 2
	vor gewirts	0 - 1 - 0
1764	**Johannes Endres** alt [Sr.]	
May 12	1 b: wein	0 - 1 - 2
26	1/2 lb. Pulver	0 - 2 - 0
	2 lb: Zucker	0 - 1 - 8
29	1 halss tuch	0 - 5 - 6
Juny 18	sein dochter [his daughter] 3 yd: Camelot 2 strang seiten un 1 seiten nestel	0 -12- 11
	1 strang seiten	0 - 0 - 10
	2 yd: floret	0 - 0 - 8
Juny 20	1 wetstein	0 - 1 - 0
28	1 sichel	0 - 3 - 5
July 3	2 sichel	0 - 6 - 9
13	4 lb: Reiss	0 - 1 - 2
16	1/4 alspeis	0 - 0 - 6
	12 fisch	0 - 2 - 6
	Sein dochter [his daughter:] 1 1/2 viertel Camlot	0 - 2 - 1
	1/4 yd shalon	
	sein dochter [his daughter] 1 messer	0 - 0 - 8

No 62		
1763	**Michel Meÿser**	4 - 0 - 2
	1 beint maderÿ wein un vor deet	7 - 0 -11
14 Junÿ	Iber Ein lott und rend vor den Bareck und Aus den	1 - 0 - 0
	alden buch [for a deed for one lot and rent for the hill	5 - 0 - 5
	and from the old book]	2 - 5 - 0
1763	**Michael Meisser**	
No 5	1 q: Br: wein 1 q: seiter	0 - 1 - 4
De: 24	1 q: seol	0 - 0 - 8
May 1764 15	1 lb Zucker	0 - 0 - 10
21	1 q: seiteröl	0 - 0 - 8
22	1 q: bir	0 - 0 - 6
1764		
Decen: 6	1 b: seiteröl	0 - 0 - 4
1765		
Mertz 27	1 b: seiteröl	0 - 0 - 4
1765		
Mertz 27	1 b: seiteröl	0 - 0 - 4
May 27	1 b: seiteröl	0 - 0 - 4
July 2	1 q: seiteröl	0 - 0 - 8
Nov: 29	3 Par schnallen	0 - 1 - 6
1766		
Jan: 1	1 Bottel	0 - 0 - 9
May 17	1 q: Br: wein	0 - 1 - 0

19	1 q: seiteröl	0 - 0 - 8
	gelehnt an gelt vor Lorents Arnold	0 - 1 - 3
	[lent in money for Lorent Arnold]	
1763	**Jacob Berger**	
Sep 5	1 b: m: wein	0 - 2 - 0
	1 Wagen voll geschirr in Tolbenhacken geführt	
	[Driving one wagon load of things to Tulpehacken]	
April 25	1 w: schling un 5 weck	0 - 1 - 2
28	1 q: bir	0 - 0 - 6
May 27	1 b: seideröl	0 - 0 - 4
1765		
July 26	1 b: wein un 1 muschcaten nuss	0 - 1 - 6
Sep 27	1/4 lb: Pulver	0 - 0 - 11
Octo: 16	11lb: Negel	0 -11- 0
1766		
Jan: 15	1 q: Rom	0 - 1 - 0
May 17	1 feil	0 - 1 - 6

No 63		
1763	**Friedrich Walser**	
14 Jeny	1 bsalder	0 - 2 - 3
	Friedrich Walsser	
February 24	1 b: seitereol	0 - 0 - 4
April 27	1 b: wein	0 - 1 - 2
May 23	1 q: Tram	0 - 1 - 0
	Friedrich Walser	
July 28	3 yd. floret und natheln	0 - 1 - 0
October 28	1 q: tron	0 - 1 - 0
Dec: 23	1 q: thron	0 - 1 - 0
	1/2 gill Rom	0 - 0 - 2
	d: 11t May 1764 abgrechnet mit Frietrich Walsser. Bleibt nichts mehr [11 May 1764 settled with Friedrich Walser. Owes no more.]	
August 18	1 lb. schrott	0 - 0 - 7
November 15	2 q: Rom	0 - 2 - 0
1764	**Jacob Zartman**	
Decem: 19	1 1/2 q: seiter	0 - 0 - 6
1771		
Febr: 14	1 R. schling 1/2 gill Rom	0 - 0 - 8
1765	**George Conrad**	
Mertz 6	10 1/2 lb. fleisch vor schuck's Tochtermann	0 - 3 - 6
	[for Schuck's son-in-law]	
1765	**George Conrad**	
Augst 15	1 b: wein	0 - 1 - 2
Sebt 12	Vor schab gut	0 - 8 - 8
	1 b: m: wein	0 - 2 - 0
	1 b: wein	0 - 1 - 2
Octo: 10	1 licht	0 - 2 - 6
19	1 Kapp 1 Par strümb 1 buch	0 - 9 - 8
25	2 lb: Reiss	0 - 0 - 6
Nov 23	1 b: wein un 1 weck	0 - 1 - 3

No 64

1763	**Jacob Seltzer**	
18 Jan	1 tschil tram	0 - 0 - 4
	1 bsalder	0 - 2 - 3
Mertz 31	von bernhards Vendu 1 : strümpff [from Bernhard's sale 1 pair of stockings]	0 - 6 - 9
	vor Trinken Beÿ weinkauff [for drinking at the wine sale]	0 -17- 0
May 4	Jacob Seltzer bleibt schuldig von bernhards vendue [Jacob Seltzer still owes from Bernhard's sale]	0 - 6 - 9
Juny 7	1 b: m: wein	0 - 2 - 0
12	1 fuchs schwantz	0 -15- 0
Aug 20	1 q: Br: wein	0 - 1 - 2
Sept 27	5 buschel speltz	
Dec: 22	13 q Honig	0 -13- 0
22	1/2 viertel thee	0 - 1 - 3
26	Bezahlt vor Jacob Schenck [paid for Jacob Schenck]	3 - 0 - 0
1764	**Jacob Seltzer**	
Mertz 12	3 b: m: wein	0 - 6 - 0
April 28	1/2 b guten Rom	0 - 0 - 6
	1 strengel Camel garn un vor naths	0 - 0 - 9
July 12	7 1/2 lb: fleisch	0 - 1 - 10
16	1 q: Rom	0 - 1 - 0
	1 q: Rom	0 - 1 - 0
Aug: 12	1 q: Br: wein	0 - 1 - 0
1765	**Jacob Seltzer**	
Febru: 13	1 b: m: wein	0 - 2 - 0
Mertz 6	24 lb: fleisch	0 - 8 - 0
20	vor ein Diet	0 - 9 - 6
July 2	4 Buschel kleien	0 - 5 - 0
Decem 15	Haut Wigt 60 lb:	0 -12- 6
	abgerechnet mit Jacob Seltzer d: 15 February 1766 Bleibt er Schultig [settled with Jacob Seltzer 15 February 1766. He still owes.]	4 - 9 - 2
	bleibt noch schuldig vor der rechnung [still owes for the settlement]	0 -15- 0

No 65

1763	**Peder Gudman**	
22 Jan	Ein hut	0 -17- 6
1764	**Peter Gutman** alte	
Mertz 14	1 1/4 yd: Braun Thuch	0 -17- 6
19	2 feilen	0 - 1 - 0
Aprill 4	1 b: Rom	0 - 0 - 10
1766	**Peter Gutman** alte	
Juny 23	3 1/2 gill Rom	0 - 1 - 2
July 5	1/2 gill Rom	0 - 0 - 2
1767		
Augst 15	2 gill Br: wein	0 - 0 - 6
1768		
May 31	3 q: seiter	0 - 1 - 0

1763	**Wielen Färmer**	
22 Jan	1 tschill rom 1 q: seider	0 - 0 - 8

1765	**Johannes Schuhmacher**	
May 28	8 yd: bet Barget	2 - 0 - 0
	Bezahlt an geld	1 - 0 - 0
Octo: 7	vor 1 hut	0 - 3 - 6
	John Schuhmacher	
	Credit	0 -15- 0

No 66		
1763	**Henrich Leÿnenweder**	
18 Jan	1 q bier	0 - 0 -6
22 Jan	1 halb beint rom	0 - 0 - 6
Febru: 9	Auss Zug vom alte Buch fol: 129	1 - 5 - 5
	[Extract from the old book, p. 129]	
	2 q: Rom 1 q: m: wein 1 q: thron 1/2 hut Zucker vor 1/0 saffron	0 -10- 1
26	1 b: seitereol	0 - 0 - 4
April 27	1 tippig	0 -18- 6
Sep: 27	2q: Thron	0 - 2 - 0
Octobr 23	2 1/2 b: m: wein 1/2 beck haber 4 weck 1 peiff	0 - 4 - 0
	abgerechnet mit Henrich Leinenweber d: 13 Mertz 1764 bleibt no rest [settled with Henrich Leinenweber 13 March 1764. No balance remains.]	
1764		
May 15	1 q: wein	0 - 2 - 4
	1 band geschrieben [wrote one bond]	0 - 0 - 9
July 13	1 sichel	0 - 3 - 3
	1 q: bir	0 - 0 - 6
30	gelent an geld [lent in money]	0 - 1 - 10
1765		
Febru 17	1 1/2 lb hut zucker 3 kleine feilen un grosse feil 2 mittel gading	0 - 7 - 5
Mertz 6	1 q: bir	0 - 0 - 6
18	6 lb reiss 1 q: bir	0 - 2 - 3
30	2 b: m: wein 3 q: bir	0 - 8 - 6
Aprill 13	1 lb: zucker	0 - 0 - 10
19	2 b: m: wein	0 - 4 - 0
	1 yd: Kelsch un bendel	0 - 4 - 5
	1 q: Rom	0 - 1 - 0
	vor schnir un nodeln	0 - 1 - 0
May 1 1765	2 lb: zucker	0 - 1 - 8
	1 gill Rom	0 - 0 - 4
6	1/2 gill Rom	0 - 0 - 2
9	vor tram 1 q: seiter	0 - 0 - 7
	18 panes of glass	0 -13- 6
	2 q: Rom	0 - 2 - 0
1765	2 q: Rom 1 q: seiter	0 - 2 - 4
	muss Henrich Leineweber hauss rent zahlen [Henrich Leineweber must pay house rent]	9 - 0 - 0
1765	ist eingezogen 15 April 1765 [moved in 15 April 1765]	

No 67

1763	**Christian Berhart**	
24 Jan	1 q tram	0 - 1 - 0
25 Jan	1 q seider	0 - 0 - 4
25 Jan	1 q tram	0 - 1 - 0
26	1 q bier	0 - 0 - 6
27 Jan	1 q seider	0 - 0 - 4
29 Jan	vor seider	0 - 0 - 6
1763	d: 21 Feb Habe gerechnet mit Christian Bernhard bleibt schuldig nach der rechnung [February 21 settled with Christian Bernhard. Still owes after the settlement.]	5 -15- 11
	Christian Bernhart Extra	
Febru: 26	1 q: tram	0 - 1 - 0
Mertz 5	2 b: seitereol 2 q: seiter	0 - 1 - 4
15	1 q: tram	0 - 1 - 0
April 7	1 b: Rom 1 B: tram	0 - 1 - 4
13	1 b: Brandwein	0 - 0 - 6
23	1 b: Brandwein	0 - 0 - 6
Sep 10	1 q: Rom	0 - 1 - 6
1764		
July 2	1 q: seiter	0 - 0 - 4
1766		
Aprill 25	1 q: seiter	0 - 0 - 4

1767	**Andereas Mohr**	
Junuary 13	1 1/4 yd: gestrefelt Zeug	0 - 4 - 10

July 1766	**Henrich Simon**	
9	1/2 b: m: wein 3 q: haber	0 - 1 - 6

No 68

1763	**Johannes Weber**	
24 Jan	1 q bier	0 - 0 - 6

1767	**John Clerck**	
Septem: 25	1/4 lb Pulver	0 - 0 - 11
	1 gill Baumöhl	0 - 0 - 8
	1 bottel un 3 flintenstein	0 - 1 - 4
	1 w: schling 1/2 b: wein	0 - 1 - 4
1767	**John Klerck**	
October 12	1/2 b: wein	0 - 0 - 7
	John Clerck	
	1/4 lb Pulver 1/2 lb schrot 1 flintinstein	0 - 1 - 6

1763	**Daniel Clerck**	
July 19	1 q seiter	0 - 0 - 4
	sein dochder [his daughter] 6 weck	0 - 0 - 6
	1/4 lb: Peffer 1/4 lb: alspeis	0 - 1 - 6
Decem: 13	sein John vor 1 schnall	0 - 0 - 10
	sein Daniel 1 R: schling un 3 Peiffen	0 - 0 - 9
Decem: 25	1 lb: zucker un 1 b: wein un 1 bottel John	0 - 2 - 10
	sein Dannel 1 q: Bir und 1 B: Rom	0 - 1 - 1
1766		
Aprill 14	sein Danel 1 q: bir	0 - 0 - 6
May 20	sein Danel 2 gill Rom	0 - 0 - 8
July 28	ein Danel 1 sentz	0 - 4 - 0

Augst 25	sein Danel 2 q: Bir	0 - 1 - 0
Decem: 8	1/4 lb: Pulver 4 flintenstein 1 lb: schrot	0 - 1 - 11
1767		
May 1	sein Danel 2 q: Rom	0 - 2 - 0
Octo: 20	alt 1 q: Rom	0 - 1 - 0
	1 q Rom	0 - 1 - 0

No 69

1763	**Johannes Flicker**	
27 Jan	2 gallen rom	0 - 12- 0
1763	**Johannes Flicker**	
Dec: 17	1 q: Rom	0 - 1 - 6
1768	**Paul Lepo**	
Febrary 5	1 b: m: wein und Essen vor zweÿ mann [food for two men] un 1 q: bir	0 - 4 - 2
1768		
January 11	1 gill Rom	0 - 0 - 4
1763	**Johannes Dinjus**	
Sep 27	6 q: thron 1 q: Br: wein	0 - 7 - 0
Octo 17	1 q: Br: wein 2 Peiffen	0 - 1 - 2
24	1 q: Br: wein	0 - 1 - 2
	1 q: Rom	0 - 1 - 6
1765	**Adam Bach**	
Feb: 4	1 zinner bottel 1/2 b: Rom	0 - 3 - 6

No 70

1763	**Georg Medes**	
29 Jan	vor duch	0 - 9 - 6
Febr: 12	1 beint seideröill	0 - 0 - 4
	1 b seitereol	0 - 0 - 8
1766	**Filbina Beustlerin**	
Mertz 17	1 b: wein	0 - 1 - 2
	gelehnt vor ein Haltz Tuch [lent for a neckarchief]	0 - 5 - 9
Aprill 7	1 stuck weisen schnir	0 - 0 - 10 [blotched]
	2 yd: Bendel	0 - 0 - 4
1763	**Phillib Kiesecker**	
29 Jan	gelend an gelt [lent in money]	4 - 0 - 0
	Bezahlt in geld [paid in money]	2 - 0 - 0
	Phillip Kiesecker	
July 25	1 q: seiter	0 - 0 - 4
January 29	1 yd Cattun 2 yd floret	0 - 6 - 2
1764	**Phillip Kiesecker**	
May 7	ist schuldig wegen Wilhelm Besch [owes on the account of Wilhelm Besch]	<u>3 -12- 0</u>
October 9	Bezahlt an geld [paid in money]	<u>2 -12- 0</u>

1765	**Phillip Kiesecker**	
Febr: 4	1/2 b: m: wein	0 - 1 - 0
9	gelehnt an geld in Leditz [lent in money in Lititz]	0 - 1 - 0
Aprill 10	sein tochter [his daughter] 1/2 yd: Lahn	0 - 6 - 0
	Bezahlt [paid]	0 - 6 - 0
Decem: 29	1/2 lb alspeis	0 - 1 - 2
	sein tochter 1 q wein un 1 bottel gelehnt [his daughter borrowed. . .]	0 - 2 - 4

No 71		
1763	**Jacob Widmer**	
29 Jan	1 q seider	0 - 0 - 4
Juny 24	1 sichel 1 yd flored	0 - 3 - 11
1763	**Jacob Wittmer**	
Nov: 4	1 b: Br: wein	0 - 0 - 6
	2 Bol m: senckery wegen dem Babelbaum von Michel Trion [2 bowls M. Sangrea wine, on account of Michel Trion's poplar tree]	0 - 4 - 6
1769		
February 2	2 lb: Butter	0 - 1 - 2
		0 - 6 - 2
1764	**Jacob Witmer**	
July 23	2 q: seiter	0 - 0 - 8
	4 q seiter	0 - 1 - 4
Aug 10	1 Neb bunsch	0 - 0 - 6
Decem: 1	1 q: Bir 1 weck	0 - 0 - 7
19	1 yd: Catun	0 - 5 - 6
Octo: 1	1 b: thron	0 - 0 - 6
7	1 1/2 q: thron	0 - 1 - 6
25	1 b: wein	0 - 1 - 2
1763	**Adam Meisser**	
Febr: 8	1 licht	0 - 2 - 6
1763	**Stras borger schneitern** [Strasburg tailor]	
Juny 8	1 lb zucker	0 - 0 - 9
Octob 8	vor Cattun und bendel	0 - 1 - 6
1764	**Adam Meisser**	
November 19	6 lb Negel	0 - 6 - 0
21	3 b: seiteröl	0 - 1 - 0
24	2 lb negel	0 - 2 - 0
26	1/2 buschel Har	0 - 0 - 7

No 72		
1761 [sic]	**Georg Meisser**	
Decem: 16	1/2 beint ma. wein u: 5 quart bier	0 - 3 - 1
1763		
Jan: 18	2 beint Matherÿ wein	0 - 4 - 0
24	vor wein	0 - 1 - 5
29	1 schling und gill rom und zweÿ lb zucker	0 - 2 - 4
Febru: 2	1 beint materÿ wein	0 - 2 - 0
25	1/2 b: M: wein	0 - 1 - 0

1763	**Georg Meisser**	
Dec 15	6 B: m: wein	0 -12- 0
	2 weck	0 - 0 - 2
	noch schuldig von schuttin mätsch [still owes from the shooting match]	0 -10- 0
	vor saffran 1 lb zucker	0 - 1 - 4
		1 - 3 - 6
1765	**George Meisser**	
Novem 10	1 lb Pulver un 3 lb: Bleÿ un 2 q: seiter	0 - 5 - 8
1766		
July 7	1 buschel Buchweitzen	0 - 2 - 6
28	4 1/2 4 yd: Zwillig 1/2 b: m: wein	0 -17- 0
1763	**Jacob Scheurer**	
Sep 24	Vor schap gut	0 - 9 - 0
1765	**Felden Urich**	
Octo 25	1 q: m: wein	0 - 4 - 0
1766		
May 1	1 gill Rom 3 q: Bir	0 - 1 - 10
1767		
Mertz 23	1 1/2 gill Rom	0 - 0 - 6
1768		
Apr: 26	1 gill Rom 1 q: Bir	0 - 0 - 10

No 73		
1760	**Abraham Stumpff**	
24 Nov:	Bleibt schuldig in der abrechnung [still owes in the settlement]	1 -16- 7
Decem:	die Vendu ist nicht Verrechnet [the sale is not accounted for]	
28	vor Bendel	0 - 1 - 1
29	Vor allspeiss und Imber	0 - 1 - 9
1761		
18 Jan:	1 beint Molasses und 1/2 gill Baumoel	0 - 0 - 10
28 Juny	2 quart tram	0 - 2 - 0
8 Julÿ	1 quart und 1 beint tram	0 - 1 - 6
9	7 gallen tram gebrendt [distilling 7 gallons whiskey]	0 - 8 - 2
29	1/2 lb: Pfeffer	0 - 1 - 6
12 Aug:	1 beint wein und 1 muscatnuss	0 - 1 - 2
1762		
4 April	1 beint Rom und safferan	0 - 1 - 10
27 May	1 beint mathery wein	0 - 2 - 0
4 April	1 q wein	0 - 2 - 0
27 July	1 quart malasses	0 - 1 - 0
25 Aug	1 q Rom	0 - 1 - 3
6 Octo:	3/4 Blau tuch und 2 dutzend Knöpff	0 -10- 10
		3 -13- 6
	fon der Vendu vom 24t Novem: 1759 [from the sale of 24 Novem. 1759]	0 -13- 11
	auss dem vendu zettel von 27. Dec: 1758 [from the sale bill of 27 Dec. 1758]	0 - 3 - 0
1763		
Mertz 19	1 b: seitereol	0 - 0 - 4

1763	den 9 tag maÿ gerechnet mit Abrahm Stumpff bleibt schultig [9 May settled with Abraham Strumpff. Still owes]	3 - 1 - 9
April 30	2 bol mimm	0 - 2 - 0
May 7	1 b: seitereol	0 - 0 - 4
	Bezalt an geld [paid in money]	3 - 0 - 0
1763		
July 9	1 lb: zucker	0 - 0 - 10
Octo 25	1/2 b: wein	0 - 0 - 7
No: 29	1/4 lb: Peffer un 1/4 lb: alspeis	0 - 1 - 7
	Credit vor 1 Raconen Haut [Credit for one raccoon skin]	0 - 2 - 6
	abgerechnet mit Abraham Stumb d: 24tn Juny 1766 Bleibt nichts [Settled with Abraham Stumb 24 June 1766. Owes nothing.]	
July 1	1 q: m: wein	0 - 4 - 0
Augst 11	1 q: Rom 1 q: thron	0 - 2 - 0
1764		
July 23	2 bol senckery	0 - 3 - 0
25	6 q: Br: wein	0 - 4 - 6

No 74

1760

Casper Iba

24 Dec:	Ein Hut	0 -13- 0
1761		
20 April	1 gill tram	0 - 0 - 3
20 April	1 quart seiter	0 - 0 - 4
6 Febr:	2 beint materÿ wein	0 - 4 - 0
13 Febr:	2 quart Beir	0 - 0 - 10
13 Febr:	1 beint wein	0 - 1 - 0
30 Junj	1 quart Bier	0 - 0 - 5
1762		
29 Febr:	1 qart Ditto	0 - 0 - 6
18 Mertz	6 qart Honig	0 - 6 - 0
18 Mertz	5 yd beÿ und farb	0-17- 11
12 Aug:	2 beint m: wein	0 - 4 - 0
23 Aug:	1 beint matherÿ wein	0 - 2
12 Sep:	1 Bohl mimm	0 - 1 - 0
27	1 b: wein	0 - 2 - 0
1 Octo:	1 beint ma: wein	0 - 2 - 0
26 Nov:	1 quart seiter	0 - 0 - 4
30 Nov:	2 yd schallun	0 - 5 - 8
11 Dec:	1/2 gill Rom	0 - 0 - 2
30 July	1/2 lb. Pulfer	0 - 2 - 3
1763		
18 Jan:	1 quart Bier	0 - 0 - 6
18 Jan:	Vor seiter	0 - 0 - 3
	Credit	0 - 1 - 8

No 75

1763

Michael Leckes

Februa: 7	1/2 Viertels lb the und 2 lb zucker	0 - 2 - 10
	1 quart seiter	0 - 0 - 4
	1 schnupf tuch von der Vendue [from the sale]	0 - 2 - 9

	Georg Strohm	
1767		
July 6	1 b: Baumöl	0 - 1 - 2
1771		
Juny 24	1 q: seiteröl 1 gill Rom	0 - 1 - 0

	Georg Magnus Conrad	
1763		
Febru: 8	4 quart seiter	0 - 1 - 4
	auss zug vom alten buch folio 15 [extract from the old book, page 15]	3 - 1 - 11
	Mehr von folio 162 [more from page 162]	0 -16- 5
24	1 q: fisch thron	0 - 1 - 0
26	1 b: seitereol	0 - 0 - 4
5 Mertz	4 b: Ditto 1 q: seiter	0 - 1 - 8
7	1 q: seiter	0 - 0 - 4
12	2 q: seiter	0 - 0 - 8
19	4 1/2 q: seitereol	0 - 3 - 0
3 April	1 1/2 q: seitereol	0 - 1 - 0
22 Mertz	3 q: seiter	0 - 1 - 0
22 Mertz	2 buschel weitzen a 6/0	0 -12- 0
	1 q: fisch tron	0 - 1 - 0
12	1 q: seitereol	0 - 0 - 8
April 18	1 q: Ditto 1 q: Rom	0 - 2 - 4
21	1 q: bir	0 - 0 - 6
28	2 buschel weizen	0 -12- 0
30	1 b: seitereol	0 - 0 - 4
May 2	gelent [lent]	0 -15- 0
23	1 q: bir	0 - 6 - 0

	Casper Ipa	
No 75 [sic]		
Febru: 1763		
15	Bleibt schuldig nach der abrechnung [Still owes after the settlement]	3 -17- 0
Aug: 6	1 bol mim	0 - 1 - 0
Sep: 10	1 q: seiter	0 - 0 - 4
30	1/2 b: wein	0 - 0 - 7
	1 q: Br: wein	0 - 1 - 0
	1 Bol. senckery	0 - 1 - 6

	Casper Iba	
1766		
23 juny	1 q: Br: wein	0 - 1 - 0
Augst 15	1/2 b: m: wein	0 - 1 - 0
Sebt 3	1 q: seiter	0 - 0 - 4
Octob: 7	1/2 gill Rom	0 - 0 - 2
Novem: 1	1 b: Br: wein	0 - 0 - 5
Febrary 5	gelehnt an geld [lent in money]	1 - 5 - 0
1767		
Aprill 28	1/2 b: m: wein	0 - 1 - 0
May 20	1 q: seiter	0 - 0 - 4
	Cridit	1 - 0 - 0
Septem: 21	1 b: wein	0 - 1 - 2
Novem: 10	Credit vor weck	0 - 3 - 0
18	1 q: Rom	0 - 1 - 0
1768		
January 14	1 q: m: wein	0 - 4 - 0
February 6	1/2 gill Rom	0 - 0 - 2
8	1 gil rom	0 - 0 - 4
Mertz 14	1 q: Rom	0 - 1 - 0

	Jacob Wolff	
1764		
October 11	1/2 yd. kelsch	0 - 2 - 6
1765		
January 14	1 1/2 yd: flenel 1/2 lb Zucker	0 - 5 - 8

No 76

	Dewalt Schanck	
Jan: 7	1 beint m: wein	0 - 2 - 0
	und das ist Bezahlt [and that has been paid]	
	hundsfut und spitzbub [mild, but coarse expletives]	
April 1	Vor trinken bei Handel	0 -14- 4
Mertz 24	1 q: seitereol	0 - 0 - 8

1763	**Der gross Schwob** [The tall Swabian]	
May 20	1 par schnallen	0 - 1 - 6
	[above entries crossed out]	

1763	**Conrad Kratzinger**	
May 20	1 par schnallen	0 - 1 - 6
Juny 2	1 b: Rom	0 - 0 - 10
July 3	1 gallen Rom 1 1/2 q: s. eol	0 - 7 - 9
Decem: 19	1 1/2 lb Pulfer 1 lb: schrot 4 feÿerstein 2 beint seideröl	0 - 7 - 10
	Conrad Kratzinger bleibt schuldig vor 4 q: fisch tron	0 - 0 - 11
	[Conrad Kratzinger still owes for 4 qt. fish oil]	

1763	**Dewald Schanck**	
October 12	Bleibt schuldig in der abrechnung	2 -16- 4
	[Still owes in the settlement]	
	1/2 lb Pulver	0 - 2 - 0
	2 b: m: wein	0 - 4 - 0
	1/2 b: Rom 1 gill Rom	0 - 0 - 10
	gaul bei heu [horse at hay]	0 - 0 - 6
		3 - 3 - 0
1766		
December 6	abgerechnet mit Devald Schanck d: 6 December 1766	
	Bleibt er schultig [settled with Devald Schanck 6 December 1766. He still owes.]	0 -10- 4
1767		
Marz 9	vezehrt	0 - 3 - 0
Aprill 10	1 q: Rom 1 q: seiter 1/2 beck Haber un 1 Bottel	0 - 2 - 9
Juny 8	2 q Bir 1 q: seiter	0 - 1 - 4
1767		
Augst 25	1 b: m: wein	0 - 2 - 0
	verzehrt	0 - 4 - 0
Nov: 10	4 b: m: wein 1 glas verbrochen [1 broken glass] 4 q: seiter 4 q: haber	0 -12- 0

No 77

1763	**Peter Bohre**	
Mertz	übertrag von folio 23 [brought over from page 23]	0 - 4 - 5
4	1 b: seiter eol	0 - 0 - 4
7	1 q: seiter	0 - 0 - 4

25	1 q: seiter	0 - 0 - 4
29	1 1/2 b: seitereol	0 - 0 - 6
1 Apr:	1/2 gill anis	0 - 0 - 3
April	1 b: seitereol	0 - 0 - 4
12	1 q: seiter 1 b: seitereol	0 - 0 - 8
Juny 12	Credit vor 1 kalbhaut wgt 6 1/2 lb [Credit for 1 calf's skin weighing 6 1/2 pounds]	
	1 q: seiter	0 - 0 - 4
July 6	2 lb Pulver zum Brunen [to the fountain]	0 - 8 - 6
25	1 q: seiter	0 - 0 - 4
Aug 6	1 bol mimm	0 - 1 - 0
11	1 b: wein	0 - 1 - 2
18	1 lb Pulver	0 - 4 - 3
20	1 b: seitereol	0 - 0 - 4
29	1 q: seitereol	0 - 0 - 8
7	1 gill Rom 1 b: seitereol	0 - 0 - 8
	1 hut	0 - 7 - 6
Novem:	Vor Heu	1 - 0 - 0
24	1/2 gill Rom	0 - 0 - 2
	2 buschel weitzen gelehnt [lent]	
25	1 gill Rom	0 - 0 - 4
Dec: 20	1/2 gill Rom	0 - 0 - 2
24	1 gill Rom	0 - 0 - 4
26	1 gill Rom	0 - 0 - 4
	1/2 gill Rom	0 - 0 - 2
1764		
Jan: 1	1 q: thron	0 - 1 - 0
	1 gill Rom	0 - 0 - 4
	1/2 gill Rom 1 q: seiter	0 - 0 - 6
	1/2 b: m: wein 1/2 gill Rom	0 - 1 - 2
	1 q: bir	0 - 0 - 6

No 78

1763	**Friedrich Casimir Müller** Pr[eacher]	
7 Febru:	1/2 lb: thee	0 - 5 - 6
25 Mertz	1 b: m: wein	0 - 2 - 0
	Aus Zug Vom alten buch fol: 161 [Extract from the old book, p. 161]	2 - 0 - 6
Aug 8	1/2 lb hut zucker	0 - 0 - 9
October 11	vor schap gut	5 - 6 - 1
	Frietrich Müller Bleibt shuldig in der abrechnung [Frietrich Müller still owes in the settlement]	6 - 4 - 10
1764		
Novem: 26	2 q: m: wein	0 - 8 - 0
1765		
Augst 11	1 Par strümb	0 - 6 - 0
1766		
Maj 23	1/2 buschel haber gelehnt [lent]	
29	gelehnt an gelt [lent in money]	0 -16- 0
Juny 19	1 q: Rom	0 - 1 - 0
Augst 11	1 b: m: wein	0 - 2 - 0
Sebt: 5	1/2 b: m: wein	0 - 1 - 0
	2 yd: kelsch un 4 yd: Bendel	0 - 7 - 8

1763	**Friedrich Müller** junior	
	1 pahr strüpff	0 - 5 - 0
	1 1/2 yd wercken tuch	0 - 2 - 6
	1 pahr schnallen	0 - 1 - 8
	1 hut	1 - 4 - 0
	vor kelsch und knöpff und tuch	0 - 7 - 9
	1 hut	0 - 6 - 6
	1 par schnallen	0 - 1 - 9
	vor tuch und mehr	0 -16-
	vor leintuch	0 - 0
	gelent [lent]	3 - 0 - 0
	1 b: m: wein	0 - 2 - 0
	An geld vor schneiter [money for the tailor]	0 - 2 - 0
	1 p schnallen	0 - 1 - 0
	gelent [lent]	0 - 2 - 6
	1 q: seiter	0 - 0 - 4
	Vor schap wahr	0 - 9 - 0
		7 - 1 - 11

No 79		
1763	**Henrich Keÿler**	
	übertragen von folio 22 [brought over from page 22]	7 - 5 - 6
Mertz 21	3 b: seitereol	0 - 1 - 0
Mertz 21	3 b: Ditto	0 - 1 - 0
22	1 q: seiter	0 - 0 - 4
1 April	1 q: seitereol 1 hut 2 gill Rom	0 - 6 - 4
1 April	1 q: seitereol	0 - 0 - 8
3	Bar geld	0 - 0 - 2
4	1 1/2 gill Rom	0 - 0 - 6
12	1 b: m: wein	0 - 2 - 0
	Mehr vor trinken [more for drinking]	0 - 0 - 8
13	1 fingerhut	0 - 0 - 3
	2 q: seitereol	0 - 1 - 4
19	Vor trinken und schap gut	0 - 1 - 7
May 3	1 q: seiter	0 - 0 - 8
4	1 q: seitereol	0 - 0 - 8
13	1/4 yd cattun 4 yd floret bendel	0 - 2 - 5
		8 - 9 - 7

1763	**Henrich Keÿler**	
Juny 22	1 Messer 1 b: Rom	0 - 1 - 8
23	2 lb doback 1 q: seiter 1 b: tram	0 - 1 - 8
July 30	1 1/2 q: seiter 1 b: Rom	0 - 1 - 4
July 30	1 b: seitereol	0 - 0 - 4
Aug 2	1 gill Rom 1 Rom schling	0 - 0 - 10
20	1 schling	0 - 0 - 6
21	1 q: Br: wein	0 - 1 - 2
Sep: 6	1 b: seitereol	0 - 0 - 4
7	1 yd Cattun 1 fingerhut	0 - 5 - 3
10	1 schling 1/2 gill tram	0 - 0 - 8
19	2 q: seiter	0 - 0 - 8
Octob 3	1 q: thron 2 yd bendel 2 yd floret und neths	0 - 2 - 2
17	2 q: seiter	0 - 0 - 8
18	1 b: seitereol	0 - 0 - 4

No 80

1763	**Lorentz Keller** Brouer [brewer]	
	Bracht über von folio 8 [brought over from page 8]	5 -10- 8
Mertz 5	1 b: m: wein	0 - 2 - 0
12	1 b: seitereol	0 - 0 - 4
30	1 b: m: wein	0 - 2 - 0
April 27	2 b: m: wein	0 - 4 - 0
May 19	1 bol mimm	0 - 1 - 0
1763	d: 8t Juny 1763 gerechnet mit Lorentz Keller bleibt schuldig [8 June 1763 settled with Lorentz Keller. Still owes]	3 - 3 - 3
Juny 20	1 q: seitereol	0 - 0 - 8
20	1 b: m: wein	0 - 2 - 0
22	1 bol. mim	0 - 1 - 0
24	1 q: seitereol	0 - 0 - 8
25	1 q: seitereol	0 - 0 - 8
29	1 b: seitereol	0 - 0 - 4
30	1 q: Bir	0 - 0 - 6
1 July	1/2 gill Bitters	0 - 0 - 3

1763	**Wilhelm Ewig**	
May 19	1/2 b: wein 1 weck	0 - 0 - 9
	bleibt schultig [still owes]	0 - 0 - 6

	Lorentz Keller	
July 3	1 b: seol	0 - 0 - 4
5	1 b: Ditto	0 - 0 - 4
6	1 q: Bir	0 - 0 - 6
14	1/2 gill Genever	0 - 0 - 3 (?) [page torn away]
16	1 b: m: wein 1 bol mim 2 q: bir	0 - 4 - 0
16	1/2 hut zucker 2 Lichter	0 - 1 - 0
25	1 b: m: wein	0 - 2 - 0
Aug 6	1 1/2 q: seiter 2 weck	0 - 0 - (?)
15	2 bol mimm	0 - 2 - 0
	1 q: seiter	0 - 0 - (?)
22	1 b: seitereol 1 schling	0 - (?) - (?)

No 81

1763	**John Breght**	
	Auss Zug vom alten buch fol. 104 [Extract from the old book, page 104}	0 -16- 0
Febru: 15	2 1/2 buschel weitzen	0 -10- 0
17	3 1/2 lb unschlitt	0 - 2 - 4
Mertz	1 1/2 b: m: wein	0 - 3 - 0
12	1 b: seitereol	0 - 0 - 4
19	1 b: m: wein	0 - 2 - 0
April 21	1 q bier	0 - 0 - 6
Juny 13	5 lb speck	0 - 2 - 6
	1 Hut Zucker 1 bottel Baumoehl	0 -14- 3
	1/2 virtel lb peffer	0 - 0 - 4
Nov: 14	1 1/2 b: m: wein	0 - 3 - 0
Dec: 22	1 1/2 buschel weitzen	0 - 3 - 0
		2 - 3 - 3

1764	**Johannes Brecht**	
February 17	1 boll mim	0 - 1 - 0
19	1 b: wein	0 - 1 - 2
	vor Kellers Merr	6 - 0 - 0
Sep 15	80 Leims und heu	1 -10- 0
21	1 bol leims bunsch	0 - 1 - 6
	2 q: matherÿ wein	0 - 8 - 0
1765		
January 4	vor holtz	0 - 4 - 0
Febr 1	1 b: m: wein	0 - 2 - 0
May 27	7 lb unschligt	0 - 4 - 1
Juny 12	1 q: bir	0 - 0 - 6
Augst 11	gelehnt an geld [lent in money]	3 - 0 - 0
	Bezahlt [paid]	0 - 0 - 0
Octo: 16	1/2 lb: bulver	0 - 0 - 10
1766		
Mertz 31	3 1/4 lb: hut zucker	0 - 4 - 11
	6 gallen un 1 q: un 1 b: m: wein gelehnt [lent]	
April 7	1 q: m: wein gelehnt [lent]	
10	1 q: m: wein gelehnt [lent]	
14	1 q: m: wein gelehnt [lent]	
20	3 q: m: wein gelehnt [lent]	

No 82		
1763	**Michael Hag**	
Febr: 15	Vor cattun	0 - 8 - 0
Mertz 12	1 b: wein	0 - 1 - 2
17	2 q: Brandwein	0 - 2 - 0
April 9	Vor 10 fisch 6 q haver	0 - 3 - 2
	5 Dickens	2 - 8 - 9
July 16	vor Leinen tuch	0 - 7 - 6
	gelent an geld [lent in money]	42-0 - 0
Dec: 19	3/4 yd tuch 1 p: Lederne hosen 1 p: hosen schnallen und neths und 1 hut	1 -11- 9
22	gelent vor den Heffner [lent for the potter]	0 - 2 - 8
Janu	1/2 lb Peffer 1/2 lb alspise	0 - 2 - 6
14	8 yd Camlot 1 strang seiten und vor neths	2 - 1 - 6
30	Vor eissen	6 - 0 - 0
1765	vor Br: wein Brennen 41 gallen a 1/0 [for distilling brandy, 41 gallons at 1/0]	2 - 1 - 0
January 10	1 w: schling	0 - 0 - 9
19	1 b: m: wein	0 - 2 - 0
Feb: 20	1 lb: bleÿ	0 - 0 - 6
Mertz 27	bezahlt vor ihn beÿ Peter Ried vor tuch zu machen [paid **Peter Ried** for him for making [i. e. weaving] cloth]	0 - 5 - 10
Aprill 13	1 hut	0 - 3 - 0
May 27	vor Schab gut vor sein mad [for shop wares for his maid]	2 - 0 - 10
Sebt 30	1 b: m: wein	0 - 2 - 0
	vor endego	0 - 2 - 0
Octo 16	2 lb: Bleÿ	0 - 1 - 0
Decem: 25	2 1/2 yd druget un 1 dutzet Knöp un Camel garn	0 - 8 - 0

1766		
Mertz 3	3 lb zucker	0 - 2 - 6
17	gelehnt an geld [lent in money]	0 - 7 - 6
Aprill 24	2 1/2 q: Rom	0 - 2 - 6
	1 hut	0 - 7 - 0
May 17	2 1/2 yd Kelsch	0 - 4 - 0
Juny 4	3/4 lb: Eisen	4 - 6 - 0

No 83

	Jacob Schwanger	
	Auss Zug vom alten buch fol. 110 [extract from the old book, page 110]	1 -18- 8
febru: 18	Vor schap wahr	0 - 9 - 2
Aprill 13	1 strengel seiten	0 - 1 - 0
May 15	1 par strümpff	0 - 5 - 6
	1 q: bir	0 - 0 - 6
1764		
May 21	2 yd: kelsch das sein tochter gehohlt [which his daughter fetched]	0 - 5 - 8
1771	**Jacob Schwanger**	
May 8	1 q: Bir	0 - 0 - 6
1763	**Abraham Ruland**	
May 24	Verzehrt	0 - 5 - 3
July 6	1/2 b: m: wein 1 q: bir 1 gill Rom	0 - 1 - 10
Sep: 10	Vor flintenstein und tram	0 - 1 - 0
Nov: 14	1 b: wein	0 - 1 - 2
1765	**Abraham Ruland**	
January 1	1 b: m: wein	0 - 2 - 0
May 19	1 gill Rom	0 - 0 - 4
1766	**Abraham Ruland**	
Jan 30	verzehrt	0 - 3 - 0
Febru: 1	1 q: seiter 1 gill Rom 2 q: haber 1 Brill	0 - 2 - 6
21	1 Calender	0 - 0 - 8

No 84

1763	**Matheis Albrecht**	
Febr: 21	1 yd floret	0 - 0 - 4
Ap: 2	1 b: m: wein	0 - 2 - 0
May 7	1 b: wein	0 - 1 - 2
1769	**Georg Haushalter**	
Jany 20	1 sentz	0 - 4 - 0
1771		
Mertz 16	1/2 b: m: wein	0 - 1 - 0
1763	**Nichlas Bollman** der alte [Senior]	
May 13	1/4 lb Peffer	0 - 0 - 9
Juny 24	1 sentz 1 sickel 1 wetstein	0 - 8 - 9

Lisabetha Wolferspergern

1764		
Novem 24	3 lb: zucker	0 - 2 - 6
1765		
January 14	1/2 buch Babier	0 - 0 - 9
July 2	1/2 yd Borget un 1 strang seget garn	0 - 1 - 8
	9 1/2 lb: Reiss 5 gallen br: wein	1 - 2 - 3
1766		
Aprill 25	4 yd: Bendel 2 yd: floret un vor Rosenwein	0 - 4 - 4

Catharina Wolferspergern

1766		
Mertz 17	2 yd: band	0 - 1 - 8
Ma: 2	2 yd: band	0 - 2 - 8

Lisabetha Wolfersperger

1767		
Juny 9	2 b: m: wein	0 - 4 - 0
Sebt: 12	1/2 b: m: wein bey der rechnung [at the settlement]	0 - 1 - 0
		1 -16- 6

No 85

Antony Stigel

1763		
Febru: 19	1 bol Mimm 2 q: haber	0 - 1 - 4
Mertz 22	verzehrt	0 - 2 - 0
29	3 q: haber	0 - 0 - 6
April 28	3 q: haber	0 - 0 - 6
Juny 3	3 q: haber 1 q: bir	0 - 1 - 0
8	1 fensterglas gebrochen [1 window broken]	0- 0 - 10
July 6	5 q: bir 2 q: seiter 3 q: haber 2 q: Bir	0 - 1 - 0
30	2 Bol mimm 3 q: Haber	0 - 2 - 6
Sep 15	1 bol Min	0 - 1 - 0
19	3 q: haber 2 bol mimm 1 weck	0 - 2 - 7
24	3 bol mimm 4 q haber	0 - 3 - 8
27	3 q: haber	0 - 0 - 6
30	1 bol mimm	0 - 1 - 0
Octo 4	2 bol mimm 1 b: m: wein 2 q: haber 1 weck und essen	0 - 4 - 11
6	1 bol mimm	0 - 1 - 0
12	2 q: haber 1 bol mimm	0 - 1 - 4
14	2 bol mimm 1 weck	0 - 2 - 1
Nov: 3	1 bol leims bunsch	0 - 1 - 6
Dec 1	1 bol leims bunsch 1 bol: mimm 4 weck 3 q: haber	0 - 3 - 4
3	1 bol mimm	0 - 1 - 0
20	2 bol mimm 2 q: haber	0 - 2 - 3
24	1 bol mimm	0 - 1 - 0
1764		
Febr: 2	1 bol mimm	0 - 1 - 0
	8 q: haber	0 - 1 - 4
8	3 q: Bir 3 q: Haber	0 - 2 - 0
15	1 bol mimm	0 - 1 - 0
23	1 q: bir	0 - 0 - 6
25	3 q: haber 1 q: bir 1 weck	0 - 1 - 0
	1 bol Mim	0 - 1 - 0
		2 - 4 - 8
		1 - 7 - 6

No 86

Melcher Lautermilch

1763		
	Aus altem buch fol 47 [From the old book, page 47]	0 - 2 - 9
Febru: 24	1 q: seitereol 1 weck	0 - 0 - 9

1763	**Melcher Lautermilch**	
Juny 12	2 wein schling	0 - 1 - 6
July 16	1 Bol senckery	0 - 1 - 6
Aug 8	1 Neb senckery 4 weck	0 - 1 - 1
Dec: 10	2 wein schling 2 weck	0 - 1 - 8
		0 - 5 - 9

1764	**Melcher Lautermilch**	
Sep: 10	1 lb: schrott	0 - 0 - 7

1764	**Henrich Meyer**	
Feb: 18	1 q: bir 1 weck	0 - 0 - 7
Mertz 6	1 wein schling	0 - 0 - 9
9	2 wein schling	0 - 1 - 6
Decem 14	1 w: schling 1 weck	0 - 0 - 1
1765		
Augst 13	4 lb: Negel	0 - 4 - 0
1766		
Juny 12	Bleibt schuldig vor wein wie Peter Eckart da war [still owes for wine when **Peter Eckert** was here]	0 - 5 - 0
1767		
Febrary 14	ist schultig vor spilen [owes for gambling]	0 - 0 - 10
1768		
January 1	1 b: m: wein	0 - 2 - 0
Juny 11	vor 1 watsch	0 - 3 - 6
July 15	1 w: schling	0 - 0 - 9
9	Credit vor 1 haut	0 - 9 - 6
15	1 b: wein	0 - 1 - 2

No 87	**Martin Heffelfinger**	
Mertz 4	1 q: wein	0 - 2 - 4
7	1 b: seiter 1 weck	0 - 0 - 5
July 25	1 q: seitereol	0 - 0 - 8
Aug: 7	2 yd Kelsch	0 - 9 - 8
Sep 17	1 hut	0 - 4 - 0
De 22	1 q: seiter	0 - 0 - 4
1764	**Martin Heffelfinger**	
May 28	2 q: bir	0 - 1 - 0
1765		
April 19	1 hut das Büchers Bub geholt [1 hat fetched by Bücher's boy]	0 - 4 - 0
Juny 12	1 bol mimm	0 - 1 - 0
18	vor farb	0 - 1 - 6
	2 hut un 1: bir	1 -12- 6
Sept 12	2 q: Thron	0 - 2 - 0
1766		
July 11	4 gallen Rom 2 hüt	1 - 2 - 0
	Bezahlt an geld [paid in money]	1 - 5 - 0
1767		
Jany 27	1 q: seiter	0 - 0 - 4

1765	**Bernhard Weber**	
Jany 26	1 hut	0 - 7 - 0
February 17	vor schap gut un 1 q seiter	0 -10- 3
	Bezahlt an geld [paid in money]	0 - 7 - 6
May 27	1 q bir	0 - 0 - 6
	2 hüt	1 -12- 0
Decem: 23	2 yd: halb Dück	0 - 7 - 4

1766		
Jan: 15	Verzehrt	0 - 1 - 0
	abgerechnet mit berned weber den 31ten Mertz 1766 bleibt er schuldig [settled with **Berned Weber** 31 March 1766. He still owes.]	0 - 8 - 0

No 88		
1763	**Andreas Klein**	
Merz 4	1 b: seitereol	0 - 0 - 4
1765	**Conrad Dinjus** strumbweber in Lancester [stocking weaver in Lancaster]	
Aprill 19	verzehrt	3 - 4 - 0
1763	**Regina Bäustlerin**	
Merz 11	vor schap gut	0 - 0 - 6
1764	**Friedrich Person**	
Novem. 26	1 1/2 q: Bir 4 q: haber	0 - 1 - 5
1765		
Febr: 2	1 b: wein	0 - 1 - 4
20	1 b: Bir 1 gill Rom	0 - 0 - 7
1766	**Friedrich Person**	
May 23	verzehrt	0 - 4 - 5
24	1 b: Bir	0 - 0 - 3
July 1	2 q: Bir 1 b: seiter	0 - 1 - 2
28	3 b: Bir	0 - 0 - 9
Augst 2	3 b: Bir	0 - 0 - 9
16	1 b: Bir	0 - 0 - 3
25	2 q: Bir un 1 glas verbrochen [1 broken glass]	0 - 4 - 0

No 89		
1763	**Ludwig Kohl**	
Merz 5	4 b: m: wein 3 weck	0 - 8 - 3
April	1 1/2 b: m: wein	0 - 3 - 0
25	1 q: bier	0 - 0 - 6
27 Juny	4 q: Bir 3 weck	0 - 2 - 3
30	1 q: Bir 1 q: seiter 1 weck	0 - 0 - 11
1764	**Ludwig Kohl**	
Juny 10	1 q: bir	0 - 0 - 6
1768	**Jacob Gemberling**	
Augst 1	1 q: thron	0 - 1 - 0
1769 Feb: 14	1 q: Rom	0 - 1 - 0
Sep: 1	1 b: wein	0 - 1 - 2
Decem: 30	1 q: Br: wein	0 - 1 - 0
1770		
January 15	1 1/2 yd: Catun	0 - 9 - 0
	1 q: Br: wein	0 - 0 - 10
	1 b: wein	0 - 1 - 2
	Credit vor spinen [credit for spinning]	0 - 2 - 6
Merz 28	Credit vor spinen	0 - 5 - 3

1764	**Wilhelm Schreiner**	
April 20	verzehrt	0 - 3 - 0

1768	**Katolisch Doctor** [The Catholic doctor]	
February 20	1 bottel gelehnt	
Merz 21	2 q: Rom	0 - 2 - 0
May 7	2 q: Rom	0 - 2 - 0
1769		
Sep: 1	1 b: wein	0 - 1 - 2
1771		
Juny 24	1/2 b: wein 1 b: seiter	0 - 0 - 10

No 90

1763	**Ruthÿ Bollinger**	
Merz	aus altem buch fol: 196 [from the old book, page 196]	0 - 1 - 2
12	2 1/2 dtz knöpff	0 - 2 - 2
25	1/2 b: wein	0 - 0 - 7
Aug 6	1 q: Bir	0 - 0 - 6
1763	**Ruthÿ Bollinger**	
Dec: 24	1 b: wein	0 - 1 - 2
1764		
Sep 7	vor Endigo	0 - 0 - 6

1768	**John Clerck**	
October 29	1/2 b: wein	0 - 0 - 7
	Vor schab gut	0 -15- 3
	1 q: W: Rom 1 botel un 1 w: schling	0 - 3 - 9
Novem: 6	1 Par strumbendel un 1 strang Camelgarn	0 - 1 - 3
1769	**John Clerck**	
January 23	1 q: W: Rom	0 - 1 - 6

1765	**Casper Oberman**	
Sebt 13	1 b: wein	0 - 1 - 2
1767		
January 31	3 q: seiterol	0 - 2 - 0
February 2	1 q: seiter	0 - 0 - 4
5	1 q: seiter	0 - 0 - 4
11	1 q: seiter 1 gill Rom	0 - 0 - 8

No 91

1763	**Lautermilch Godfred**	
March 19	Vor Trinken	0 - 3 - 3

1763	**Jacob Lautermilch**	
July 25	1 bol: senckery	0 - 1 - 6
No: 26	1 wein schling	0 - 0 - 9
	1 b: seol 1 weck	0 - 0 - 5

Date	Entry	Amount
1764	**Jacob Lautermilch**	
Jan 29	1 b: seol	0 - 0 - 4
July 23	2 wein schling 1 rom schling 1/2 gill rom	0 - 2 - 2
1765		
Feb: 4	1 q: bir	0 - 0 - 6
Merz 4	Credit vor riegel machen [Credit for splitting rails]	0 - 7 - 0
8	1 bole mim	0 - 1 - 0
June 13	gelehnt an geld [lent in money]	0 - 6 - 0
1764	**Gottfried Lautermilch**	
May 15	1 q: bir	0 - 0 - 6
1765		
Feb: 29	1/2 gill rom 1 q: seiter	0 - 0 - 6
Merz 4	Credit Vor to mak Riel [credit for splitting rails]	0 - 7 - 0
	ist schuldig vor Jacob Hammen seiner Vendu [owes from **Jacob Hammen**'s sale]	0 - 6 - 0
1766	**Gottfried Lautermilch**	
January 5	9 b: m: wein	0 -18- 0
July 5	1 q: Tar	0 - 0 - 6
1767	Credit	0 - 2 - 6
Juny 27	1 q: seiter	0 - 0 - 4

Date	Entry	Amount
No 92		
1763	**Jacob Hetzel**	
Merz 21	2 yd ossnabrick	0 - 3 - 0
April	1 Psalter	0 - 2 - 3
1	1 lb zucker	0 - 0 - 9
1763	**John Clerck**	
Juny 27	1 b: wein	0 - 1 - 4
1763	**Jacob Hetzel**	
Aug 27	1 q: Rom 1/4 lb Peffer	0 - 2 - 6
Sep 27	Vor Endigo und Neths	0 - 1 - 2
October 18	1/2 lb Peffer 1/2 lb alspeis	0 - 2 - 8
1764	1 q: Wein	0 - 2 - 4
Jan 8	1 q: Rom	0 - 1 - 6
		0 -10- 2
1763	**Friedrich Person**	
Mertz 25	Vor Trinken und 1 Fässgen	0 - 6 - 10
	bleibt schultig in der abrechnung [still owes at the settlement]	0 - 1 - 2
	Friedrich Person	
	2 weck	0 - 0 - 2
	1 schnuptuch gelehnt [lent]	
1764	**Jacob Hetzel**	
May 21	1 lb: zucker un 1/4 lb: alspeis das vergessen [which was forgot]	0 - 1 - 4
November 21	1 q: Thron	0 - 1 - 0
1765		
Sebt 16	1 q: thron	0 - 1 - 0
April 1767	**Jacob Hetzel der Jung**	
17	1 hut 1/2 lb: roth holtz	0 - 7 - 8

No 93

1763	**Georg Hetzeler**	
Mertz 29	vor trinken und Essen [for drinking and eating]	1 -10- 9
	Bezahlt an geld [paid in money]	0 - 1 - 0
December 25	200 schuhnagel	0 - 0 - 11
	Georg Hetzeler aus alten Buch das nicht verrechnet ist von 1762 Jahr [**George Hetzeler** from the old book which has not been paid, from the year 1762]	
26: Mertz	2 b: wein	0 - 2 - 0

1763	**Jacob Gass**	
April 21	1 schling	0 - 0 - 6
23	1 schling 1 b: M: wein 1/2 b: m: wein	0 - 2 - 8
25	1 b: seiter eol	0 - 0 - 4
	Jacob Gass bleibt schuldig[Jacob Gass still owes]	0 - 7 - 2
	1 sickel	0 - 4 - 1
	1 feil	0 - 0 - 6
		0 -11- 9
1763	**Jacob Gass**	
July 16	1 Boll senckery	0 - 1 - 6
1765	**Jacob Gass**	
Nov: 23	1 Par strümb	0 - 5 - 6
	1/2 lb pulver	0 - 1 - 9
1766		
Merz 27	7 lb fleisch	0 - 1 - 9
29	1 q: Bir	0 - 0 - 6

No 94

1763	**Sebastian Barget**	
Mertz 29	3 q: Rom 4 lb zucker	0 - 8 - 0
	1 1/4 yd Cattun	0 - 6 - 3
1765	**Sebastian Borgert**	
May 6	2 q: Tar 1 q: Thron	0 - 1 - 6
Juny 1	1 q: thron 1 lb zucker 2 q: Essig	0 - 2 - 0
July 2	8 q: Rom un 3 q: Essig	0 - 8 - 6
13	1 q: seiter un 1 b: Rom	0 - 0 - 10
		0 -12- 10

1763	**Johannes Fertig**	
April 21	1 q: seiter	0 - 0 - 4
Sep. 6	1 Messer	0 - 0 - 6
Octo 14	1 q: seiter	0 - 0 - 4
1764	**Johannes Fertig**	
Juny 9	2 q: seiteröl	0 - 1 - 4
	1 lb zucker	0 - 0 - 8
	1/4 lb Peffer	0 - 0 - 10
1765		
Feb: 17	1 Catecismus	0 - 1 - 0
Octo: 25	Vor Baumöl	0 - 0 - 5
Decem: 19	1 q: Thron	0 - 1 - 0
Mertz 7	1 q: Thron	0 - 1 - 0

No 95

1763	**Adam Bolender**	
April 1	1 q: seitereol	0 - 0 - 8
3	Bezahlt [paid]	0 - 0 - 10
May 20	1 q: bir	0 - 0 - 6
1763	**Adam Bolender**	
Aug 8	1 bol. senckerÿ	0 - 1 - 6
October 11	vor Neths	0 - 0 - 5
24	1 q: seiter	0 - 0 - 4
Dec: 10	1 wein schling	0 - 0 - 9
1764		
Febr: 17	1 gill Rom	0 - 0 - 4
19	1 b: seiter eol	0 - 0 - 4
Mertz 19	1 bol senckerÿ	0 - 1 - 6
	1 Cam un 1 lb: zucker	0 - 2 - 6
April 13	1 Backen Buch	0 - 1 - 3
26	vor Bunsch	0 - 0 - 10
1764	abgerechnet mit Adam Bolender d: 17t September 1764 bleibt no rest [settled with Adam Bolender 17 September 1764. No balance remains.]	
Sep: 26	2 b: wein	0 - 2 - 4
28	1 par hemderknöpff	0 - 0 - 8
	vor Endigo	0 - 1 - 0
Octo.	1 lb pech	0 - 0 - 4
31	2 par schnallen	0 - 0 - 10
	1 q: Br: wein	0 - 1 - 0
	1/2 lb Peffer 1/4 lb alspeis 1 Namenbuch 100 schunägel	0 - 3 - 1
	abgerechnet mit Adam Bolender d: 12. February 1765 bleibt no rest [settled with Adam Bolender 12 Feb. 1765. No balance remains.]	
January 21	das vergessen [this forgotten] 1 b: wein 1 b: M: wein 1 bole senckery	0 - 5 - 10
May 27	1 q: bir	0 - 0 - 6
Sebt 12	1 b: Thron	0 - 0 - 6
Nov: 20	1 q: Thron	0 - 1 - 0
Decem: 12	1 Messer	0 - 0 - 10
25	vor Baumwolle	0 - 0 - 6
1766		
Jan 30	1 hut	0 - 7 - 0
Febrar 15	1 b: wein	0 - 1 - 2

No 96

1763	**George Stroh**	
April 3	Vor Trincken	0 - 0 - 9
May 2	1 hut	1 -15- 0
Juny 6	1 b: M: wein	0 - 2 - 0
Aug 29	1 b: M: wein	0 - 2 - 0
Nov: 3	Bezahlt an geld [paid in money]	1 -10- 0
1764	**George Stroh**	
Aprill 13	1 q: seiter	0 - 0 - 4

1763	**Müller** auf der alten Forness [Müller, or the miller, at the old furnace]	
May 4	2 yd Cattun	0 -10- 0
Octo 24	bezahlt an geld [paid in money]	0 - 6 - 0

1765	**George Lautermilch**	
May 27	1 bole senckery	0 - 3 - 0

No 97		
1763	**Wilhelm Ewÿ**	
	bleibt schuldig [still owes]	0 - 0 - 6
Apr 9	Vor Trinken	0 - 5 - 0
May 19	1/2 wein 1 weck	0 - 0 - 9
July 25	1 q: seiter 1/4 lb Pulver 1 wein schling	0 - 2 - 2
Aug 7	1 b: wein 2 weck	0 - 1 - 4
1764	4 q: bir	0 - 2 - 0
Juny 10	3 herhüter Peiffen 1 b: seiter	0 - 1 - 8
Sep: 21	sein sohn [his son] 1 q: seitereol	0 - 0 - 8
1765		
January 14	Verzehrt	0 - 0 - 6
1766		
Febry 11	1 1/2 q: Br: wein	0 - 1 - 6
1763	**Ewÿ Georg**	
Juny 7	Verzehrt	2 - 1 - 7
1764	**Georg Ewig**	
Mertz 26	Vor Catun Vor 1 Halss Tuch 1 lb: pulfer	0 - 6 - 9
	Vor Essen 2 Peiffen 3 q: Bir	0 - 3 - 0

No 98		
1763	**Frantz Eckert**	
April	Auss Zug Vom alten fol: 135	0 -13- 7
	[Extract from the old book, page 135]	
9	1 b: seitereol	0 - 4 - 0
1763	**Frantz Eckert**	
Juny 8	1 lb zucker	0 - 0 - 9
25	Vor fluss Corellen	0 - 8 - 0
	d: 8t November gerechnet mit Frantz Eckert bleibt nichts	
	[8 November settled with Frantz Eckert. Owes nothing.]	
1766	**Christian Ewig**	
July 11	1 q: seiteröl	0 - 0 - 8
1764	**Thorst Thomas** junior	
Mertz 3	1 q: seitereol	0 - 0 - 8
Sept 20	1 Licht	0 - 2 - 6
	1 b: m. wein	0 - 2 - 0
Novem 24	1 q: Thron	0 - 1 - 0
Decem 6	1 Kap	0 - 3 - 0
	Bezahlt an geld [paid in money]	0 - 7 - 6
		0 - 9 - 2
		0 - 7 - 6
		0 - 1 - 8
		0 - 1 - 8

1766	**Dorst Thomas** junior	
Augst 29	1/2 gill Rom	0 - 0 - 2

Date	Entry	Amount
No 99		
1763	**Andreas Miller**	
Ap: 12	1 q: Tarr	0 - 0 - 5
1763	**Jacob Fotler**	
Aug 20	1 b: seitereol	0 - 0 - 4
1765		
April 19	1 gill Rom	0 - 0 - 4
1766		
February 20	1 b: seiteröl	0 - 0 - 4
1763	**Jacob Herlÿ**	
Aug 20	1 b: seitereol	0 - 0 - 4
1765		
April 19	1 gill Rom	0 - 0 - 4
1766		
February 20	1 b: seiteröl	0 - 0 - 4
1771	**Jacob Herly**	
Juny 16	gerechnet Bleibt Schultig [settled: still owes]	0 - 0 - 3
1766	**Adam Ewig**	
Janu: 26	1/4 lb Peffer un 1 Calender 4 yd Bendel	0 - 2 - 7
No 100		
1763	**John Mohr**	
Ap: 13	gelend an geld [lent in money]	4 - 0 - 0
	1 schling	0 - 0 - 6
Meÿ 25	1 q: bir	0 - 0 - 6
Juny 12	1 b: seitereol	0 - 0 - 4
	d: 9 November gerechnet mit Johannes Moor Bleibt Nichts [9 November settled with Johannes Moor. Owes nothing]	
1765	**Johann Moorr**	
Juny 12	1 bole Mimm	0 - 1 - 0
July 24	1 b: M: wein	0 - 2 - 0
1766		
January 22	1 b: Rom	0 - 1 - 0
24	1 q: Rom	0 - 2 - 0
1763	**Bast Henrich**	
May 19	1 hut	0 - 7 - 6
1764	**Jacob Spengler**	
Decem: 20	1 hut	0 - 4 - 0
No 101		
1763	**Henrich Miller** auf Dorsten Mühl [Henrich Miller at Dorst [Thomas's] mill]	
April 18	Vor Trincken	0 - 0 - 9
1763	**Friedrich Kapp**	
April 18	Vor druget	0 - 3 - 7
1766	**Johnnes Frantz**	
Augst 15	2 q: seiter	0 - 0 - 8
1764	**Daniel Conrad**	
July 6	1 sichel 1 q: Rom 1 bottel 1 hut zucker	0 -14- 0

No 102		
1763	**John Lauser**	
April 6	1 yd Cattun	0 - 5 - 0
1764		
Febru: 26	1 b: wein	0 - 1 - 2
Mertz 10	1 b: seitereol	0 - 0 - 4
19	1 q: seitereol	0 - 0 - 8
	1 q: seitereol	0 - 0 - 8
April 4	1 b: seitereol	0 - 0 - 4
6	1 p: schnallen	0 - 1 - 3
20	1 Engen Cam 1 yd floret 1 b: seitereol	0 - 2 - 4
26	1 b: seitereol	0 - 0 - 4
Meÿ 28	1 q: Rom	0 - 1 - 2
1763	**Peter Drucke Müller**	
April 18	1 q: Tram	0 - 1 - 0
23	1 b: seitereol	0 - 0 - 4
May 2	1 q: Br: wein	0 - 1 - 0
	Peter Drucken Müller	
Junÿ 25	1 sichel 1 q: tram	0 - 4 - 11
30	1 q: tram	0 - 1 - 0
July 3	1 b: wein	0 - 1 - 2
	d: 31t Octob gerechnet mit Peter Druckenmüller bleibt nichts [31 October settled with Peter Druckenmüller. Owes nothing]	
October 4	1 b: Persig tram	0 - 0 - 7
	1 b: thron	0 - 0 - 6
	sein Tochter [his daughter] 1 p: schnallen	0 - 1 - 8
1764		
Jan 7	1 Calender	0 - 0 - 8
1764	**Peder Druckenmüller**	
22 Oct	hat noch zu fodern an Alexander Schafer [has coming from **Alexander Schaeffer**]	1 - 3 - 0

No 103		
1763	**Henrich Wm Stiegel**	
April 22	sein arbeits leut [laborers] 1 q: Rom	0 - 1 - 8
23	verzehrt	0 - 4 - 8
26	sein arbeits leut [laborers] 1 q: Rom	0 - 1 - 8
28	sein arbeits leut [laborers] 1 q: Ditto	0 - 1 - 8
30	2 b: M: wein 2 bol Mimm	0 - 6 - 0
May 2	sein arbeits leut [laborers] 1 q: rom	0 - 1 - 8
May 2	1 1/2 q: Rom	0 - 2 - 6
4	sein arbeits leut [laborers] 1 q: rom	0 - 1 - 8
7	sein arbeits leut [laborers] 1 1/2 q: rom	0 - 2 - 6
	13 fuhr stein geholt 1 fuhr holz geholt auf Henlys Platz 14 bleck in die Mill gefierd vor jeder 4 schilling 6 bens [13 loads of stone fetched 1 load of wood fetched from Henley's place, 14 logs driven to the mill, each at 4 shillings, 6 pence]	3 -17- 0
	wieder bosten gefierd von des Henlis blatz 21 1/2 dag un 1 man [again posts fetched from Henly's place 21 1/2 days, 1 man]	2 - 0 - 0
1763		
17 Meÿ	1 halb vertel stroh das der seltzer geholt hat [which Seltzer fetched]	0 - 2 - 6

19	3 bol Mimm 2 weck Mittagessen [noon meal]	0 - 3 - 8
20	4 bol mimm 2 weck 2 q: haber	0 - 4 - 8
Juny 7	noch schuldig vor 4 Deet [still owes for 4 deeds]	3 - 0 - 0
	4 bol mimm 1 b: M: wein und Essen vor 4 Mann	0 - 9 - 4
12	2 bol mimm 1 weck	0 - 2 - 1
	posten geholt auf Henlÿs platz und 30 lb Nagel auf der forness [posts fetched from Henly's place and 30 pounds of nails to the furnace]	0 - 4 - 0
9	sein schreiner [his joiner] 1 q : rom	0 - 1 - 8
9	sein schreiner [his joiner] 1 q: rom	0 - 1 - 8
13	sein schreiner [his joiner] 1 q: rom	0 - 1 - 8
	sein schreiner 1 q: Rom	0 - 1 - 8
22	4 Bol mim 2 weck	0 - 4 - 2
	vor stein welcher Simon Leible gebrochen [for stone broken by **Simon Leible**]	0 - 5 - 0

No 104
1763

Adreas Ricker

April 23	1 b: seitereol 1/2 b: wein	0 - 0 - 11
27	1 b: seitereol 1/2 b: wein	0 - 0 - 4
28	1 q: seitereol 1/2 b: wein	0 - 0 - 8
May 2	1 q: seitereol	0 - 0 - 8
4	1 b: seitereol	0 - 0 - 4
23	1 q: bir	0 - 0 - 6
25	1 q: Thron 2 q: seiter 1 fisch	0 - 2 - 0
Juny 2	1 1/2 q tram 5 q: seiter 1 wein schling 1 weck	0 - 4 - 0
6	2 q: 1/2 b: seitereol 1 q: seiter 1/2 b: M: wein	0 - 3 - 1
13	1 q: tram	0 - 1 - 0
20	1 b: M: wein 1 q: seiter 3 1/2 b: s. eol	0 - 3 - 6
	1 q: seiter	0 - 0 - 4
25	4 q: s. eol 1 weck	0 - 2 - 9
27	2 q: seitereol	0 - 1 - 4
July 3	2 b: seitereol 1 weck 1/4 lb Peffer 1/4 lb alspeis	0 - 2 - 2
5	Vor Kelsch wegen der Schräcken [on Mrs Schrach's account]	0 - 6 - 0
13	3 q seiter	0 - 1 - 0
14	gelent an geld [lent in money]	0 - 2 - 9
	1 b: seol	0 - 0 - 4
16	1 b: seitereol	0 - 0 - 4
	2 1/2 q: seiter 1 q: seitereol	0 - 1 - 6
30	2 q: seiter 1 q: seitereol 1 weck	0 - 1 - 5
	vor seitereol	0 - 0 - 2
Aug	2 q: seiter 1 b: seitereol 1 weck	0 - 1 - 1
12	vor Indigo	0 - 1 - 0
15	2 q: seiter	0 - 0 - 8
15	gelent [lent]	0 - 0 - 1
18	1 q: seitereol	0 - 1 - 4
	gelent an geld [lent in money]	0 -16- 0
20	2 q: seitereol	0 - 1 - 4
	1 b: seitereol	0 - 0 - 4

No 105
1763

William Besch

April 23	1 b: seitereol	0 - 0 - 4
May 4	5 q seiter	0 - 1 - 8

May14	3 q: seiter	0 - 1 - 0
25	3 q: seiter	0 - 1 - 0
Juny 7	1/2 b: wein 1/2 B: M: wein	0 - 1 - 7
22	1 q: seiter	0 - 0 - 4
	2 q: seiter 1 lb doback	0 - 1 - 1
	bezahlt an geld [paid in money]	1 - 1 - 6
July 30	3 q: seitereol	0 - 2 - 0
Augus 6	1 q: seiter	0 - 0 - 4
7	1 q: seiter	0 - 0 - 4
15	3 q: seiter 1 b: tram	0 - 1 - 7
20	3 B: seitereol	0 - 1 - 0
24	1 1/2 q: seitereol	0 - 1 - 0
27	1 q: seitereol	0 - 0 - 8
	1 wein schling	0 - 0 - 9
Sep. 11	1 b: seitereol	0 - 0 - 4
19	1 b: s. eol	0 - 0 - 4
	3 q: seiter	0 - 1 - 0
21	1 bol senckerÿ	0 - 1 - 6
	1 q: seiter	0 - 0 - 4
30	2 q: seitereol	0 - 1 - 4
Octo. 3	1 q: seitereol	0 - 0 - 8
	1 schling	0 - 0 - 6
	1/2 gill Rom	0 - 0 - 2
6	1 q: seiter	0 - 0 - 4
11	2 q: seiter	0 - 0 - 8
12	2 bol. Mimm	0 - 2 - 0
	1 p: schuh	0 - 7 - 0
13	4 q: seiter 1 q: thron 1 gill Rom 1 peiff	0 - 2 - 9
	2 q seiter	0 - 0 - 8
17	3 q: seiter	0 - 1 - 0
20	1 bol Mimm	0 - 1 - 0

No 106

1763	**Casper Schweitzer** Na: Schmitt [nail smith]	
April 30	1 gill schimber 1 q: seiter	0 - 0 - 10
Meÿ 25	1 q: seiter	0 - 0 - 4
	1/2 gill schimber 1 b: M: wein	0 - 2 - 3
	d: 8 Meÿ 1763 gerechnet mit Casper schweÿtzer bleibt keinem dem andern nicht schultig [8 May 1763 settled with Casper Schweytzer. Neither owes the other anything]	
1763	**Caspar Schweitzer**	
Juny 12	1 q: seiter 1 b: M: wein	0 - 2 - 4
	1/2 b: wein	0 - 0 - 8
20	Vor Trincken Bey handel zwischen Bernt Jacob	0 -12- 0
24	1 P: strümpff 1 q: seiter	0 - 7 - 4
30	3 q: seiter	0 - 1 - 0
July 16	3 b: M: wein 1 q: bir 4 b: M: wein 1 q: seitereol	0 - 6 - 6
18	1 q: seiter	0 - 9 - 0
Aug 3	1 b: m: wein	0 - 2 - 0
7	3 q: seiter	0 - 1 - 0
9	2 schling 1 q: seiter	0 - 1 - 4
21	1 gill Tram	0 - 0 - 3
27	3 1/2 b: m: wein 1 weck	0 - 7 - 1
29	2 b M: wein 1 seitereol	0 - 4 - 4
Sep 19	1 B: m. wein 2 q: seiter	0 - 2 - 8
21	3 q: seiter	0 - 1 - 0

27	2 q: seiter	0 - 0 - 8
30	4 b: M: wein	0 - 8 - 0
October 10	1 b: wein 2 q: seiter	0 - 1 - 10
11	5 q: seiter	0 - 1 - 8
14	1/2 lb pulver	0 - 2 - 0
Nov: 3	1 q: seiter	0 - 0 - 4
Dec: 6	2 b: m: wein bleibt dran schuldig [owes on 1 b: m: wein]	0 - 2 - 6
9	1 b: M: wein	0 - 2 - 0

No 107

1763	**Adam Hiltebeitel**	
May 2	1 hut	1 - 5 - 0
	Bezahlt an geld [paid in money]	0 -15- 0
1765	**Tobias Hack**	
Juny 13	1 sentz	0 - 4 - 0
1768	**Tobias Hack**	
July 7	1 q: seiter un 1 weck	0 - 0 - 5
1763	**Joseph Finck**	
May 7	1 hut 1 par strümpff	1 - 9 - 6
1763	**der junge losser**	
Meÿ 24	1 lb zucker	0 - 0 - 9
1765	**Henry Stoner**	
Decem: 12	1 b: M: wein un 1 bol: senckery un 1 Peiff	0 - 3 - 7

No 108

1763	**Benjamen Nathan**	
May 16	1/2 b: anis	0 - 0 - 6
24	1 B: anis	0 - 1 - 0
Juny 20	1 b: bir	0 - 0 - 3
1763	**Benjamen Nadan**	
Dec: 12	1 gill gatsel	0 - 0 - 6
	1/2 gill Rom	0 - 0 - 2
	1/2 gill Br: wein	0 - 0 - 2
1764		
Aug. 28	1 strang seiten	0 - 0 - 10
Oct 15	1 gill gatsel 1 b: seiter	0 - 0 - 8
1763	**Stiegels schreiner** [joiner]	
Sep 24	Henrich 1/2 b: rom Essen	0 - 1 - 0
1764	**dem Kieffer**	
Decem: 6	1 gill Rom 1 q: seiter	0 - 0 - 8
1764	**Kapler**	
Decem 6	1 b: Rom	0 - 0 - 6

1765	**Friedrich Wolfersperger**	
October 25	bezahlt an Hock[?]	3 -13- 0
	bezahlt an Horsch	0 - 7 - 6
1765	**Friedrich Wolfersperger**	
October 25	Bezahlt an Horsch	0 - 7 - 6

No 109 geh zurück

1763	**Carl Seÿbold Doctor**	
April 30	Vor Trincken	0 - 1 - 0
	bezahlt an geld [paid in money]	0 - 7 - 6
May 10	bezahlt an geld [paid in money]	1 - 0 - 0
18	1 1/2 gill Rom	0 - 0 - 6
19	1/2 b: wein 1 gill tram	0 - 0 - 11
20	2 1/2 gill Rom	0 - 0 - 10
24	2 gill Rom	0 - 0 - 8
	Credit	0 - 7 - 4
Juny 12	1 gill Rom	0 - 0 - 4
14	1 1/2 gill Rom	0 - 0 - 6
	1 q: seiter 1 gill Rom	0 - 0 - 8
20	1 1/2 gill Rom 1 b: seiter	0 - 0 - 8
22	1 1/2 gill Rom	0 - 0 - 6
23	1 gill romm 1 b: seiter	0 - 0 - 6
July 5	2 gill Rom	0 - 0 - 8
6	1 gill tram	0 - 0 - 3
	1 Tag August 1763 gerechnet mit Carl Seÿbold beibt er schuldig vor [1 August 1763 settled with Carl Seybold. He is in debt for]	4 -17- 6

1765	**Jacob Bäcker**	
Nov: 20	4 b: m: wein	0 - 8 - 0
1765		
January 5	scheiben glas	0 - 3 - 6
1766		
Febery 27	vor fensterglas das er verbrochen [for a window he broke]	0 - 2 - 6

No 110	**Georg Urich**	
1763		
24 May	bleibt schuldig in der abrechung [owes on settlement]	0 - 6 - 0
29 Juny	1 q: bir	0 - 0 - 6
	1 b: wein 1 lb doback	0 - 1 - 7
Sep 3	1/2 viertel throt	0 - 2 - 3
Octo 8	vor Cattun und bentel	0 - 1 - 6
1764		
Sep: 7	1 lb schrot	0 - 0 - 7
1765		
July 10	1 b: wein	0 - 1 - 2
Oct: 7	2 q: thron	0 - 2 - 0
Novem: 6	6 nagelborn un 1 lb: schrot	0 - 3 - 7
	1 hut	0 - 6 - 6

1766		
Juny 16	1 q: B: wein	0 - 1 - 0
17	1 q: Br: wein	0 - 1 - 0
18	1 q: Br: wein	0 - 1 - 0
July 18	1 hut	0 - 7 - 6
	Bezahlt an geld [paid in money]	0 -10- 0
Aug 15	1 q: Br: wein	0 - 1 - 0
Sebt 1	1 q: Br: wein	0 - 1 - 0
Sebt 17	1 q: Rom	0 - 1 - 0

1763	**Abraham Bollman**	
Sep 3	vor dinten pulver	0 - 1 - 0
	1 dintenfass	0 - 2 - 6
Dec: 10	1/2 gill Rom	0 - 0 - 2
1766	**Abraham Bollmann**	
Decem: 19	1/2 gill Rom	0 - 0 - 5
23	1 gill Rom	0 - 0 - 4
29	1/2 b: Rom	0 - 0 - 5
1768		
May 1	1 w: schling 1/2 tram	0 - 0 - 11

No 111

1763	**Jacob Levy**	
May 14	1 q: Rom 2 lb zucker	0 - 3 - 2
April 27	1 b: m: wein	0 - 2 - 0
Mey 10	1 b: m: wein	0 - 2 - 0
	1 b: 1 gill anis	0 - 1 - 6
	2 lb zucker 1 b: s. eol	0 - 1 - 10
20	1 b: anis 1 b: Essig 2 lb zucker	0 - 2 - 8
24	1 b: anis	0 - 1 - 0
25	2 lb zucker	0 - 1 - 6
1763	bleibt schuldig in der abrechnung [owes at settlement]	0 -19- 0
	Jacob Levy	
Juny 6	1 b: Rom	0 - 0 - 10
13	4 lb zucker	0 - 3 - 0
1764	**Jacob Levÿ** Jud	
Sep: 26	1 muscaternuss	0 - 0 - 4
	1/4 lb Peffer	0 - 0 - 10
November 19	3 lb zucker	0 - 2 - 6
	1/2 lb hut zucker	0 - 0 - 5
May 19	1 gill Baumöl	0 - 0 - 8
	1 gill Baumöl	0 - 0 - 8

1768	**Nicoluas Wissler**	
Aprill 2	2 seuger	0 - 5 - 6

No 112

1763	**Michael Reger**	
febru: 8	1 b; M: Wein 1 lb. Zucker	0 - 2 - 9
9	1 q: Tram	0 - 1 - 0
10	1 q: seiter	0 - 0 - 4
12	1 gill bitters 3 q: seiter	0 - 1 - 6

18	2 q: seiter 1 q: Tram	0 - 1 - 8
19	2 q: Ditto 1 gill Rom	0 - 1 - 0
24	Vor Trincken u. Nahmen buch	0 - 2 - 5
25	1 q: seiter	0 - 0 - 4
26	1 b: Wein	0 - 1 - 2
27	1 q: seiter 1 q: Tram	0 - 1 - 4
Mertz 5	5 b: seitereol 1 Weck	0 - 1 - 9
	1/2 gill Rom 1 lb. schrot	0 - 0 - 8
8	1 /2 gill schimber	0 - 0 - 3
11	Vor Trincken und Weck	0 - 2 - 2
	1 bol. senckerÿ	0 - 1 - 6
12	1 1/2 gill Rom 1/2 lb. schrot	0 - 0 - 5
	1 b seeol. 1 weck	0 - 0 - 5
	Von bernhards Vendue 2 par strümph [2 pairs of stockings from Bernhard's sale]	0 - 6 - 8
17	1 q: brand Wein	0 - 1 - 0
19	1/2 lb. bley	0 - 0 - 3
	gelent [lent]	0 - 2 - 6
	Vor Trincken	0 - 1 - 8
	Vor Schap Wahre	3 - 5 - 0
21	1 b: seitereol 1 q: seiter	0 - 0 - 8
	Vor Trincken u. u: 1 fisch	0 - 0 - 11
22	1 q: seitereol	0 - 0 - 8
24	gelent an geld [lent in money]	0 -15- 0
29	1/2 gill Rom	0 - 0 - 2
April 1	1 q: seitereol	0 - 0 - 8
	1/2 gil Rom	0 - 0 - 2
3	1 q: seitereol	0 - 0 - 8
	1 q: Tram	0 - 1 - 0
7	1 gill Tram 1/2 lb. Peffer	0 - 1 - 9
	1 q: Tram	0 - 1 - 0
9	1 b: Wein 1 gil Rom 1 weck	0 - 1 - 7
12	1 b: M: Wein 1 Wein schling	0 - 2 - 9
13	1/2 gil Rom 1 b seitereol	0 - 1 - 6
18	2 b: Wein 2 : Weck	0 - 2 - 6
	siehe ferner Fol: 114 [see further page 114]	6 - 7 - 9

No 113

1763	**Gertraut die Nähern beÿ Wolffesb:** [Gertraut the seamstress at Wolfersberger's]	
febr: 15	1 b: Wein 1 lb. Zucker 1/2 lb. hut Zucker	0 - 2 - 8
18	1 q: Thron	0 - 1 - 0

1763	**Juny der auff der fornis die Bücksen raus Thut** [the person at the furnace who puts out the guns?]	
July 18	2: bir 1 gill Rom	0 - 1 - 4
1764 20	2 q: bir 1 gill Rom	0 - 1 - 4

1765	**Samuel Harnisch**	
Decem: 23	Bezehlt an Samuel [paid to Samuel]	2 - 9 - 8

1763	**George Shwengel**	
Abril 30	Vor Camlot	0 - 1 - 4
	1 hut	0 - 7 - 0

	Samuel Harnisch	
	Bezahlt auff die Vendue [paid at the sale]	4 - 0 - 0

1764	**Michael Schregle**	
Mertz 13	1 q: bir un 1/2 Beck Haber	0 - 1 - 0

No 114		
1763	**Michael Reger**	
April 21	Vor Wachs bech und unschlit	0 - 2 - 6
22	1 q: bir 1/2 gil Rom	0 - 0 - 8
23	1 q: seitereol	0 - 0 - 8
25	2 b: Wein 1 q: bir	0 - 2 - 10
27	Vor Trincken	0 - 6 - 2
	1/2 b: Wein 2 q: seiter	0 - 1 - 3
28	gelent Vor dem jud [lent for the Jew]	1 - 6 - 0
	3 yd bendel 1 dutzend Knöpff	0 - 2 - 0
29	1 b: Wein 2 buschel Weitzen 1 yd: bendel	0 -13- 4
	gelent	0 -15- 11
	1/2 gill Rom	0 - 0 - 2
30	1 schling	0 - 0 - 6
May	1 gill schember 1 weck	0 - 0 - 7
2	2 q: brandwein	0 - 2 - 0
	50 flintenstein 38 lb Mehl	0 - 6 - 0
30	1 beck haber und Vor Trincken	0 - 2 - 1
Juny 2	1 q: Tram	0 - 1 - 0
6	1 q: bir	0 - 0 - 6
8	1 q: und 1 bint seitereol	0 - 1 - 0
	2 q: brande wein	0 - 2 - 0
9	1 q: Tram	0 - 1 - 0
12	6 1/2 q: Br: Wein	0 - 6 - 0
	1 q: bir 1 gill Rom 1 weck	0 - 0 - 11
	1 1/2 gill Rom 1 q: saltz	0 - 0 - 8
	2 q: seiter	0 - 0 - 8
13	1 gill Rom	0 - 0 - 4
14	1 gill Rom	0 - 0 - 4
	1/2 gill Rom 2 q: seiter	0 - 0 - 10
18	1 bottel 1 q: Tram 1 Cam 1 b: seitereol	0 - 2 - 10
20	1 schling 1 b: serol 1 q: seiter 3 weck	0 - 2 - 5
	2 sicheln	0 - 6 - 7
26	Bezahlt Vor Michael Reger an Jacob Levÿ [paid Jacob Levy for Michael Reger]	1 - 6 - 8
	1 gill Rom 1 weck	0 - 0 - 5
		5 -16- 10

No 115		
1763	**Ulrich Risser**	
April 22	Bezahlt auff der Vendue [paid at the sale]	2 - 5 - 0
July 14	1/2 lb. alspeis	0 - 1 - 0
18	sein dochter [his daughter] vor 1 spellen und natheln	0 - 0 - 4
Aug 6	1 bol. wein 1 weck	0 - 1 - 1
Sep 27	1 bol wein	0 - 1 - 0
30	1 q: Thron	0 - 1 - 0

Octo 23	1 b: wein	0 - 1 - 2
Dece 10	1 Calender	0 - 1 - 8
1764		
Jan 1	1 hut	0 - 7 - 0
	sein Tochter [his daughter] Vor Corallen	0 - 8 - 0
Mertz 30	1 q: seiter	0 - 0 - 4
May 1	1/4 camlot	0 - 1 - 4
	1 lb Zucker	0 - 0 - 10
31	1 b: wein	0 - 1 - 2
July 6	1 sichel un neths	0 - 3 - 11

1763	**Jacob Wagner**	
July 16	1 zinern schüssel	0 - 7 - 10
	bezahl an seiner schult [paid on his dibt]	0 - 4 - 3

1765	**Ulrich Risser**	
Febr. 20	1 q: Rom	0 - 1 - 6
d. 10 Nov.	Vor Endego	0 - 1 - 6
1766	Bezahlt an geld [paid in money]	1 - 5 - 0
January 10	1/2 lb Baumwolle	0 - 0 - 8
Febrary 27	1/2 gill Rom	0 - 0 - 2
Aprill 24	Bezahlt an geld [paid in money]	0 - 7 - 6
	Bezahlt an geld [paid in money]	1 - 0 - 0
	1 bo: Leins Bunsch	0 - 1 - 6

No 116		
1763	**Magnus Conrad**	
1 July	gerechnet mit Magnus Conrad bleibt schuldig [settled with Magnus Conrad. Still owes]	0 -11- 9
	1 sichel	0 - 3 - 10
	1 buschel weitzen	0 - 5 - 6
	2 q: seiter	0 - 0 - 9
3	1 q: seiter	0 - 0 - 4
6	1 q: seiter	0 - 0 - 4
	1 q: Ditto	0 - 0 - 4
13	Vor Kelsch	0 - 1 - 0
October 8	1/4 lb. Imber 1 Muscatnus	0 - 0 - 9
De: 23	1 q: seiter	0 - 0 - 4
February 1	gelehnt an geld Vor Viemann [paid in money for Viemann]	0 - 5 - 0
2	1 q: seiter	0 - 0 - 4
Mertz 19	1 gill Rom	0 - 0 - 4
26	1 q: seiter	0 - 0 - 4
1764		
Aug 29	1 hut	0 - 4 - 0
1765		
Decem: 25	2 q: seiter	0 - 0 - 8
1766		
January 1	1 q: seiter	0 - 0 - 4
Mertz 8	1 q: bir 1 q: seiter	0 - 0 - 10
May 20	1 q: bir	0 - 0 - 6
1767		
February 20	1 q: seiter	0 - 0 - 4
April 20	1 q: bir	0 - 0 - 6
May 1	1 q: seiter	0 - 0 - 4

1768		
May 16	1 q: seiter	0 - 0 - 4
July 15	1 q: seiter	0 - 0 - 4
1769		
Febr: 1	1 q: Mallisses	0 - 0 - 10
14	1 Calender	0 - 0 - 8
21	1 q: Malassis	0 - 0 - 10
Mertz 3	1/2 gill Baunöl 1 yd: floret	0 - 0 - 7
6	1 hut 1 buch Babir	0 - 8 - 9
	2 buschel weitzen	0 -10- 0
20	1 hut	0 - 4 - 0
Aprill 20	1 q: Malassis 1/2 Peffer 1/4 Imber 1/4 lb. alspeis	0 - 2 - 4
		3 - 7 - 1

No 117

1763	**Magdalena Weissin**	
Juny 28	2 sintzen 1 sichel 1 wetzstein 3 yd. Cattun 1 strohut	1 -10- 11
1763	**Melcher Kuhnÿ**	
Aug: 6	1 par schnallen 4 Thelöffel	0 - 2 - 6
No 5	1 gill Rom	0 - 0 - 4
7	1 gill Rom 1 q: seiter	0 - 0 - 8
January 13	1/2 gill Rom	0 - 0 - 2
1764		
Juny 24	1 q: Rom	0 - 1 - 2
July 27	1/2 b: Wein	0 - 0 - 7
1766	**Abraham Haid**	
Augst 6	Verzehrt	0 - 6 - 6
1764	**Magdalena Weissin**	
Jan: 18	18 Vorhang Ring	0 - 1 - 6

No 118

1763	**Simon Leible**	
Juny 4	1 q: Tram	0 - 1 - 0
14	2 Gallen Tram	0 - 8 - 0
	Vor stein	0 - 4 - 3
22	1 sichel 1 lb Doback	0 - 3 - 8
1763	**Simon Leibel**	
Aug 11	1 q: seiter	0 - 0 - 4
15	1 q: Tram 1 b: seitereol	0 - 1 - 6
18	1 q: Thron	0 - 1 - 0
20	3 b: seitereol	0 - 1 - 0
21	1 q: Br: wein 12 q: seitereol	0 - 2 - 6
24	1 q: Br: wein	0 - 1 - 2
30	2 q: seiter	0 - 0 - 8
Sep: 7	1 q: Rom	0 - 1 - 6
10	4 q: seiter	0 - 1 - 0
15	1 q: Thron	0 - 1 - 0
Octo 7	1 lb: Pech	0 - 0 - 4
8	1 q: Tram	0 - 1 - 0
10	1 q: Ditto	0 - 1 - 0

13	1 q: Tram	0 - 1 - 0
15	2 q: seiter 1 q: Tram	0 - 1 - 8
19	1 q: Tram	0 - 1 - 0
20	2 q: Thron	0 - 2 - 0
23	2 q: Br: wein	0 - 2 - 0
28	2 q: Ditto	0 - 2 - 0
Nov: 7	2 q: Ditto	0 - 2 - 0
	2 lb unschlit	0 - 1 - 4
14	2 galle Tram	0 - 8 - 0
24	1 bol. senckery	0 - 1 - 6
Dec. 15	2 q: seiter	0 - 0 - 8
16	2 q: seiter	0 - 0 - 8
	2 wein schling 1 weck	0 - 1 - 7
	Vor schreiben	0 - 1 - 6

No 119		
1763	**Jacob Zimerman**	
Juny 6	2 gill bitters 2 gill Rom	0 - 1 - 8
20	1 1/2 gill Rom	0 - 0 - 6
22	1/2 gill Rom	0 - 0 - 2
27	1 gill Rom	0 - 0 - 4
Julÿ 4	1 b: seiter 1 gil Rom	0 - 0 - 6
5	3 1/4 yd. Kelsch 1 gill Rom	0 -10- 1
6	1 q: bir 1/2 gill Rom	0 - 0 - 8
1764	**Jacob Zimerman**	
Nov: 24	1 bole mim	0 - 1 - 0
	1/2 gill Rom	0 - 0 - 2
1763	**Beltz der Zimmerman** [Beltz, the carpenter]	
July 6	3 q: seiter 1 gill Rom	0 - 1 - 4
1766		
Metz 31	1 q: seiter	0 - 0 - 4
1766	**Ludwig derr an der schwader** [on the Swatara]	
July 30	Verzehrt	0 - 3 - 6

No 120		
1763	**Johannes Hoffer**	
Juny 8	1/2 b: M: wein	0 - 1 - 0
1764		
Febru: 2	1 q: M. wein	0 - 4 - 0
Augst 1766	**Jacob Ried** über dem Berg [across the mountains]	
20	2 Messer 1/2 gill Rom	0 - 2 - 4
1763	**Johannes Schneiter**	
Nov: 14	1 Neb Bunsch	0 - 0 - 6
1767	**Betz der Jung** [Jr.]	
May 6	2 Geil Beÿ Heu [2 horses at hay]	0 - 1 - 8

No 121

1763	**Andrias Knauer**	
Juny 12	2 q: Br: wein	0 - 2 - 0
No 24	3 q: seiter	0 - 1 - 0
1766		
Augst 11	2 q: bir	0 - 1 - 0
1767		
April 2	1 b: seiter	0 - 0 - 2
1765	**Adam Knauer**	
Sebt 27	1 bol: mimm	0 - 1 -
1768	**Lutz schumacher ins steitzen** [shoemaker in Steitzen = Lebanon]	
Sebt 18	2 1/2 q: seiter 1/2 gill Rom	0 - 1 - ?
1763	**die Brunen Compagnÿ** [the fountain company]	
Aug 22	vor schreiben Ein accord [writing an agreement]	0 - 3 - 0
	1 q: seitereol	0 - 0 - 8
July 28	3 q: seiteroehl un 1 q: seiter	0 - ? - 4
1767		
May 16	die Jury verzehrt wein es ausgemacht [the jury ate, wine, it comes to]	0 -10-
	darauf hat friederich Miller was die Jury verzehrt bezahlt [Friederich Miller paid what the jury ate]	0 - 2 - ?

No 122

1763	**Johannes Enderes** der Jung [Jr.]	
12 Junÿ	1 1/2 q: Rom	0 - 2 - 6
Aug 8	5 q: seiter	0 - 1 - 8
1764	1 hut (crossed out)	1 - 0 - 0
Novem 30	1 hut 1/2 yd: 1/4 yd: Blau Tuch 1 dutzend Knöp un 1 stran Camel garn	0 -16- 11
1769		
January 23	2 gill rom	0 - 0 - 8
1763	**Henrich Meisser**	
Aug 9	Vor Kelsch	0 -11- 0
1766	**Jacob Scheiner**	
Augst 11	1 wetzstein	0 - 1 - 0
Decem: 2	1 q: Thron 1 gill Rom	0 - 1 - 7
1768		
Augst 6	2 q: mallassis	0 - 1 - 8
Sebt. 18	2 R schling 1 q: seiter	0 - 1 - 4
1767	**Adam Scheiner**	
Febrary 28	ist schultig vor schiesen	0 - 7 - 0
Mertz 27	2 hüt un 12 fisch	0 -10- 0
	Credit	0 -15- 0
1769		
Sebt: 4	1 b: wein	0 - 1 - 0

No 123

1762	**Abraham Dürr**	
21 Ocdo:	1 hut	0 - 7 - 6
	1 1/2 yd. Kelsch 1 w. schling	0 - 6 - 0
1764	**Abraham Dürr**	
Decem: 6	1 Colender 1 hut	0 - 8 - 2
1765		
July 2	2 sicheln	0 - 6 - 9
1763	**Michel Kintzel**	
Sep 19	1 Neb bunsch	0 - 0 - 6
1764		
Jan: 4	1 q: thron	0 - 1 - 0
	2 q: Rom	0 - 2 - 4
	2 Weck 1 Peiff	0 - 0 - 3
15	1 b: Rom	0 - 0 - 9
	1 gill Rom	0 - 0 - 4
	1 b: Rom	0 - 0 - 9
	1 q: seiter	0 - 0 - 4
	2 q: Haber	0 - 0 - 4
1767		
January 25	2 q: seiter	0 - 0 - 8
31	1 1/2 q: seiteröl 1/2 gill Rom	0 - 1 - 2

No 124

1763	**Gerhardt Weick**	
August 8	1 hut	0 - 7 - 6
1763	**Henrich Kring**	
July 25	1 bol. senckery	0 - 1 - 6
Dec: 16	1 lb Zucker	0 - 0 - 10
1764		
Feb: 21	1 Messer	0 - 0 - 8
May 29	2 q: bir	0 - 1 - 0
Sep: 6	3 Hüt	0 -15- 6
Oct. 15	1 gill Rom 1 q: seiter	0 - 0 - 8
1765		
Jana: 29	sein Vatter [his father] 1 kapp	0 - 3 - 0
Merz 8	1 b: Wein	0 - 1 - 2
18	1 gill Rom	0 - 0 - 4
May 27	1 q: bir	0 - 0 - 6
1766		
October 7	1 kap	0 - 3 - 0
1767		
Mertz 12	1 w: schling 1 gill rom 2 Perssen	0 - 1 - 3
Augst 5	1 q: wein 1 lb: zucker	0 - 3 - 2
6	1 lb: zucker 1/2 lb Piffer	0 - 3 - 6
Augst 15	1 q: wein 1 lb: zucker	0 - 3 - 2
Sebtem: 7	1/2 b: wein	0 - 0 - 7
	d: 10tn Juny 1769 Henrich Kring gerechnet bleibt nichts [settled with Henrich Kring. Owes nothing]	

No 125

1763	**Adam Weÿand**	
30 Meÿ	1 q: Rom	0 - 1 - 8
July 5	1 Zinnern schüssel	0 - 2 - 9
1764	**Adam Weÿand**	
Febru:	1 Licht	0 - 2 - 6
13	1 1/2 yd. Tuch	0 -16- 9
26	1/2 yd. Tuch	0 - 5 - 9
Mertz 5	1 1/4 y. flennel	0 - 4 - 6
19	1 w: schling	0 - 0 - 9
Aprill 26	2 q: wein	0 - 4 - 8
30	1 q: wein	0 - 2 - 4
	bezahlt an geld [paid in money]	1 -12- 0
	1 schnup tuch	0 - 3 - 0

1763	**Abraham Schneÿter**	
Sep. 19	1 Neb senckerÿ	0 - 0 - 9
Mar	1 Par strumb bentel	0 - 0 - 8
7	Bezahlt vor Parren [paid for the pastor['s salary] ?]	0 - 3 - 0
1764		
Dece: 3	1 1/4 yd Blau Tuch	0 -13- 0
	1 q: Rom	0 - 1 - 0

No 126

1763	**Christian Kreiter**	
Juny 20	1 b: seitereol	0 - 0 - 4
27	1 schling	0 - 0 - 6
Aug 8	1 wein schling	0 - 0 - 9
April 4	1 haut wigt 5 1/4 lb:	0 - 1 - 9
1764		
Juny	1 schaf haut	0 - 1 - 0
18	1 haut wigt 7 lb	0 - 2 - 4
	1 tag Rünnen geführt [1 day hauling bark]	0 -13- 0
	1 haut wigt 6 1/2 lb:	0 - 2 - 2
20	2 sicheln	0 - 6 - 4
July 3	1 haut wigt 7 1/2 lb:	0 - 2 - 6
1765	schuldig vor schiessen von Reyers schuttin matsch [owes for shotting at Reyer's shooting match]	0 - 4 - 6
January 10	vor holtz	0 - 5 - 0
26	1 haut wigt 9 1/4 lbs.	0 - 3 - 1
Febr 20	1 haut wigt 9 lb	0 - 3 - 0
Mertz 6	1 haut wigt 83 lb:	0 -18- 3
	1 haut wigt 7 lb:	0 - 2 - 4
8	1 haut wigt 71/2 lb:	0 - 2 - 6
	1 haut wigt 6 3/4 lb:	0 - 2 - 3
Aprill 6	1 haut wigt 7 3/4 lb:	0 - 2 - 7
May 6	1 haut wigt 6 3/4 lb:	0 - 2 - 3
July 10	1 haut wigt 7 3/4 lb:	0 - 2 - 7
Sebt 30	1 q: Thron	0 - 1 - 0
1766		
January 23	Christian Kreiter bleibt schuldig in der abrechnung [Christian Kreiter still owes in the settlement]	1 -17- 0
Mertz 29	1 q: bir	0 - 0 - 6
Octo: 27	sein Bruder bleit schuldig für ein bottel [his brother still owes for one bottle]	0 - 0 - 5
	1 haut wigt 9 3/4 lb:	0 - 3 - 3

Decem: 12	1 kalbs haut 1 haut wigt 76 lb:	1 -15- 4
	abgerechent mit Christian Kreiter d: 26: tg:	
	January 1768 bleibt schultig [settled with Christian	0 - 9 - 3
	Kreiter 26 January 1768. Still owes]	
1769		
Juny 1	1 bottel 1 q: 1 w: Rom	0 - 2 - 9

No 127
1763

Michael Reger

Juny 22	1 q: bir	0 - 0 - 6
24	1 b: seeol	0 - 0 - 4
27	1 q: Tram	0 - 1 - 0
July	1 q: bir	0 - 0 - 6
30	1 gill Rom	0 - 0 - 4
	1/2 lb. Doback	0 - 0 - 7
July 1	1 gill Rom	0 - 0 - 4
3	1 q: seiter	0 - 0 - 4
4	1 gill Rom	0 - 0 - 4
5	1 q: seiter 1 q: Tram	0 - 1 - 4
6	2 q: seiter	0 - 0 - 8
	1 q: bir 1/2 gill Rom	0 - 0 - 8
16	2 gill Rom 1 licht	0 - 3 - 2
	2 1/2 b: wein	0 - 2 - 11
	4 lb bleÿ	0 - 2 - 0
25	1 q: seiter 1 feil	0 - 2 - 0
	2 gill Rom	0 - 0 - 8
28	3 q: seiter 1 q: Rom 5 flintenstein 2 Peiffen	0 - 3 - 0
30	2 q: seiter 1 b: M: wein	0 - 2 - 8
Aug 6	1 q: Per Tram 4 q: seiter	0 - 2 - 6
8	1 q: seiter	0 - 0 - 4
9	2 q: seiter 1 weck	0 - 0 - 9
11	1/2 gill Rom 1 b: seiter	0 - 0 - 4
20	1 q: seeol 1/2 gill Rom	0 - 0 - 10
	sein sohn [his son] 1 Neb senckery	0 - 0 - 9
27	1 hut 2 b: seeol 1/2 b: wein 1 weck	0 - 8 - 10
Sep: 10	1 q: seiter	0 - 0 - 4
17	2 b: wein 2 weck	0 - 2 - 6
24	1 q: seiter 1 flintenstein	0 - 0 - 5
	2 q: seiter	0 - 0 - 8
30	1 q: seiter 2 bogen babir	0 - 0 - 5
		2 - 2 - 0

No 128
1763

Georg Trautmann

Juny 27	1 sentz	0 - 4 - 0
	1 fässgen gelent [1 little barrel lent]	
Octo 15	1 par affter geschirr	1 - 2 - 6
Nov: 14	1 Hut	0 - 7 - 6
	1 Engen Kamm	0 - 1 - 8
26	1 q: thron	0 - 1 - 0

De: 26	1 b: thron	0 - 0 - 6
	1 q: thron das vergessen worden in der rechnung [which was forgotten in settlement]	0 - 1 - 0
	Georg Trautmann	
	1 q: Thron das vergessen worden in der rechnung [which was forgotten in settlement]	0 - 1 - 0
1765	**Georg Trautmann**	
Febr 20	1 Dutzent Knöp 1b: Bir	0 - 1
1765	**Georg Trautmann**	
Decem: 12	1 b: wein	0 - 1 - 2
1769	**Georg Trautmann**	
January 25	1 b: wein 1 2/4 The	
	1 b: mallassis	0 - 2 - 4
July 20	1 w: schling	0 - 0 - 9

No 129		
1763	**Henrich Wm. Stiegel**	
Juny 29	1 q: Rom das Matheis albrecht geholt [which Matheis Albrecht fetched]	0 - 1 - 8
July 5	1 q: tram das sein Leut geholt wie sie das gerüst an dem haus gemacht [which his workers fetched when they put up scaffolding for the house]	0 - 1 - 0
	mehr 2 q: Rom das petter boren geholt [which Petter Boren fetched]	0 - 3 - 4
	1 fuhr Lathen und bort auff den Berg geholt und 1 fuhr gerüst stangen gegeben und zu dem Hauss geführt [1 load of lath and boards fetched to the hill and 1 load of scatfolding given and fetched to the house]	0 - 6 - 0
	1 mantellbiss geholt auff Henly's Blatz und sieben gebundt stro gegeben [1 mantelpiece fetched from Henley's place and seven bundles of straw given]	0 - 4 - 0
	8 fuhr stein gebrochen und geführt [8 loads of stone broken and hauled]	1 -10- 0
25	sein Schreiner [joiner] 1 q: Rom	0 - 1 - 8
28	sein Schreiner [joiner] 1 q: Rom	0 - 1 - 8
Aug: 2	sein Schreiner [joiner] 1 q: Rom	0 - 1 - 8
4	sein Schreiner [joiner] 1 q: Rom	0 - 1 - 8
	1 q: Br: wein das Matheis Albrecht geholt [which Matheis Albrecht fetched]	0 - 1 - 2
6	3 1/2 Bol Mimm 1 q: seiter vor weck und vor Heu	0 - 5 - 0
9	1 gal seiter 1 1/2 bol mim 2 weck	0 - 3 - 0
11	1 q: Rom das boren geholt zum stein brecher [which Boren took to the stone breaker]	0 - 1 - 8
15	1 bol mim	0 - 1 - 0
23	1 schling	0 - 0 - 6
	1 b: Rom das Matheis Albrecht geholt [which Matheis Albrecht fetched]	0 - 0 - 10
24	1 q: Rom das boren geholt [which Boren fetched]	0 - 1 - 8
	1 q: Rom das boren geholt [which Boren fetched]	0 - 1 - 8
29	sein Schreiner [joiner] 1 q: Rom	0 - 1 - 8
	1 lb Pulver 1 q: N: wein	0 - 8 - 0

No 130		
1763	**Johannes Busch**	
1 July	1 hut	0 - 7 - 6
1763	**Johannes Busch**	
Sep 24	1 lb pulver	0 - 4 - 0
1764	**Johannes Busch**	
Nov: 6	1 q; Thron 1/4 lb Pfeffer und schnuf toback	0 - 1 - 11
1765		
January 1	1 Calender	0 - 0 - 8
Aprill 19	1 gill Rom	0 - 0 - 4
Octob: 23	1 q: Rom	0 - 1 - 6
1766		
Febr 20	1 b: seitereöl	0 - 0 - 4
1767	**John Busch**	
Sebtemb: 14	1 q: Rom 1 gill Rom	0 - 1 - 4
1768		
January 14	1 q: Rom	0 - 1 - 0
1764	**George Ameson**	
Feb: 26	Vor knöpff	0 - 3 - 0
1767	**Felden Ilg**	
Decem: 8	1 b: wein	0 - 1 - 2
1768		
January 1	1 b: M: wein	0 - 2 - 0
Mertz 4	1 gill Rom	0 - 0 - 4
1765	**Brochnickel**	
Nov: 18	1 b: wein	0 - 1 - 2
1766		
Juny 16	1 b: seiteröl 1 b: seiter un 1 weck	0 - 0 - 7

No 131		
1763	**Friederich Müller**	
July 3	2 lb Pulver zum Brunen [to the fountain]	0 - 8 - 6
14	Vor flored Bendel	0 - 0 - 10
Aug 20	1 b: seitereol	0 - 0 - 4
	gelent	0 - 8 - 0
	1 p: strümpff	0 - 5 - 0
	vor schapp War	1 -10- 6
	gelent an geld [lent in money]	0 - 7 - 6
1764	**Friederich Müller**	
September 24	1 B: wein	0 - 1 - 2
November 24	1/4 Imber 1/4 alspeis 1/4 lb Pfeffer	0 - 1 - 9
1765		
January 1	1 Calender	0 - 0 - 8
Febr: 2	1 b: Wein	0 - 1 - 2
5	1 q: Rom	0 - 1 - 0
13	1 q: Thron	0 - 1 - 0
Mertz 30	1 q: Thron	0 - 1 - 0
Aprill 19	1 gill Rom	0 - 0 - 4

1766	**Friederich Müller**	
Febrary 14	1 b: wein	0 - 1 - 2
20	1 b: seiteröl	0 - 0 - 4
	Abgerechnet mit Friedrich Müller D: 19 May 1766 Bleibt nichts Friederich Miller gerechnet d: 26: t Novem: 1768 bleibt nichts [settled with Freiderich Müller 19 May 1766. Owes nothing. Friederich Miller settled 26 Novem. 1768. Owes nothing]	
1769		
May 15	1 b: wein	0 - 1 - 2

No 132		
1763	**Jacob Schencke**	
July 6	1 q: Rom 1 q: seiter	0 - 2 - 0
Aug 8	1 sentz 1 q: seiter	0 - 4 - 4
27	1 b: seitereol	0 - 0 - 4
Sep: 11	1 q: seiter	0 - 0 - 4
21	1 b: wein	0 - 1 - 2
27	1 q: seiter	0 - 0 - 4
Octo: 8	1 q: seiter	0 - 0 - 4
Dec 13	1 b: M: wein	0 - 2 - 0
	1 q: seiter	0 - 0 - 4
26	1 q: Persig Tram 1 q: seiter	0 - 1 - 6
		0 -12- 8
		2 - 4 - 5
		15- 6
		1 - 4
		2 -13- 11
1764		
Febr: 7	Jacob Schenck bleibt schuldig in der abrechnung [Jacob Schenck owes at settlement]	0 -14- 3
Mertz 1	1 strang seiden 2 sträng Camel garn	0 - 1 - 6
February	5 q: seiter 1 gill Rom ist ver gessen worden in der Rechnung [forgotten in the settlement]	0 - 1 - 11
21	4 1/2 q: seiter	0 - 1 - 6
Mertz 6	2 1/2 yd. drugget 1 strengel Camel garn	0 - 9 - 6
Aprill 4	vor Tuch	0 - 2 - 3
Juny 9	2 lb zucker un 1 q: seiter	0 - 2 - 0
25	1 q: seiter	0 - 0 - 4
July 6	1 sichel	0 - 3 - 9
	2 sichel	0 - 6 - 7
Aug: 12	sein sohn [his son] 1 hut	0 - 7 - 6
Octo 11	1/2 b: wein	0 - 0 - 7
	1 q: Br: wein	0 - 1 - 0
	Bezahlt vor ein sau [paid for a saw]	0 -10- 0
Decem: 6	5 lb: Negel das Boren geholt [which Boren fetched]	0 - 5 - 0
17	sein sohn [his son] vor schab gut	1 -19- 3
	Bezahlt darauf [paid thereon]	1 -15- 0

No 133		
1763	**Martin Weber**	
July 11	12 yd Kelsch und vor Neths	2 - 2 - 6
Febr 19	3 q: bir	0 - 1 - 6

Date	Entry	Amount
1764	**Martin Weber**	
Aprill 6	1 1/2 gill Rom	0 - 0 - 6
	vor Trincken	0 - 2 - 6
	1 gill Rom	0 - 0 - 4
1764	**Martin Weber**	
Novem. 26	4 gill Rom 2 1/2 q: Bir	0 - 2 - 7
1768		
May 20	4 q: bir 1 gill Rom	0 - 2 - 4
1770	**Martin Weber**	
Merz 7	Bleibt schultig in der Rechnung	0 - 2 - 5
	3 q: bir 1 gill Rom vergessen [forgotten]	0 - 1 - 10
20	4 gill Rom	0 - 1 - 4
1765	**Adam Lautermilch**	
Decem: 12	1/2 lb: Pulver	0 - 1 - 9
23	1 lb: Bley	0 - 0 - 6
	d: 10 t Novem: 1766 Jacob Geib bleibt schultig in der abrechnung [Jacob Geib owes at settlement]	0 - 3 - 7
1767	**Jacob Geib**	
Sebtem: 23	1 lb: zucker	0 - 0 - 10
1769	**Adam Lautermilch**	
May 1	vor fisch	0 - 0 - 5
Decem: 6	1 q: seiter	0 - 0 - 4
30	1 1/2 b: wein 1 w: schling	0 - 2 - 6

Date	Entry	Amount
No 134		
1763	**Adam Hoffmann**	
July 13	2 yd Kelsch 1 doz. Knöpff und 2 grosse	0 -10- 9
14	2 yd Kelsch	0 - 9 - 8
Aug 15	vor Zinern geschirr	1 - 5 - 7
Octo 10	vor seiten und Neths	0 - 2 - 6
	3 B: M: wein	0 - 6 - 0
		2 -14- 6
		0 - 7 - 6
		3 -12- 0
1764	**Adam Hofmann**	
Decem: 6	1 q: seiteröl 1 lb: schrot 2 lb: zucker 1/2 lb: Caffe	0 - 3 - 8
1765		
Janua 10	1 yd: Kelsch 1 yd: Catun 2 yd: Bendel	0 -10- 10
Febr. 20	1 q: wein 1 q: bir 1 lb: Cafee	0 - 4 - 4
	vor schiessen von Reyers Schutenmetsch [for shooting at Reyer's shooting match]	0 - 7 - 0
	Bezahlt an geld [paid in money]	1 -10- 0
Juny 24	1 lb: negel	0 - 1 - 0
Sebt 12	4 q: Thron	0 - 4 - 0
Decem: 7	1 Messer	0 - 1 - 4
1766		
January 23	Vor wein un zucker un Bottel	0 - 8 - 9
Mertz 17	2 q: Rom	0 - 2 - 4
18	4 q: Thron	0 - 4 - 0
24	1 q: Rom 2 q: seiteröl und 2 lb: zucker	0 - 5 - 0
	Bezahlt an geld [paid in money]	0 -15- 0
Augst 26	4 q: Thron 2 q; Rom un 2 lb: zucker	0 - 7 - 8

Sebt 3	1 q: wein	0 - 2 - 4
Sebt 3	1 q: wein un 1 lb: Zucker	0 - 3 - 2
6	4 lb: zucker	0 - 3 - 2
10	1 b: wein 1/2/4 Baumwolle	0 - 1 - 8
25	2 lb: zucker	0 - 1 - 8
October 3	1 b: wein	0 - 1 - 2
Novem: 17	1 q: wein	0 - 2 - 4
Decem: 15	1 hut	0 - 7 - 6
1767		
Febrary 2	1 hut un 1 Enge Kam	0 -10- 0
Mertz 12	1 w: schling	0 - 0 - 9
May 25	1 lb: zucker	0 - 0 - 10

No 135

1763	**Henrich Wm. Stiegel**	
September 3	sein schreiner [his joiner] 1 q: Rom	0 - 1 - 8
5	2 q: Rom das boren geholt [which Boren fetched]	0 - 3 - 0
	sein schreiner [his joiner] 2 q: Rom	0 - 3 - 0
7	2 q: M: wein	0 - 8 - 0
	sein Moler [his painter] 1 q: Rom	0 - 1 - 6
10	1 b: seitereol 4 q: Haber	0 - 1 - 0
15	sein Moler [his painter] 1 b: Rom	0 - 0 - 9
	sein schreiner [his joiner] 1 q: Rom	0 - 1 - 6
16	sein Moler [his painter] 2 b: Rom	0 - 1 - 6
	Vor essen Vor Jacob Eigelberger 2 1/2 Tag	0 - 2 - 6
17	sein Moler [his painter] 1 b: Rom	0 - 0 - 9
19	sein Moler [his painter] 1 b: Rom	0 - 0 - 9
	sein schreiner [his joiner]	0 - 1 - 6
20	sein Moler [his painter] 1 b: Rom	0 - 0 - 9
21	Ditto 1 b: Rom	0 - 0 - 9
22	Ditto 1 b: Rom	0 - 0 - 9
vom 23 bis zum 27 Sep:	sein Moler [his painter] 3 b: Rom	0 - 2 - 3
27	1 b: M: wein 2 bol Mimm	0 - 4 - 0
28	1 b: Rom sein Moler [his painter]	0 - 0 - 9
29	1 b: Rom sein Moler [his painter]	0 - 0 - 9
30	2 b: Rom sein Moler [his painter]	0 - 1 - 6
Octo. 3	sein schreiner [his joiner] 2 q: Rom	0 - 3 - 0
	sein Moler [his painter] 1 b: Rom	0 - 0 - 9

d. 4 October sind die 2 mauere und der Hand langer wo im Thorn schaffen komen [4 October the 2 masons and the helper came who work at the Thorn = tower]

	sein Mauer [his mason] 1 q: Rom	0 - 1 - 6
	sein Mauer [his mason] 2 gill Rom	0 - 0 - 8
4	1 q: Rom das Ibach geholt [which Ibach fetched]	0 - 1 - 6
	sein Moler [his painter] 1 b: Rom	0 - 0 - 9
6	sein schreiner [his joiner] 1 q: Rom	0 - 1 - 6
	sein Moler [his painter] 1 b: Rom	0 - 0 - 9
7	sein Mauer [his mason] 1 q: Rom	0 - 1 - 6
	sein Moler [his painter] 1 b: Rom	0 - 0 - 9
8	sein Moler [his painter] 1 b: Rom	0 - 0 - 9

No 136		
1763	**Stiegels Moler** [Stiegel's painter]	
Sept. 15	1 gill Rom	0 - 0 - 4
16	1 b: M: wein	0 - 2 - 0
17	1 wein schling 1 q: seeol	0 - 1 - 5
19	1 gill Rom	0 - 0 - 4
	1 b: M: wein	0 - 2 - 0
	1/2 b: m: wein	0 - 1 - 0
	Vor Essen Vor sein Frau und vor ein Gaul [Food for his wife and for a horse]	0 - 6 - 4
23	1 b: M: wein	0 - 2 - 0
24	1 b: M: wein 1 B: seitereol	0 - 2 - 4
	1/2 b: M: wein	0 - 1 - 0
27	1 q: seiter	0 - 0 - 4
30	2 1/2 b: wein 2 gäul beÿ Heÿ [2 horses at hay]	
	2 Mahl Essen vor 2 Weiber [2 times food for 2 women]	0 - 9 - 0
October 3	3 1/2 b: wein	0 - 4 - 1
	1 b: M: wein	0 - 2 - 0
	1 gill Rom	0 - 0 - 4
4	1/2 b: m: wein	0 - 1 - 0
6	1/2 b: wein	0 - 0 - 7
7	1/2 b: wein	0 - 0 - 7
8	1/2 b: wein	0 - 0 - 7
10	1/2 b: wein	0 - 0 - 7
12	1 b: wein	0 - 1 - 2
14	3 b: wein	0 - 3 - 6
15	1/2 b: warme wein	0 - - 9
	1/2 b: wein	0 - 0 - 7
17	1 1/2 b: wein	0 - 1 - 9
	3 gill Br: wein 1 q: seiter	0 - 1 - 1
	1 b: warme Wein	0 - 1 - 4
18	2 b: m: wein	0 - 4 - 0
19	1/2 b: wein	0 - 0 - 7
	1 q: seiter	0 - 0 - 4
	1 q: seiter	0 - 0 - 4
	2 b: wein	0 - 2 - 4
		2 -15- 7

No 137		
	Henrich Stiegel	
October 9	sein Moler [his painter] 1 b: Rom	0 - 0 - 9
10	1 b: Rom sein Moler [his painter]	0 - 0 - 9
	1 q: Rom das boren geholt [which Boren fetched]	0 - 1 - 6
11	sein Mauer [his mason] 1 q: Rom	0 - 1 - 6
	1 q: Rom das boren geholt [which Boren fetched]	0 - 1 - 6
	sein Moler [his painter] 1 b: Rom	0 - 0 - 9
12	sein Moler [his painter] 1 b: Rom	0 - 0 - 9
	sein schreiner [his joiner] 1 q: Rom	0 - 1 - 6
13	sein Mauer [his mason] 1 q: Rom	0 - 1 - 6
	sein Moler [his painter] 1 b: Rom	0 - 0 - 9
14	sein Moler [his painter] 1 b: Rom	0 - 0 - 9
15	sein Mauer [his mason] 1 q: Rom	0 - 1 - 6
	sein Moler [his painter] 1 b: Rom	0 - 0 - 9

17	sein schreiner [his joiner] 1 q: Rom	0 - 1 - 6
	sein Mauer [his mason] 1 q: Rom	0 - 1 - 6
	sein Moler [his painter] 1 b: Rom	0 - 0 - 9
18	sein Mauer [his mason] 1 q: Rom	0 - 1 - 6
	1 q: Rom das lautenschlager geholt [which Lautenschlager fetched]	0 - 1 - 6
20	sein Mauer [his mason] 1 q: Rom	0 - 1 - 6
	gelent 100 Negel [lent 100 nails]	
	sein Moler [his painter] 1 b: Rom	0 - 0 - 9
	sein Moler [his painter] 1 b: Rom	0 - 0 - 9
22	sein Mauer [his mason] 1 q: Rom	0 - 1 - 6
	sein Moler [his painter] 1 q: Rom	0 - 1 - 6
	sein schreiner [his joiner] 1 Q: Rom	0 - 1 - 6
	1/2 lb. Rothen Miny	0 - 0 - 5
25	2 q: Rom das boren geholt [which Boren fetched]	0 - 3 - 0
No. 3	1 1/2 q: Rom das boren geholt [which Boren fetched]	0 - 2 - 3
Sep. 30	sein schreiner [his joiner] 1 q: Rom	0 - 1 - 6
October	1 q: Rom das boren geholt [which Boren fetched]	0 - 1 - 6
18	gelent 100 Nägel [lent 100 nails]	
24	sein Schreiner [his joiner] 1 lb zucker	0 - 0 - 10
Nov: 14	1 q: Rom das boren geholt [which Boren fetched]	0 - 1 - 6
	sein Mauer [his mason] 1 b: Rom	0 - 0 - 9
	sein schreiner [his joiner] 1 q: Rom	0 - 1 - 6

No 138

1763	**Stiegels Mauer** [Stiegel's mason]	
Octo 11	1 gill Rom	0 - 0 - 4
14	Tribschu 2 b: wein	0 - 2 - 4
18	1 q: seiter	0 - 0 - 4
	Tribschu 1 b: seiter	0 - 0 - 4
	1 q: seiter	0 - 0 - 4
20	Tribschu 1 q: seiter	0 - 0 - 4
Dec: 6	1 gill Rom	0 - 0 - 4

1767	**Keÿser in Ridin fuhrmann** [Keyser in Reading, driver]	
Aprill 2	2 1/2 bushel Haber 2 q: Bir	0 - 8 - 6

1763	**Stiegels Moler** [Stiegel's painters]	
Octo 22	2 b: wein	0 - 2 - 4
	1/2 gill Rom	0 - 0 - 2
	1 q: seiter	0 - 0 - 4
	Hoff: 1 q: seiter	0 - 0 - 4
24	1 q: seiter	0 - 0 - 4
	Hoff: 1 q: seiter	0 - 0 - 4
25	1/2 b: wein 1 1/2 gill Rom	0 - 1 - 1
	Hoff: und Gretsch 1 gill rom 1 1/2 q: seiter 3 b: wein	0 - 4 - 4
	Hoff: und Gr: 1 q: seiter	0 - 0 - 4
	Hoff: 2 q: seiter	0 - 0 - 8
	Hoff. 1 b: seiter	0 - 0 - 2
	Hoff. und Gretsch 1 q: seiter	0 - 0 - 4
	Hoff. und Gretsch 1 1/2 q: seiter	0 - 0 - 6
26	Hoff. Gr: 1 b: wein 1 q: seiter	0 - 1 - 6
	Hoff: 1 Q: seiter	0 - 0 - 4
Nov: 28	1 b: wein 1 b: seiter gr:	0 - 1 - 4
Dec: 6	1 wein schling	0 - 0 - 9
10	1 gill rom	0 - 0 - 4
		0 -10- 6

No 139		
1763	**Jacob Düy**	
July 25	1 wein schling	0 - 0 - 9
1765	**Henrich Minnig**	
Decem: 15	1 bottel un 2 q: rom	0 - 5 - 4
	2 b: M: wein	0 - 4 - 0
	un vor Rossen Rein	0 - 0 - 10
	William Dinus	
	2 q: seitereol	0 - 1 - 4

No 140		
1763	**Jacob Kreiter**	
July 28	1 q: seiter	0 - 0 - 3
1765	**Sem Tempel**	
Decem: 15	1 gill rom	0 - 0 - 4
1766	**Georg Lechner** [,] Miller	
October 28	1 q: Bir	0 - 0 - 6
1763	**Georg Kob**	
Sep 17	1 hut vor Cattun	0 - 8 - 10
	vor senckery	0 - 0 - 9
	Bezahlt [paid]	0 - 7 - 6
1765	**Georg Kob**	
Sebt 27	100 kleine schunegel	0 - 0 - 5
	150 grosse schunegel	0 - 0 - 11
1766	**Georg Kob**	
Febrary 8 (?)	1 b: wein	0 - 1 - 2
1765	**Friedrich Würtz**	
Sebt 6	9 1/2 1/2/4 lb: Negel	0 - 9 - 8
1766	**Georg Kob**	
Febrary 8	1 b: wein	0 - 1 - 2
Aprill 14	2 q: rom	0 - 2 - 4
1767 Juny 4	1 lb: zucker	0 - 0 - 10

No 141		
1763	**Lorentz Keller**	
Augus 22	1 b: rom	0 - 0 - 10
	1 b: M: wein	0 - 2 - 0
	1 1/4 yd Cattun	0 - 6 - 10
	1/2 bu: seitereol	0 - 0 - 2
29	1 b: seitereol	0 - 0 - 4
Sep. 5	2 1/2 q: seitereol	0 - 1 - 8
7	1 b: seitereol	0 - 0 - 4
9	1 bol Mimm	0 - 1 - 0
19	1 1/2 bol mimm 1 b: seitereol	0 - 1 - 10
	2 q: seiter	0 - 0 - 8
22	1 Nob: Mimm	0 - 0 - 6
24	1/2 gill gatsel	0 - 0 - 3

27	1 q: Thron	0 - 1 - 0
	1 q: seiter	0 - 0 - 4
30	1 b: seitereol	0 - 0 - 4
October	1 b: 1 gill Br: wein	0 - 0 - 7
3	1 1/2 bol. mimm	0 - 1 - 6
3	1 schilling	0 - 0 - 6
4	1 b: M: wein	0 - 2 - 0
7	1 q: seiter	0 - 0 - 4
12	1 bol mimm	0 - 1 - 0
14	2 q: seiter	0 - 0 - 8
	1 bol. Mimm	0 - 1 - 0
	1/2 b: Br wein	0 - 0 - 4
	1 gill Ditto	0 - 0 - 3
15	1 bol. Mimm	0 - 1 - 0
	1/2 gill Br wein 1 weck	0 - 0 - 3
17	1 b: rom	0 - 0 - 9
18	1/2 gill rom	0 - 0 - 2
27	2 q: seiter	0 - 0 - 8
28	1 q: seiter 1/2 b: M: wein	0 - 1 - 4
Nov: 3	1 bol. leims bunsch	0 - 1 - 6
		1 -11- 11

No 142

	Der alt Eirisch von der Forness wo den Winter in die Schtubb gesägt [The old Irisher from the furnace who urinated in the stove room in the winter]	
Aug 22	3 bol Mimm 2 weck	0 - 3 - 2
1766	**Georg Druck**	
Decem: 8	1 Messer un 1 Peif	0 - 1 - 4
1768	**Georg Druck**	
Decem 7	vor Soleder	0 -18- 5
	Credit vor 1 haut	0 - 3 - 3
1770	**George Druck**	
Novem: 14	gerechnet Bleibt schultig [settled. Still owes]	0 - 0 - 7
1763	**Jacob Mettler** der Butscher ins Eckerts haus [the butcher in Eckert's house]	
Nov: 27	1 q: rom	0 - 1 - 2
1764		
Jan 16	2 lb zucker 1 Calender	0 - 2 - 4
22	2 lb zucker	0 - 1 - 8
	Vor saffran 1/2 lb hut zucker	0 - 1 - 3
Aprill 25	1 b: Rom	0 - 0 - 8
	vor schab gut	0 - 1 - 8
	1 b: thron	0 - 0 - 6
1766	**Danjel Altig**	
December 29	Verzehrt	0 - 2 - 3
1766	**Heiss Junge**	
May 20	1 q: seiteröl	0 - 0 - 8

No 143

1763	**Andreas Rücker**	
August 27	1 b: seitereol	0 - 0 - 4
Sep: 3	4 lb Bleÿ 1 seitereoil 1 weck	0 - 1 - 5
	2 q: seitereol	0 - 1 - 4
7	1 q: Thron	0 - 1 - 0
17	1 b: seitereol 1 weck	0 - 0 - 5
	1 Messer	0 - 0 - 10
	1/2 gill gatsel	0 - 0 - 3
27	1/2 gill Rom	0 - 0 - 4
Octo 3	1 b: Thron 1 b: seitereol	0 - 0 - 10
5	1 q: seiter	0 - 0 - 3
13	2 bol. Mim 1 q: seiter	0 - 2 - 4
	Vor Natheln	0 - 0 - 2
18	1 b: seitereol	0 - 0 - 4
Nov: 4	2 q: seiter	0 - 0 - 8
3	2 gill Rom	0 - 0 - 8
14	3 q: seiter 2 weck 1 b: wein 2 schling 1 q: seiter	0 - 3 - 8
Dec: 6	5 q: seiter	0 - 1 - 8
26	1 b: seitereol	0 - 0 - 4
Janua. 13	1 q: seiter 2 weck	0 - 0 - 6
	1 1/2 q: Bir 1 q: seiter 1 : Messer	0 - 1 - 11
29	1 b: seitereol	0 - 0 - 4
Febru: 10	3 q: seiter 1 q: Bir 2 weck	0 - 1 - 8
13	4 q: seiter 1 weck	0 - 1 - 5
14	1 B: Tram 1 q: seiter	0 - 0 - 11
22	gelent [lent]	0 - 2 - 0
Mertz	1 q: seiter 1 q: seitereol	0 - 1 - 0
10	2 q: seitereol	0 - 1 - 9
19	2 1/2 b: M: wein 1 b: Br: wein	0 - 5 - 7
April 4	2 q: seitereol 1 weck	0 - 1 - 5
14	1 b: seitereol	0 - 0 - 4
	2 q: seitereol	0 - 1 - 4
	1/4 yd. Cattun	0 - 1 - 4
	2 q: seiter	0 - 0 - 8
20	1 q: seiter	0 - 0 - 4
	1 gill rom 2 weck	0 - 0 - 6
	1 b: seitereol	0 - 0 - 4

No 144

1763	**Ludwig Mauss**	
Aug 29	1/2 virtel lb Peffr 1/2 V: lb allpeis 1/2 zucker	0 - 1 -
1765	**Wendel Lautermilch**	
July 24	1 q: Bir	0 - 0 -
1766	**Schel Butscher auf die Hammer** [butcher at the forge]	
February 21	3: Haber und 2 gill rom	0 - 1 -
1765	**der alt schweitzer** [The old Swisser]	
July 24	verzehrt	0 - 1 -
1766	**Wendel Lautermilch**	
October 18	1 b: M: wein	0 - 2 - 0

No 145

1763	**Mr. Henrich Walter**	
10	1/2 lb Pulver 3 Mahl Essen [3 times eaten] 1/2 beck Haber gaul beÿ Heu [horse at hay]	0 - 5 - 0
1765	**Henrich Walter**	
9	4 buschel gerst	0 -14- 0
August 26	verzehrt	0 - 3 - 0
Octo 25	1 b: m: wein	0 - 2 - 0
Sebt: 1	verzehrt	0 - 3 - 0
1766		
Decem: 29	verzehrt	0 - 3 - 6
1769	**Henrich Waltel**	
Decem: 6	Cedit [sic] in rechnung	1 - 4 - 7
1764	**Carl Muckenfüs**	
October 8	1 q: Thron 1/2 bol. bunsch	0 - 1 - 6
10	vor Natheln und 3 Peiffen	0 - 0 - 5
	1q: Thron	0 - 1 - 0
Decem: 6	1 q: thron	0 - 1 - 0
1765		
Feb: 13	1 q: rom 1 w: schling 1 q: seiter	0 - 2 -
17	2 yd: Bender 2 Nethel 1 streng Neths	0 - 1 - 0
20	1 q: seiter 1 Peif un vor Nodeln	0 - 0 - 6
	1 q: Rom	0 - 1 - 0
	3 lb: Reiss	0 - 0 - 10
29	2 buschel Weitzen	0 - 8 - 0
Mertz 20	vor Nodeln 1/2 beck Saltz	0 - 0 -
April 4	1 q: Rom 1 q: bir	0 - 1 - 0
19	1 q: seiter	0 - 0 -
	1 q: Rom 2 gill 1 q: seiter	0 - 2 -
May 9	2 q: seiter	0 - 0 -
19	1 q: Rom	0 - 1 -
	gelehnt an geld [lent in money]	0 - 5 -
	50 schuhnegel un vor nodeln	0 - 0 -
	2 q: bir 1 b: seiteröl 1 q: seiter	0 - 1 -

No 146

1763	**John Wumelsdorff**	
Sep 21	1 schling	0 - 0 - 6
1766		
Jana: 19	1 q: Bir 1 R: schling	0 - 1 - 0
1764	**John Billing**	
April 6	vor Trincken	0 - 2 -
1764	**Adam Fritz**	
July	1 q: br: wein	0 - 1 -
	2 lb: Reiss	0 - 0 -
	hat Credit vor ein schaaff	0 -10-
	Bezahlt an geld [paid in money]	0 - 9 -
1767		
Aprill 2	4 scheiben	0 - 2
	Alberechnet mit Adam Fritz d: 4 Augst 1767. Bleibt er schultig [Settled with Adam Fritz 4 August 1767. He still owes]	0 - 6 -

No 147

1763	**Bernt Jacob**	
Sep: 21	1 gill gatsel	0 - 0 - 6
30	1 gill Rom	0 - 0 - 4
October	dem Karch mit stein geholt [the wheelbarrow fetched with stone]	
3	2 b: M: wein 2 boten Babir	0 - 4 - 2
10	1 grosen fisch	0 - 1 - 0
17	8 b: M: wein	0 -16- 0
Dec 12	1 gill gatsel	0 - 0 - 6
15	1 b: M: wein	0 - 2 - 0
1764		
Febr: 17	2 q: bir	0 - 1 - 0
April 4	2 tag 1 gaul gelehnt [1 horse lent 2 days]	0 - 4 - 0
13	1 q: Tar	0 - 0 - 6
Juny 9	1 b: m: wein	0 - 2 - 0
July 30	1 q: bir 1 q: Taer	0 - 1 - 0
Octo 15	1 q: seiter	0 - 0 - 4
Nov: 3	1 1/2 gill gatsel	0 - 0 - 8
1765	hat gut von Friedrich Miller wegen dem [? a surname]	0 - 5 - 0
January 26	8 lb: unschlicht	0 - 4 - 8
20	2 b: M: wein	0 - 4 - 0
30	1 gallen seiter	0 - 1 - 4
1	1/2 b: M: wein	0 - 1 - 0
19	1 b: M: wein	0 - 2 - 0
Juny 1	1 gill Baumöl	0 - 0 - 8
	1 q: Bir 1 gill Baumöl	0 - 1 - 2
4	50 Zigel gelehnt	
8	1 b: M: wein	0 - 2 - 0
12	1/2 b: M: wein	0 - 1 - 0
	3 q: bir	0 - 1 - 6
18	2 gill Baumöl	0 - 1 - 4
July 2	1 lb: Negel	0 - 1 - 0
26	1 1/2 q: bir	0 - 0 - 9
Augst 13	1 q: bir un 1 b: wein	0 - 2 - 6
15	1 bol: mim	0 - 1 - 0
23	vor wein un 1/2 gill Rom	0 - 0 - 8
Seb: 6	1 q: bir un 1 gill gatchel	0 - 1 - 0

No 148

1763	**Andreas Heffer**	
Sep 21	Vor Trincken	0 - 0 - 7
Octo 23	1 1/2 lb schrot	0 - 0 - 11
1764	**Andreas Heeffer**	
Mertz 19	2 q: bir	0 - 1 - 0
30	1 w: schling	0 - 0 - 9
April 25	2 w: schling	0 - 1 - 6
28	1 w: schling	0 - 0 - 9
July 9	1 1/2 q: M: wein	0 - 6 - 0
Aug 29	1 boll Mim	0 - 1 - 0
Sep. 6	1/4 lb Peffer 1/2 virtel lb alspeis	0 - 1 - 2
Octo. 8	1 1/2 yd. Bendel	0 - 0 - 7
Decem: 6	1/2 lb Peffer 2 yd: schnir 1 yd: floret	0 - 2 - 2
1766		
Febrary 14	1 b: M: wein	0 - 2 - 0

1767		
Febru 28	ist schultig vor schiesen	0 -11- 0
	Credit vor schisen	0 -12- 0
April 25	vor wein	0 - 0 - 6

No 149

Lorentz Keller

1763		
Nov: 3	1 Bärrel seiter	0 -10- 0
	12 lb Rind fleisch	0 - 2 - 6
	1 q: wein	0 - 2 - 4
	1 b: M: wein	0 - 2 - 0
	2 lb: Butter	0 - 1 - 2
14	5 1/2 b: M: wein	0 -11- 0
15	1/2 b: M: wein	0 - 1 - 0
	1 schling	0 - 0 - 6
21	1 q: seiter	0 - 0 - 4
	1 gill Br: wein	0 - 0 - 3
24	1 q: Br: wein	0 - 2 - 4
	1 q: seiter 1/2 gill Tram	0 - 0 - 6
25	1 b: M: wein	0 - 2 - 0
Dec: 4	1 q: Br: wein	0 - 1 - 2
6	1 schling	0 - 0 - 6
	1 q: seiter	0 - 0 - 4
	1 wein schling	0 - 0 - 9
7	1 b: M: wein	0 - 2 - 0
10	1 Bol Mim 1/2 gill Rom	0 - 1 - 2
	1 b: M: wein	0 - 2 - 0
12	1 q: Bersig Tram	0 - 1 - 2
13	1 Rom schling	0 - 0 - 6
16	2 q: seiter	0 - 0 - 8
19	1 q: seiter	0 - 0 - 4
20	1 q: seiter 1 Bol Mimm	0 - 1 - 4
23	1 b: M: wein 1 schling	0 - 2 - 6
	1 q: seiter	0 - 0 - 4
24	2 b: M: wein	0 - 4 - 0
	1 schling	0 - 0 - 6
26	1 gill gatsel	0 - 0 - 6
		8 - 8 - 6

No 150

Henry Wm. Stiegel

1763		
Nov: 14	sein Maure [his mason] 1/2 b: Rom	0 - 0 - 5
17	Tag sind 3 Maure so im Thorn geschafft in Kost gangen [meals for 3 mason who worked at the Thorn]	2 -19- 6
	4 Tag einer 4 Tag zwey 1 Tag einer [4 days one, 4 days 2, 1 day one]	0 -15- 2
	sein schreiner [his joiner] 1 lb. zucker	0 - 0 - 10
21	sein schreiner [his joiner] 1 q: Rom	0 - 1 - 6
Dec: 6	1 1/2 b: Rom sein Moler[his painter]	0 - 1 - 3
8	sein Moler [his painter] 1/2 b: Rom	0 - 0 - 6
	sein Maure [his mason] 1 b: Rom	0 - 0 - 9

8	sein Maure [his mason] 1 q: Rom	0 - 1 - 6
	sein Maure [his mason] 1 q: Rom	0 - 1 - 6
17	sein Mahler 1/2 b: Rom [his painter]	0 - 0 - 5
	die Zwei wo am Brau Haus geschafft sind in Kosten gegangen der eine Zwey Tag der andere 3 Tag [Meals for the two who worked at the brew house, one for two days, one for 3 days]	
1764	**Henry Wm. Stiegel**	
Mertz 12	an die suskahanne gefahren vor stein	1 -10- 0
	[Drove to the Susquehanna for stone]	0 - 4 - 0
19	1/2 b: Rom das sein Moler geholt [which his painter fetched]	0 - 0 - 5
26	1 q: Bir	0 - 0 - 6
April 4	1 q: Rom das Boren Geholt wie er die fenster an dem Hauss aus geschnitten [which Boren fetched when he cut out the windows in the house]	0 - 1 - 2
9	1 q: bir 2 bogen Babir	0 - 1 - 2
	3 q: Rom das Boren geholt [which Boren fetched]	0 - 3 - 6
	2 q: haber	0 - 0 - 5
10	2 q: Bir	0 - 1 - 0
	die Mauer seÿn in die Kost gangen 1/2 Tag [meals for the masons 1/2 day	0 - 1 - 9
	der Baltzer in Kost gegangen [meals for Baltzer]	0 - 1 - 2
		2 - 4 - 11

No 151		
1763	**Michael Regen**	
Septem 30	1 q: Rom	0 - 1 - 6
Octo 6	1 gill Rom	0 - 0 - 6
7	1 q: seiter 1 lb. Zucker	0 - 1 - 2
20	1 b: Wein	0 - 1 - 2
25	2 q: seiter	0 - 0 - 8
Nov: 5	1/2 gill Rom	0 - 0 - 2
7	1 gill Rom	0 - 0 - 4
	1/2 b: Rom	0 - 0 - 6
	2 gill Rom	0 - 0 - 8
	1 Zollstab	0 - 1 - 0
21	1/2 gill Tram	0 - 0 - 2
24	1 gill Rom	0 - 0 - 4
26	1 q: seider	0 - 0 - 4
Dec 9	3 q: seider 1/2 gill Rom	0 - 1 - 2
15	1 q: seider	0 - 0 - 4
20	2 q: seider 2 gill Rom	0 - 1 - 4
22	1 q: seider un 1 gill Rom	0 - 0 - 8
23	1 b: m: wein	0 - 2 - 0
24	1 gill Rom 1 schling	0 - 0 -10
	3 b: seideröl 2 gill Rom	0 - 1 - 8
	1 gill Rom	0 - 0 - 4
	noch schuldig von schuttin matsch [still owes from the shooting match]	0 - 9 - 0
	sein sohn von schuttin mätsch [his son from the shooting match]	0 - 3 - 0
1764		
Jan: 2	1 gill Rom	0 - 0 - 4
	1 q: bir	0 - 0 - 6
9	1 b. wein	0 - 1 - 2
	2 q: seiter	0 - 0 - 8
		1 -11- 6

No 152

1763	**Adam Bollman**	
August 28	2 q: Thron	0 - 1 - 8
	3 b: M: wein	0 - 6 - 0
	Zalt [paid]	0 - 5 - 0
1762		
Febr:	1 b: wein	0 - 1 - 6
10	2 b: M: wein	0 - 4 - 0
Octo: 27	1 lb Pech	0 - 0 - 4
Dece 10	1 yd. schechter 1 strengel seiten 3 strengel Neths	0 - 1 - 10
August 8	1 1/2 B: M: wein	0 - 3 - 0
	1 b: M: wein 1 lb zucker	0 - 2 - 9
24	1 lb. Peffer	0 - 0 - 10
Octo 4	1 b: Wein	0 - 1 - 2
1766	**Adam Bollman**	
January 21	2 q: Tar un 1/2 b: Thron	0 - 1 - 3
Aprill 18	1 q: Tar un 1 b: Thron	0 - 1 - 0
Decem: 12	2 q Tar	0 - 1 - 0
1768		
January 1	1 b: m: wein	0 - 2 - 0
1764	**Adam Bolmann** Junge [Jr.]	
	2 bol: senckery un 3 b: wein	0 - 5 - 10
1766	**Adam Bolmann** jung [jr.]	
October 25	1 b: wein	0 - 1 - 2
1767		
January 22	7 b: wein	0 - 8 - 2
May 28	1 w: schling	0 - 0 - 9
Decem 8	1 b: wein 1 w: schling	0 - 2 - 0

No 153

1763	**Wilhelm Besch**	
October 24	4 q: seiter	0 - 1 - 4
	1 hut	0 - 7 - 6
28	1 1/2 q: seiter	0 - 0 - 6
	1 q: seiter	0 - 0 - 4
Novem: 21	1 gill rom 1 q: seiter	0 - 0 - 8
	1 schling	0 - 0 - 6
24	1 q: seider	0 - 0 - 4
26	1 gill Brand wein	0 - 0 - 4
Dec:	1/2 b: Br: wein	0 - 0 - 4
12	1 q: seiter	0 - 0 - 4
13	1 b: Tram	0 - 0 - 6
	1 q: seiter	0 - 0 - 4
15	1 q: seiter	0 - 0 - 4
23	1 gill Rom	0 - 0 - 4
1764		
Jan:	1 q: seol	0 - 0 - 8
13	2 q: seiter vor fisch	0 - 1 - 2
15	1 q: seiter	0 - 0 - 4
20	4 q: seiter	0 - 1 - 4
22	1 b: M: wein 2 q: seiter 1 q: seol	0 - 3 - 4
23	1 b: seol 1 b: seiter	0 - 0 - 6

February	1 q: seiter	0 - 0 - 4
1	2 1/2 q: seiter 1 q: Bir 1/2 gill Rom	0 - 1 - 6
	1 1/2 q: seiter	0 - 0 - 6
	1 b: Rom	0 - 0 - 8
17	2 q: seol	0 - 1 - 4
	1 b: M: wein	0 - 2 - 0
	1 q: Bir 1 q: seol	0 - 1 - 2
26	1 q: seiter	0 - 0 - 4
Juny 25	Bezahlt an geld [paid in money]	1 - 0 - 0
	1 q: seiter	0 - 0 - 4
28	3 b: seitereol	0 - 1 - 0
Mertz 5	1 q: seiter 1 b: seitereol	0 - 0 - 8
	2 q: seiter 1 gill gatsel	0 - 1 - 2
9	2 q: bir	0 - 1 - 0
	2 q: seiter	0 - 0 - 8

No 154

1763 **Jacob Schaub**

November 14	1 gill Rom rom 2 q: seiter	0 - 1 - 0
25	2 q: seiter 1 gill Tram	0 - 0 - 11
26	2 q: seiter	0 - 0 - 8
Dec: 6	1 q: seiter	0 - 0 - 4
10	1 b: seiter	0 - 0 - 2
	3 q: seiter	0 - 1 - 0
19	1 q: seiter	0 - 0 - 4
22	Vor Cattun floret	0 - 2 - 6
24	noch schuldig vor hosen	0 - 9 - 0
	1 p: schnallen	0 - 0 - 5
24	1 schling	0 - 0 - 6
26	3 seol 1 gill Tram	0 - 1- 3
30	1 q: seol	0 - 0 - 8
1764		
Jan: 8	1 B: M: wein	0 - 2 - 0
9	1 q: seiter	0 - 0 - 4
13	2 q: seiter	0 - 0 - 8
16	1 q: seiter	0 - 0 - 4
21	1 gill Rom	0 - 0 - 4
29	2 q: Bir	0 - 1 - 0
30	1 b: seol	0 - 0 - 4
febr: 1	1 b: seiter	0 - 0 - 2
3	1 q: seiter	0 - 0 - 4
17	2 q: seiter	0 - 0 - 8
21	1 schling 1/2 gill Rom	0 - 0 - 8
28	6 q: haber und 1 gaul bey heu [horse at hay]	0 - 1 - 6
Mertz 2	1 b: wein 1 q: Rom	0 - 2 - 8
9	1/2 viertel thee	0 - 1 - 1
	1 q: bir 1 weck	0 - 0 - 7
	1 gill lein eol (?)	0 - 0 - 3
12	1 lb Zucker	0 - 0 - 10
14	2 q: seiter	0 - 0 - 8
19	1 gill Rom	0 - 0 - 4
30	1 lb. zucker	0 - 0 - 10
April 10	1/2 gill tram	0 - 0 - 2

No 155

1763	**Henrich Keÿler**	
October 28	8 lb. fleisch	0 - 1 - 8
Nov. 14	vor Trincken	0 - 0 - 3
	4 1/2 q: seiter 1 gill Rom 2 q: haber	0 - 2 - 2
Dec: 23	1 q: seiter	0 - 0 - 4
24	1 q: seiter 1 b: seol	0 - 0 - 8
26	1 b: wein	0 - 1 - 2
1764		
Jan: 8	4 1/2 q: bir	0 - 2 - 3
13	3 b: Bir	0 - 0 - 9
16	1 q: seiter	0 - 0 - 4
21	1 q: seiter 1 Calender	0 - 1 - 0
	1 q: Bir	0 - 0 - 6
22	1 b: seol 1 q: seol 1 q: Bir	0 - 1 - 6
23	1 q: seiter	0 - 0 - 4
	1 gill Rom 1 q: seiter	0 - 0 - 8
29	1 b: seol 1 q: seiter	0 - 0 - 8
Febr: 2	1/2 gill Rom 1 q: seiter	0 - 0 - 6
6	1 1/2 gill Rom	0 - 0 - 6
8	gelent	0 - 0 - 9
13	1 q: seiter	0 - 0 - 4
17	2 q: seiter	0 - 0 - 8
	1 q: 1/2 b: seol	0 - 0 - 10
	2 lb zucker	0 - 1 - 8
19	1 yd. floret	0 - 0 - 4
	1 q: seiter	0 - 0 - 4
	1 gill Rom	0 - 0 - 4
26	1 q: seiter	0 - 0 - 4
	1 Messer	0 - 0 - 10
28	2 lb. zucker	0 - 1 - 8
Mertz 3	1 q: seiter	0 - 0 - 4
6	3 q: seiter	0 - 1 - 0
9	2 buschel weitzen	0 - 8 - 0
	1/2 gill Rom	0 - 0 - 2
9	2 gill Rom	0 - 0 - 8
	1 q: seiter	0 - 0 - 4

No 156

1763	**Jehu Borckhart**	
October 21	vor schap gut	2 -12- 3
1767	**Martin Heil**	
January 17	1 lb: Pulver das Georg Conrad geholt [which Georg Conrad fetched]	0 - 3 - 6
1765	**George Gabriel**	
Febr 29 [sic]	2 q: seiter	0 - 0 - 8
1765	**Martin Schutÿ**	
Augst 17	6 q: Rom	0 - 6 - 0
29	4 q: Rom	0 - 4 - 0
Sebt 2	6 q: Rom	0 - 6 - 0
6	6 q: Rom	0 - 6 - 0
	4 q: Rom un 8 lb: Negel	0 -12- 0
27	6 q: Rom	0 - 6 - 0

Octo 10	4 q: Rom	0 - 4 - 0
16	6 q: Rom	0 - 6 - 0
	1 Cafe	0 - 1 - 8
23	4 q: Br: wein	0 - 4 - 0
25	7 gallen Br: wein	1 - 4 - 6
	6 lb: zucker	0 - 5 - 0
Novem: 23	6 q: Tram	0 - 6 - 0
1766		
Jan: 1	4 q: Rom	0 - 4 - 8
26	4 q: Rom 1 q: Br: wein 3 lb: zucker	0 - 9 - 2
28	4 q: Br: wein 2 lb: Reiss	0 - 4 - 7
February 21	4 q: Br: wein	0 - 4 - 0

No 157

1763 **Henrich Schramm**

October 23	1 1/2 q: Thron	0 - 1- 6
	1764 January 11 hab ich mit Henrich Schram Abgerechnet bleibt schuldig [1764 January 11 I settled with Henrich Schram. Still owes]	1 - 4 - 0

1764 **Henrich Schram**

February	Vor Bir	0 - 0 - 4
3	1 q seiter	0 - 0 - 4
	1 q: bir	0 - 0 - 6
17	Vor schreiben	0 - 3 - 0
	Vor schreiben	0 - 1 - 0
	4 b: Wein 2 q: bir 2 Weck	0 - 6 - 0
Mertz 19	1 q: bir 1 weck	0 - 0 - 7
	1/2 b: m: wein	0 - 1 - 0
	gelehnt [lent]	0 - 5 - 0
	1 b: Bir	0 - 0 - 3
May 29	1 1/2 q: br: wein	0 - 1 - 6
Juny 18	1 q: bir	0 - 0 - 6
24	1 q: bir	0 - 0 - 6
July 3	1 sichel	0 - 3 - 1
27	1 sentz 1 q: bir	0 - 4 - 6
	gelent in Läncaster [lent in Lancaster]	0 -15- 0
Nov: 3	1 b: Wein	0 - 1 - 2
6	1/2 gill Rom	0 - 0 - 2
1765 May 27	3 q: bir 1 b: seiteröl	0 - 1 - 10
July 2	1 q: seiteröl	0 - 0 - 8
1766 Mertz 27	1 q: Bir	0 - 0 - 6
July 7	1 sichel	0 - 3 - 2
25	1 q: Thron	0 - 1 - 0
1767		
July 20	6 q: Br: wein	0 - 4 - 6
25	1 1/2 q: Br: wein	0 - 1- 2
October 12	vor wein	0 - 7 - 6
		3 - 4 - 9

No 158

1763 **Jacob Miller**

October 23	1 lb. Pech	0 - 0 - 4
Nov: 5	1 q: seiter	0 - 0 - 4
De: 12	1 lb Pech	0 - 0 - 4
15	1 b: M: Wein	0 - 2 - 0

1764	**Jacob Miller**	
April 25	1 q: seiter	0 - 0 - 4
	1 lb: Bech	0 - 0 - 4
28	1 w: schling	0 - 0 - 9
May 26	1 w: schling	0 - 0 - 9
	1 w: schling un 2 weck 29	0 - ? - ?
	2 lb Bech	0 - 0 - 8
	1 w: schling	0 - 0 - 9
Juny 18	1 b: Wein	0 - 1 - 2
28	1 b: Rom	0 - 0 - 7
July 2	1 q: seiter	0 - 0 - 4
3	1 q: seiter	0 - 0 - 4
	1 lb: zucker	0 - 0 - 10
9	1 Eimer	0 - 1 - 6
13	1 fisch	0 - 0 - 2
23	1/2 buschel saltz	0 - 2 - 0
Aug: 16	1 q: Rom	0 - 1 - 0
Sep: 3	1 q: Ditto	0 - 1 - 0
4	2 q: Rom	0 - 2 - 0
6	1/4 lb Peffer	0 - 0 - 10
	1 q: Rom	0 - 1 - 0
10	1 q: Rom	0 - 1 - 0
15	1 q: Ditto	0 - 1 - 0
19	1 q: Ditto	0 - 1 - 0
21	1/2 gill Rom	0 - 0 - 2
22	1 q: Rom	0 - 1 - 0
Octo 15	6 lb Nägel	0 - 6 - 0
November 6	1 q: Thron	0 - 1 - 0
10	1 q: seiter 5 lb: negel	0 - 5 - 4
Decem: 6	1/4 lb: Peffer 1/4 lb: Alspeis 1/2 buschel Saltz	0 - 4 - 5

No 159		
1763	**Michael Winter**	
October 24	1 q: seiter	0 - 0 - 4
	1 b: seiter	0 - 0 - 2
Nov: 14	1 h: schnallen	0 - 1 - 5
	2 Wein schling	0 - 1 - 6
25	1 paar strümp un 1 wein schling	0 - 6 - 3
De: 20	1 b: Rom	0 - 0 - 7
1764	**Michael Winter**	
Aprill 28	1 q: seiter	0 - 0 - 4
	1/2 b M Wein	0 - 1 - 0
July 9	1 b: Wein	0 - 1 - 2
	Abgerechnet mit Michael Winter d: 13 t: January 1768 bleibt schultig [Settled with Michael Winter 13 January 1768. Still owes]	0 - 6 - 7
	Aberechnet mit Michael Winter d: 9 t: December 1768 Bleibt nichts [Settled with Michael Winter 9 December 1768. Owes nothing]	
Decem: 22	1 Erdenen Haffen	0 - 1 - 4
	Michael Winter	
	gerechnet d: 13 t: Aprill 1770 bleibt nichts [Settled 13 April 1770. Owes nothing]	
	Michael Winter	
	gerechnet d: 4 t: May 1771 bleibt nichts [Settled 4 May 1771. Owes nothing]	

No 160

	Petter Tasher Henrich Schäffer	
1763		
October 28	1 Hut 2 lb Zucker 1 q: M: wein	0 - 4 - 0
		1 - 9 - 8
	Vor den schul Tisch: 58 fus Bord 1 1/4 - 1/2 viertel lb Nägel [for the school table: 58 feet boards]	
Nov: 14	1 q: Thron 1 b: seiter	0 - 1 - 2
	vor schap war	0 -11- 9
	Bezalt das ist Wahr in der stadt [paid for goods in the city]	0 - 5 - 0
	3 y: Leinen Tuch 1/4 yd Drugget und Neths	1 - 0 - 3
27	1/2 lb thee 1 lb Cafe 1 lb Zucker 1 1/2 yd flored	0 - 6 - 4
28	1 q: Thron	0 - 1 - 0
Dec: 9	vor schap gut 2 lb zucker	0 -19- 0
10	Vor Natheln	0 - 1 - 6
13	3 lb zucker	0 - 2 - 6
	1 q: Thron	0 - 1 - 0
13	1/2 buch Babir	0 - 0 - 9
22	1 p: strümpff	0 - 7 - 0
23	1/2 Viertel lb. Peffer 1 q: Tron	0 - 1 - 5
24	1 p: strümpff	0 - 1 - 8
1764	2 lb zucker	0 - 1 - 8
Jan: 1	1 q: Thron	0 - 1 - 0
	2 lb zucker	0 - 1 - 8
9	1 Kapp	0 - 3 - 3
	1 Calenter 1 b: Bir	0 - 0 - 11
23	2 1/1 Buschel Weitzen	0 -10- 0
	1/2 yd Cattun	0
	1 1/2 yd floret	0 - 2 - 9
25	1 q: Thron	0 - 1 - 0
febr: 6	1 q: Thron	0 - 1 - 0
	3 lb zucker 1 Engen Cam 2 p: hemder knöpff	0 - 4 - 10

No 161

	Phillip Ohlinger	
1763		
Nov: 5	1 b: wein	0 - 1 - 2

	Willem Fiel	
1765		
Decem: 25	3 q: seiter	0 - 1 - 0
1768		
Aprill 23	1 q: seiter	0 - 0 - 4

	John Fiel	
1767		
July 9	1 sichel	0 - 3 - 2

	Nickolaus Wissler	
1763		
No: 21	Bleibt schultig [Still owes]	0 - 1 - 9

	Jacob Wissner	
1765		
Sebt 2	2 q: Rom	0 - 2 - 0
6	1 q: seiter	0 - 0 - 4

	Jacob Wissner	
1770		
October 22	gerechnet Bleibt schultig [settled. Still owes]	0 - 4 - 3

No 162

1763	**Der Versoffene Gerber** [The drunken Tanner]	
October 28	Vor Trincken	0 - 5 - 0
1768	**Der Versoffene Gerber** [The drunken Tanner]	
Aprill 23	1 q: seiter 1/2 gill Rom 1 Peif	0 - 0 - 7
	2 1/2 gill Rom un 1 b: seiter	0 - 1 - 0
26	1 gill Rom	0 - 0 - 4
Juny 21	2 gill Rom	0 - 0 - 8
July 2	1 gill Rom	0 - 0 - 4
Augst 6	1/2 gill Rom	0 - 0 - 2

1763	**Andreas Knauer**	
Nov: 24	3 q: seiter	0 - 1 - 0
1766	**Jacob Xander**	
Jann 26	1 b: M: wein un 3 q: bir	0 - 3 - 6

No 163

1763	**Christoph Kapp**	
Nov 27	1 hut 1 1/2 yd floret	0 -12- 6
	gelend [lent]	3 - 0 - 0
Dec: 13	1 feil	0 - 1 - 8
Jan: 15	1 Calender	0 - 0 - 8

1767	**Johann Michael Trautmann**	
February 5	1 w: schling	0 - 0 - 9

1764	**Simon Leible**	
Jan 1	1 Calender	0 - 0 - 8
	1 q: seiter	0 - 0 - 4
	1 feil	0 - 0 - 6
	2 q: seiter	0 - 0 - 8
	1 Catechismus	0 - 1 - 0
1	1 q: Br: wein	0 - 1 - 2
3	1 q: Ditto	0 - 1 - 2
5	1 b: Wein	0 - 1 - 2
	1 b: Wein	0 - 1 - 2
	1 q: Br: Wein	0 - 1 - 2

No 164

1763	**Stiegels Moler** [Stiegel's painters]	
Dec:	1 b: wein	0 - 1 - 2
12	1 gill Rom	0 - 0 - 4
13	1 gill gatsel	0 - 0 - 6
	1 gill Rom	0 - 0 - 4
	2 gill Tram	0 - 0 - 6
	1 gill Rom	0 - 0 - 4
19	2 gill Rom 1 wein schling 1 q: seiter	0 - 1 - 9
20	1 gill Rom	0 - 0 - 4
22	1 gill rom 1 q: seiter	0 - 0 - 8
	1/2 gill Rom	0 - 0 - 2
	gelend gretsch [lent to Gretsch]	0 - 7 - 6
	1 1/2 q: seiter	0 - 0 - 6

23	1 gill Tram	0 - 0 - 3
26	1 gill gatsel 4 gill Rom 4 q: seiter	0 - 3 - 2
	1 b: wein	0 - 1 - 2
1766	**Johannes Geiger**	
May 9	4 lb: zucker 1 q: seiter un Vor spellen 1 Peif	0 - 4 - 1
Juny 12	6 lb: zucker 12 q: seiter	0 - 5 - 8
July 11	4 lb: zucker	0 - 3 - 4
Augst 2	2 q: seiteröl 2 q: haber	0 - 1 - 8

No 165

1763	**Caspar Schweitzer**	
December 10	1 b: M: wein	0 - 4 - 0
1765	**Jacob Krinter Kiffer** [cooper]	
Mertz 17	4 1/2 yard schwartze Borschet un 1 halss tuch un 2 1/2 yd: Tuch un 2 yard: schalun 1 Dutzent Knöp un schechter un 2 yd: Tuch un 1 q: m: wein 1/2 lb: weisse zucker un 1 q: wein 6 q: haber 1 b: Thron	3 -12- 0
	bezahl an geld [paid in money]	0 - 5 - 0
1766	**Ernst Schwertzler**	
July 14	1 ambel 1 q: wein un 2 q: Thron	0 - 6 - 10
Augst 6	2 q: Rom 4 lb: zucker 1 schnubtuch 1 gorg	0 - 7 - 3
26	1 q: Rom	0 - 1 - 0
1768	**Ernst Schwertzler**	
Augst 6	1 q: wein 2 q: Rom un 2 lb: zucker	0 - 5 - 10
	2 q: Rom un 5 lb: zucker	0 - 5 - 9
	Credit	0 - 7 - 6
1765	**Speck Hanss** [a nickname: "Bacon John"]	
Augst 29	3 b: seiter	0 - 0 - 6

No 166

1763	**Henrich Kayler**	
De: 23	1 q: seiter	0 - 0 - 4
24	1 q: seiter 1 B: seol	0 - 0 - 8
26	1 b: wein	0 - 1 - 2
1766	**Johannes Gossweiler**	
Aprill 5	1 w: schling 1 gill Rom 2 weck	0 - 1 - 3
1766	**Michael Weber**	
May 29	1 b: Rom 1/2 b: wein	0 - 1 - 2
Juny 5	1 b: wein	0 - 1 - 2
25	1 stroh hut	0 - 2 - 10
Sebtem 6	1 q: Thron	0 - 1 - 0
29	1/2 b: Rom	0 - 0 - 5
1768	**Michael Weber**	
Feb: 12	1/2 b: baum öhl	0 - 1 - 2

No 167

	Lorentz Arnold	
1763		
Dec: 24	1 hut	0 - 4 - 0
1764		
Febru:	Aus altem Buch fol. 87 [from the old book, page 87]	1 - 1 - 1
6	1 br wein 1 lb zucker	0 - 2 - 0
Merz 30	1 lb: zucker	0 - 0 - 10
April 4	1 1/4 yd: Tuch 1 1/4 yd: schalun 1 Messer	1 -12- 0
	1 q: Bir	0 - 0 - 6
Juny 28	3 q: seiter	0 - 1 - 0
	1 b: Wein 1 B: leineohl	0 - 1- 11
Sept 8	1 q: Rom	0 - 1 - 6
10	1 lb schrot	0 - 0 - 7
28	1 yd flenell	- 3 - 3
Octo	1 b: Thron	0 - 0 - 6
11	1 hut	0 - 7 - 0
	gelent an geld [lent in money]	1 - 0 - 0
1765	Abgerechent mit Lorentz Arnold d. 16 ten February	
d. 16 Feb	Bleÿbt er schuldig [Settled with Lorentz Arnold 16 February. He still owes]	1 - 3 - 4
	Bleÿbt schultig wegen Peter Tascher [Still owes on account of Peter Tascher]	0 -19- 0
Mertz 18	1 q: Thron	0 - 1 - 0
27	1 q: seiter	0 - 0 - 4
Aprill 6	1 beck flags saamen gelehnt	
Juny 13	1 sentz	0 - 4 - 0
Nov: 18	1 1/2 lb kreiten	0 - 0 - 6
20	1 Kap	0 - 3 - 3
	1 Namen Buch	0 - 0 - 9
	1 lb: schnub tuback	0 - 1 - 4
1766		
Febray 4	1 Catecismus	0 - 1 - 6
1769		
Augst 22	Lorentz Arnold gerechnet Bleibt schultig [Lorentz Arnold settled. Still owes]	1 - 0 - 3

No 168

	Frietrich Müller	
	Noch schultig vor schiessen [Still owes for shooting]	0 - 4 - 0
	1/2 lb Pulver	0 - 2 - 0
	gelent vor schuhmacher [lent for shoemaker]	0 - 8 - 0
	1 p: strümpff	0 - 5 - 0
	vor schapp gut vor Canisol	1 - 10 - 0
	gelent vor schneiter [lent for tailor]	0 - 7 - 6
	2 y. kelsch	0 - 5 - 0
July 12	2 1/2 yd: Tuch un macher Lohn vor 1 hem [2 1/2 yd cloth and seamstress fee for 1 shirt]	0 - 7 - 3
	gelent vor schuhmacher [lent for shoemaker]	0 -10- 6
	1 par strümpff	0 - 5 - 0
	vor tuch	0 - 1- 2
	Vor Ein Camisol	1 - 4 - 0
	vor seiten und knöpff zu hosen	0 - 2 - 8
	vor schapp gut zum rock	2 -15- 0
	gelent vor schneiter [lent for tailor]	0 -14- 4
	1 par strümp	0 - 5 - 6
	Vor ein hirsch fell	0 -16- 0

1765	**Johannes Walter** bey Hursch [at Hursch's}	
Mertz 30	300 schuhnegel	0 - 1 - 8

No 169

Kattarina Leibelin hat Credit vor schlosser gschirr und 1 kist welches ich **Alexander Shafer** ihr abgekaufft hab [Kattarina Leibelin has credit for . . . which I Alexander Schaeffer bought from her]

solches bekennet
ihr
Kattarina Leibelin
marck
[Acknowledge by Kattarina Leibelin, her mark]

d: 14 1 february
1764
Andreas Rücker
Lorentz Arnold

1765	**Michael Leÿdig**	
July 15	1 q: wein 2 lb: zucker	0 - 4 - 0
1766		
Febr: 8	1 hut	0 - 7 - 6
Juny 12	2 Sentzen 1 q: Rom	0 - 9 - 0
July 20	8 1/2 gallen Br: wein 1/2 b: Br: wein	1 - 6 - 1
1768		
January 2	1 b: wein	0 - 1 - 2
Mertz 28	1 hut	0 - 4 - 0
	Michael Leidig	
Sebtem		
3 1770	Bleibt schultig in der abrechnung [Still owes in the settlement]	0 -14- 0

No 170

1764	Hab ich mit **Casper Schweitzer** Abgerechnet	0 -15- 5
febu 13	Bleibt schudig [I settled with Casper Schweitzer. Still owes]	
	1 b: m: Wein das vergessen werden in der Rechnung [which was forgotten in the settlement]	0 - 4 - 0
13	3 q: seiter	0 - 1 - 0
17	1 q: seiter 1 q: Bir	0 - 0 - 10
21	Bezalt an geld [paid in money]	0 -15- 0
26	4 q: seiter	0 - 1 - 4
	gelent [lent]	0 - 2 - 0
Mertz 3	3 q: seiter	0 - 1 - 0
6	3 q: seiter	0 - 1 - 0
9	3 Wein schling 2 q: seiter	0 - 2 - 11
9	2 Wein schling 1 q: seiter	0 - 1 - 10
	1 q: seiter	0 - 0 - 4

19	2 q: seiter	0 - 0 - 8
	3 q: seiter	0 - 1 - 0
	1 fisch	0 - 0 - 4
	2 q: seiter	0 - 0 - 4
20	1 q: bir	0 - 0 - 6
	2 b: m: wein 2 q: seiter	0 - 4 - 8
	1 q: seiter	0 - 0 - 4
30	1 bole mim	0 - 1 - 0
Aprill 13	2 q: seiter	0 - 0 - 8
	1 q: Ditto	0 - 0 - 4
25	2 q: seiter	0 - 0 - 8
1764	Hab ich mit Casper Schweitzer abgerechnet den 19den Tag Juny [I settled with Casper Schweitzer 19 June.]	

1769	**Michael Miller**, sein Miller [his miller]	
February 14	1 gesang Buch	0 - 9 - 6
	1 b: m: wein 1 w: schling 1 Par schnallen	0 - 3 - 5

No 171

1764	**Lorentz Keller**	
16 feb:	bleibt schultig in der abregnun [still owes in settlement]	3 - 7 - 10
17	2 Bol Mim	0 - 2 - 0

1764	**Michael Haack** in der Pfannen [in the pan, a place designation]	
febr: 18	1 q: seitereol	0 - 0 - 8
may 4	1 q: Bir	0 - 0 - 6

1767	**Ploferber** [Blauferber] [bluedyer]	
October 12	1 b: wein	0 - 1 - 2
27	2 q: Rom	0 - 2 - 0
29	1 q: seiter	0 - 0 - 4

No 172

	Stiegel Mohler [Stiegel's painters]	
January 1	3 q: Haber 1 gill Rom	0 - 0 - 10
	1 b: seiter 1/2 gill Rom	0 - 0 - 4
2	1 b: seiter 1 gil Rom	0 - 0 - 6
7	1 q: seiter	0 - 0 - 4
8	1 q: seiter	0 - 0 - 4
13	8 Tag in kost gangen und den gaul Beÿ heu gehabt 8 Tag-gretsch und davit pautz [8 days' meals and the horse at hay 8 days- Gretsch and David Pautz]	
	1 q: bir	0 - 0 - 6
16	1 q: seiter 2 gill Br: Wein	0 - 0 - 10
21	2 gill gatsel	0 - 0 - 10
	2 b: M: Wein	0 - 4 - 0
	1 b: Wein	0 - 1 - 2
	2 b: M: Wein	0 - 4 - 0
22	1 q: seeol	0 - 0 - 8

23	1 gill Rom	0 - 0 - 4
	1 q: seeol	0 - 0 - 8
30	1/2 b: M: Wein	0 - 1 - 0
	1 gill Rom	0 - 0 - 4
febr:	3 gill gatsel	0 - 1 - 6
1	1 Boll Mimm	0 - 1 - 0
8	1 gill Rom	0 - 0 - 4
	1 q: seiter	0 - 0 - 4
	2 q: 1/2 b seeol	0 - 1 - 6
26	1 q: seiter	0 - 0 - 4
	bezahlt [paid]	0 - 5 - 0
28	4 b: seitereol	0 - 1 - 4
	2 b: seitereol	0 - 0 - 8
Mertz 3	1 q: seiter	0 - 0 - 4
9	1 gill Rom	0 - 0 - 4
	1 q: bir	0 - 0 - 6
	1 q: bir 1 gill Rom	0 - 0 - 10
12	1 gill Rom	0 - 0 - 4
19	3 q: seiter	0 - 1 - 0
	1 1/2 gill Rom	0 - 0 - 6
	1 gill Rom	0 - 0 - 4
		1 - 2 - 8

No 173

1764	**Petter Tascher**	
February 14	1 q: Wein 1 q: Rom	0 - 3 - 10
Mertz 5	1 q: Rom	0 - 1 - 6
13	2 lb Zucker	0 - 1 - 8
	2 buschel Weitzen	0 - 8 - 0
26	1 b: Bir	0 - 0 - 3
	2 lb Zucker	0 - 1 - 8
April 6	2 p: schnallen	0 - 2 - 6
6	1 schnup Tuch	0 - 1 - 8
	1 1/2 q: bir	0 - 0 - 8
	1 q: Rom	0 - 1 - 2
13	2 buschel Weitzen	0 - 8 - 0
May 4	3 lb Zucker	0 - 2 - 6
15	2 buschel Weitzen	0 - 7 - 6
	1 q: Rom	0 - 1 - 2
21	1 lb Zucker	0 - 0 - 10
28	2 lb Zucker	0 - 1 - 8
Juny 6	1/2 yd shalun 1 strang camel garn 1 dutzent knöpff	0 - 2 - 3
		2 - 6 - 10
1764		
12 Nov:	Abgerechnet mit Peter Tascher d: 12 November Bleÿbt er mir schuldig [Settled with Peter Tascher 12 November. He still owes me]	5 - 6 - 5
Fer 13	Credit com Hannes Wolfsperger	1 - 0 - 0
November 21	Credit von Lorentz Arnold	0 -19- 0
	1 lb Cafee 1 q: Thron 1/2 b: wein	0 - 3 - 1
30	1 b: Rom	0 - 0 - 6
	1 q: Thron	0 - 1 - 0
1766	**Peter Tascher**	
May 29	1 hut un 2 yd: Kelsch	0 -14- 6
1771	**Peter Tascher**	
May 7	gerechnet Bleibt schultig [settled. Still owes]	0 - 1 - 6

No 174

1764	**Michael Reger**	
Jan: 13	1/2 gill Rom	0 - 0 - 2
	2 1/2 gill Rom	0 - 0 - 10
23	Bezahlt [paid]	0 -15- 0
	1/2 gill Rom 1 q: seiter	0 - 0 - 6
Febr: 8	1 gill Rom 1 gill Br: Wein	0 - 0 - 7
	gelent [lent]	0 - 1 - 0
	2 q: seeol 1 lb Bley	0 - 1 - 11
10	2 gill Rom	0 - 0 - 8
	2 q: seiter	0 - 0 - 8
	2 q: Bir	0 - 1 - 0
	1 Weck	0 - 0 - 1
10	2 1/2 q: Br: Wein	0 - 2 - 11
14	2 q: seol	0 - 1 - 4
	1 q: Rom	0 - 1 - 2
	1/2 lb Zucker	0 - 0 - 5
26	1 gill tram	0 - 0 - 3
27	1 gill Rom	0 - 0 - 4
28	2 q: seiter	0 - 0 - 8
	1 Br: Wein 1 Weck	0 - 0 - 4
Mertz 5	1 gill Rom	0 - 0 - 4
6	1 1/2 Buschel Weitzen	0 - 6 - 0
10	1 1/2 q: bir	0 - 0 - 9
	1 gill Rom	0 - 0 - 4
19	1 gill Tram	0 - 0 - 3
26	1 q: seiter 1/4 lb Pulver 1 lb Bley	0 - 1 - 10
April 6	1 M: Wein 1 q: bir 1 fisch	0 - 2 - 11
6	1 q: seiter	0 - 0 - 4
10	1 q: seiter	0 - 0 - 4
12	1 q: Tram	0 - 1 - 2
12	1 b: Tram	0 - 0 - 7
13	2 q: seiter	0 - 0 - 8
	1 q: seiter 5 Weck	0 - 0 - 9
20	1 q: bir 3 Weck	0 - 0 - 9
	1 Par schnallen	0 - 1 - 3
	1/2 gill Rom	0 - 0 - 2

No 175

1764	**Sebastian Hauer**	
January 14	1 yd. tuch 1 1/2 yd shalun 1 1/2 dutzent knöpff	
	1: strang seiten 14 yd schetter 1 gill Rom	2 - 2 - 8
1768	**der Mann wo ins dreers haus hat kommen sollen**	
	[the man who was supposed to move into Dreer's house]	
February 26	1 b: seiter 1 gill Rom	0 - 0 - 6
1764	**Georg Schmid** auf stiegels fornes [at Stiegel's furnace]	
December 19	2 Rom schling 4 weck 1/2 gill Rom	0 - 1 - 6
1765		
January 19	1/2 b: wein	0 - 0 - 8
agst 26	3 boli mim 1 b: wein	0 - 4 - 2
Seb: 2	1 g: Rom	0 - 1 - 0
12	1 q: Thron	0 - 1 - 0
13	1 w: schling	0 - 0 - 9

16	1 q: Thron	0 - 1 - 0
Octo. 23	1 q: Thron	0 - 1 - 0
1766		
Mertz 31	1 R: schling un b: wein 1 gill Rom 1 b: Bir	0 - 2 - 9
July 1	1 R: Schling	0 - 0 - 6
	Bezahlt an geld [paid in money]	0 -10 - 0
1767		
October 12	4 w: schling	0 - 3 - 0
1768		
February 26	1 w: schling 1 b: Bir	0 - 1 - 0
Aprill 6	2 q: westin Rom un 1 w: schling	0 - 3 - 9
	2 q: Rom	0 - 2 - 6

No 176

1764

Henrich Strack

Jan: 29	1 q: Rom 1 Q: Wein 1 Muscatnis 3 lb: Zucker	0 - 6 - 8
30	1 q: Wein 1 q: Rom saffran	0 - 4 - 4
Febru	1 Bottel gelent [lent]	
6	1 q: Wein 1: Rom 1 lb Zucker	0 - 4 - 8
10	2 lb Zucker	0 - 1 - 8
1764		
Sep: 24	1 lb Caffe 3 lb Zucker 1 Muscatenus 1 q: Wein	0 - 6 - 8
	1 q: fisch Thron	0 - 1 - 0
Octo 11	17 lb Nägel	0 -17- 0
1765		
Mertz 30	2 lb: Zucker 1/2 lb: Caffe 2 yd: Bendel	0 - 2 - 8
	Bezahlt an geld [paid in money]	1 - 5 - 0
Juny 24	2 sicheln	0 - 6 - 1
Sebt 2	1 q: Thron	0 - 1 - 0
25	1 bol: senckery	0 - 1 - 6
Octo: 25	1 q: wein un 1 bottel	0 - 4 - 1
No: 2	1 q: Rom	0 - 1 - 0
	Abrechnet mit Henrich Strack d: 15 ten Augst 1766 Bleibt nichts [Settled with Henrich Strack 15 August 1766. Owes nothing]	
Sebtem: 3	1 q Thron	0 - 1 - 0
5	3 lb: Zucker un 4 q: Bir	0 - 4 - 6
16	1 q: wein	0 - 2 - 4
October 8	2 lb Zucker un 1 b: wein	0 - 2 - 10
1767		
Mertz 20	1 lb: Weisen Zucker	0 - 1 - 8
August 24	1 b: wein	0 - 1 - 2
Sebtem 27	1 q: M: wein	0 - 4 - 0
October 5	1 b: M: wein	0 - 2 - 0
1768		
Sebtem: 26	Henrich Strack Bleibt schuldig in der Rechnung [Henrich Strack still owes in the settlement]	1 - 1 - 0

No 177

1764

Henrich Keyler

Mertz 9	2 q: Bir	0 - 1 - 0
10	3 b: seitereol	0 - 4 - 0
	1/2 lb imber 1/4 lb: alspeis 1 q: seiter	0 - 1 - 8

19	1 b: seeol	0 - 0 - 4
	2 q: Bir	0 - 1 - 0
	1 b: M: wein	0 - 2 - 0
	1 fisch	0 - 0 - 4
	2 q: seiter	0 - 0 - 8
	2 q: Bir	0 - 1 - 0
	1 glas gebrochen [1 glass broken]	0 - 1 - 0
	1 gill Rom	0 - 0 - 4
	2 q: seiter	0 - 0 - 8
	1 q: seiter 1 b: M: Wein	0 - 2 - 4
	1 q: seiter 1 q: bir und Essen	0 - 1 - 6
20	2 q: seiter	0 - 0 - 8
	1 q: seiter	0 - 0 - 4
30	1 1/2 q: seitereol	0 - 1 - 0
April 6	Vor Trincken	0 - 1 - 4
9	6 1/2 buschel Haber gelent 1/2 gill Rom	0 - 0 - 2
12	Vor neths 1 q: seiter	0 - 0 - 6
13	gelent	0 - 1 - 0
	1 gill rom	0 - 0 - 4
	2 q: seiter	0 - 0 - 8
	1 b: Rom	0 - 0 - 9
	sein dochter vor gortel	0 - 1 - 0
	vor schapp gut	0 -15- 6
20	Vor Trincken	0 - 1 - 2
	1 q: seiter	0 - 0 - 8
	1 b: Bir	0 - 0 - 3
	1 b: Rom	0 - 0 - 10
	1 q: seeol	0 - 0 - 8
25	1 q: seiter	0 - 0 - 4
28	1 gill Rom 1 q: seiter 1/2 b: Wein	0 - 1 - 4

No 178

1764	**Friedrich Müller**	
Febru 6	1 Wein schling	0 - 0 - 9
	Vor Trincken in Comp	0 - 0 - 3
Mertz 19	1 gill Bamöl un 1/4 lb: Hut Zucker	0 - 1 - 1
1764	**Petter Ohrendorff**	
October 19	1/2 b: wein	0 - 0 - 8
1765	**Jacob Witmer**	
Nov: 2	100 schunegel	0 - 0 - 7
6	1 b: Rom	0 - 0 - 6
29	50 schunegel	0 - 0 - 3 1/2
	Abgerechnet mit Jacob Wittmer d: 11 ten Aprill 1766 Bleibt nichts [Settled with Jacob Wittmer 11 April 1766. Owes nothing]	
1767		
May 20	2 lb: Reiss	0 - 0 - 6

No 179

1764	**Gibby**	
February 6	Vor Essen und Trincken und Vor Heu	0 -11- 0

1764	**Jacob Brecht**	
September 21	1 gill Rom	0 - 0 - 4
Oct 24	1 q: Thron	0 - 1 - 0
1765		
Feb: 4	1/2 gill Rom	0 - 0 - 2
Mertz 6	1 b: seiter	0 - 0 - 2
Aprill 19	1 gill Rom 1 q: seiteröl	0 - 1 - 0
	gerechnet mit Jacob Brecht d: 24 ten Juny 1765 bleibt er schuldig [Settled with Jacob Brecht 24 June 1765. He still owes]	0 - 3 - 10
July 13	1 b: seiter	0 - 0 - 2
15	1 Dutzent un 2 Grossen knop	0 - 1 - 2
	1 b: seiter	0 - 0 - 2
Augst 29	1 q: Rom un 1 lb: schrot	0 - 1 - 7
Sebt 13	1 q: Rom	0 - 1 - 0
23	1 lb: negel	0 - 1 - 0
27	1 q: wein	0 - 2 - 4
Octo 1	1 q: Thron	0 - 1 - 0
3	1 b: Rom	0 - 0 - 6
10	1 q: Rom	0 - 1 - 0
23	1 q: Thron	0 - 1 - 0
Decem: 7	1 lb: Weise Zucker un 1 q: Thron 1 b: Rom	0 - 3 - 3

No 180		
1764	**der Arnold auff der Meindhol** Arnold at the mine hole]	
Febr: 6	1 1/2 b: Wein 1 Weck	0 - 2 - 1
1765	**Arnold Schörnetz**	
July 28	1 q: Rom un 1 q: bir	0 - 1 - 6
Augst 29	1 q: Rom	0 - 1 - 0
Seb: 25	2 q: seiter	0 - 0 - 8
1764	**Tobias Bickel**	
Nov: 30	2 q: seiter 1 gill Rom 1 Bole m: senckery 1 b: m: win und vor Essen	0 - 5 - 10
Decem: 14	Vor Br: wein	0 - 0 - 6
1766	**Tobias Bickel**	
Febrary 11	Verzehrt	1 - 7 - 0
1767	**Tobias Bickel**	
January 5	Verzehrt	2 - 0 - 0
May 9	5 q: seiter 1/2 beck haber	0 - 2 - 4

No 181		
1764	**Henrich Keÿler**	
May 1	gelehnet an geld [lent in money]	0 -12- 0
	2 q: Wein	0 - 4 - 8
2	1 q: seiteröl	0 - 0 - 8
3	1 b: Wein	0 - 1 - 2
	Vor Essen	0 - 0 - 6
4	1 q: seiter	0 - 0 - 4

7	1/2 b: Br: wein	0 - 0 - 4	
	1 q: seiter	0 - 0 - 4	
	1 q: seiter	0 - 0 - 4	
12	3 q: seiter	0 - 1 - 0	
	1 Lott gezackert	0 - 4 - 0	
17	1 b: Brantewein	0 - 0 - 6	
	3 q: seiter	0 - 1 - 0	
	1 q: Bir	0 - 0 - 6	
	gelehnet an geld [Lent in money]	0 - 1 - 3	
	1/2 gill rom	0 - 0 - 2	
21	2 q: seiter	0 - 0 - 8	
22	1 gill rom	0 - 0 - 4	
26	2 buschel Weitzen		0 - 8 - 0
28	1 q: seiter	0 - 0 - 4	
Juny 6	2 q: seiter	0 - 0 - 8	
8	Vor schabgut	0 -16- 10	
	1 q: seiter	0 - 0 - 4	
9	2 q: bir un Essen		0 - 1 - 6
	1 gallen Bir	0 - 2 - 0	
	3 q: seiter	0 - 1 - 0	
	1 q: Br: wein	0 - 1 - 0	
23	2 q: seiter	0 - 0 - 8	
	1 b: Br: wein	0 - 0 - 6	
	1 lb: Zucker	0 - 0 - 10	
	1 q: seiter	0 - 0 - 4	
25	1 q: seiter	0 - 0 - 4	
	2 q: seiter	0 - 0 - 8	
July 2	1 q: seiter	0 - 0 - 4	
7	1 q: seiter	0 - 0 - 4	
9	1 b: Br: wein	0 - 0 - 6	
	1 q: seiter	0 - 0 - 4	
12	1 b: seiter	0 - 0 - 2	
13	1 q: seiter	0 - 0 - 4	

No 182		
1764	**Dieder Mercker**	
21May	vor schap gudt	0 -19- 10
	1/2 buch babier	0 - 0 - 9
1766	**Dieder Mercker**	
Sebtem: 27	Verzehrt	0 - 4 - 0
1766	**John Mercker**	
July 18	2 B: m. wein un 2 W: schling	0 - 8 - 6
1769	**John Mercker**	
January 16	1 b: m: wein	0 - 2 - 0
1765	**Alt Schumacher [The old shoemaker]**	
Nov: 2	3 gill Br: wein un 3 b: seiter	0 - 1 - 3
	2 1/2 gill Br: wein	0 - 0 - 8
Mertz 17	**Alt Schumacher [The old shoemaker]**	
1768		
Mertz 11	1 1/2 gill Br: wein un 1 q: seiter	0 - 0 - 10
	1 q: seiter	0 - 0 - 4

1764	**Adam Hoffmann über der suskahana** [Across the Susquehanna]	
Aug 16	1 b: Wein	0 - 1 - 4
1766	**Alt Schulmeister ins Schenken** [The old schoolmaster in Schenken]	
Mertz 29	1 q: Br: wein 1/2 gill Br: wein	0 - 1 - 2

No 183		
1764	**Johannes Meisser**	
February 17	1 yd. Cattun 1 1/2 q: Rom	0 - 7 - 5
28	1 1/2 q: Rom 1 b: Wein 1 lb Zucker	0 - 4 - 3
Decem. 14	1 Catecismus	0 - 1 - 6
	8 scheiben glas	0 - 6 - 8
1765 Febr 20	2 w: schling	0 - 1 - 6
Mertz 4	Credit vor Negel machen [Credit for making nails]	0 -12- 6
20	1/2 b: m: wein	0 - 1 - 0
	Bezahlt an geld [Paid in money]	0 - 7 - 6
1765	**Johannes Meyser**	
Octob: 7	1 q: Thron	0 - 1 - 0
10	1/4 lb: Pulver 2 flintenstein	0 - 1 - 2
	1 1/2 lb: Bley 1/4 lb: Pulver	0 - 1 - 8
1766		
Septem: 10	1 q: Thron	0 - 1 - 0
1767		
Augst 15	1 q: Rom	0 - 1 - 0
24	1 b: wein	0 - 1 - 2
Sebtem: 19	1/2 b: wein	0 - 0 - 7
	Johannes Meÿser	
	gerechnet d: 20 November 1769 ihm schu. [Settled 20 November 1769. Owe him]	1 - 8 - 0
1765	**Christian Brubacher**	
May 27	1 w: schling	0 - 0 - 9

No 184		
1764	**Christopher Meyer**	
February 18	1 q: seitereol 1 Weck	0 - 0 - 5
Mertz 19	2 w: schling 1 weck	0 - 1 - 7
April 26	1/2 bole Bunsch	0 - 0 - 6
28	2 w: schling	0 - 1 - 6
	Abgerechnet mit Christoph Mayer d: 17 September 1764 Bleibt No Rest [Settled with Christoph Mayer 17 September 1764. No balance remains]	
1764		
May	sein Mutter [his mother] 2 lb. zucker	0 - 1 - 8
Sep: 19	2 b: Wein	0 - 2 - 4
	1 b: M: wein	0 - 2 - 0
20	1 b: wein	0 - 1 - 2
26	2 b: Wein	0 - 2 - 4
November 4	2 b: seiteröl	0 - 0 - 8

1765 Febr. 20	2 1/2 Dutzend strang Camel garn	0 - 2 - 10
Mertz 8	1 b: M: wein 1 bole Mim	0 - 3 - 0
Juny 7	1 sentz	0 - 4 - 0
	gelehnt an geld [lent in money]	0 -10- 0
1766		
Feb: 21	gelehnt an geld Vor Tax [lent in money for tax]	0 - 2 - 6
Augst 29	2 yd. Hassen Brick	0 - 2 - 6
	ist schultig vor schisen [owes for shooting]	0 -10- 10
	agerechnet mit Chistoph Mayer d: 20 t: Mertz 1767	
	Bleib ich Allexander Shaeffer ihm schultig	6 -13- 0
	[Settled with Christoph Mayer d. 20 March 1767. I Alexander Schaeffer owe him]	
1769	**Christoph Meyer**	
July 3	ist schultig [owes]	8 -13- 0
	Bezahlt an [paid on]	

1768	**Jacob Dell**	
Sebt 12	vor Roth Holtz	0 - 0 - 4
October 20	1 lb: Endego	0 -10- 0
	1/2 b: seiteröl	0 - 0 - 2
	darauf Bezahlt [paid thereon]	0 - 4 - 6
1765 Juny 1	hab ich Allexander Shaffer von ihm gelehnt	52-0 - 0
	[I Alexander Schaeffer borrowed from him]	

No 185		
1764	**Petter Bohrer**	
Febru: 21	1 gill Rom	0 - 0 - 4
22	1/2 gill Rom	0 - 0 - 2
	1 gill Rom	0 - 0 - 4
26	1 q: seiter	0 - 0 - 4
Mertz 26	1 q: seiter	0 - 0 - 4
April 4	Vor Bäum	0 - 2 - 0
25	1 gill Rom	0 - 0 - 4
	1 fuhr stroh geholt [1 load of straw fetched]	0 - 1 - 0
28	1 gill Rom	0 - 0 - 4
May 4	1 q: Rom	0 - 1 - 2
	16 fuss walnuss bort 1/2 gill Rom	0 - 3 - 0
7	1 1/2 q: br: Wein	0 - 1 - 6
	1 b: Rom	0 - 0 - 7
	d: 9 July 1764 gerechnet mit Petter Bohrer bleibt Rest	0 - 2 - 0
	[9 July 1764 settled with Petter Bohrer. Balance remains]	
	1/2 gill Rom	0 - 0 - 2
July 12	2 q: seiter	0 - 0 - 8
16	1 b: Wein	0 - 1 - 2
	1 q: Rom	0 - 1 - 0
23	1 q: seiter	0 - 0 - 4
30	1 gall gelent in die Mühl [1 horse lent to the mill]	0 - 0 - 6
	2 fisch 1 gill Rom	0 - 0 -10
Aug: 9	1 b: Rom	0 - 0 - 6
Sep: 6	1 q: Rom	0 - 1 - 0
16	1 gill Rom	0 - 0 - 4
22	1/2 gill Rom	0 - 0 - 2
October	1 lb schrot 1/4 lb Pulver	0 - 1 - 5
11	6 knöpff	0 - 0 - 5
November 19	1/2 b Rom	0 - 0 - 5
21	1 q: Thron	0 - 1 - 0

24	1 lb: zucker	0 - 0 - 10
Decem 12	1 lb negel	0 - 1 - 0
19	1 q: Thron	0 - 1 - 0
28	1 q: Wein 1 q: Rom Vor guter Vor Neths	0 - 4 - 1
1765 Janu: 21	2 q: thron	0 - 2 - 0
Febr: 2	1 1/2 q: Rom	0 - 1 - 6
	1 q: Rom	0 - 1 - 0
20	1 b: Rom 1/2 gill Rom 1 q: Thron 2 lb: negel	0 - 3 - 8

No 186
1764

Jacob Schaub

April 12	Vor schapp Wahre	1 -17- 4
20	1/2 gill Rom	0 - 0 - 2
May 4	Vor Essen	0 - 0 - 6
12	1 1/2 q: seiter	0 - 0 - 6
15	1/2 lb: Wachs	0 - 0 - 9
	1 q: seiter	0 - 0 - 4
21	1 q: seiter	0 - 0 - 4
28	2 1/2 q: seiter	0 - 0 - 10
	1 gill tram	0 - 0 - 3
31	1 q: seiter	0 - 0 - 4
	1 b: wein	0 - 1 - 2
31	1 q: bir 3 Weck	0 - 0 - 9
Juny 6	1 q: seiter	0 - 0 - 4
9	1 b: M: Wein	0 - 2 - 0
10	2 q: seiter	0 - 0 - 8
14	3 fisch	0 - 0 - 9
18	1 q: seiter	0 - 0 - 4
20	1 q: seiter	0 - 0 - 4
21	2 q: bir	0 - 1 - 0
24	1 b: seiter	0 - 0 - 2
	1/2 gill Rom	0 - 0 - 2
28	1 q: seiter	0 - 0 - 4
	1 1/2 q: seiter	0 - 0 - 6
	1 b: seiter	0 - 0 - 2
July 7	1 q: seiter	0 - 0 - 4
12	1 b: seiter	0 - 0 - 2
	1 q: bir	0 - 0 - 6
13	2 q: seiter	0 - 0 - 8
	1 R: schling	0 - 0 - 6
19	1 b: m: wein	0 - 2 - 0
23	1 b: seiter	0 - 0 - 2
28	1 gill tram	0 - 0 - 3
	1 gill tram	0 - 0 - 3
August 20	1 b: bir	0 - 0 - 3
23	2 1/2 q: bir	0 - 1 - 3
28	1 q: bir	0 - 0 - 6

No 187
1764

Stiegels Mahler [Stiegel's painters]

April 26	1 q: bir	0 - 0 - 6
May 4	1 1/2 q: seiter	0 - 0 - 6
	4 gill Rom	0 - 1 - 4

17	1 q: bir	0 - 0 - 6
	1 q: seiter	0 - 0 - 4
21	3 q: seiter	0 - 1 - 0
26	2 q: bir	0 - 1 - 0
28	2 q: bir	0 - 1 - 0
	1 q: bir	0 - 0 - 6
29	2 q: seiter	0 - 0 - 8
	1 q: seitereol	0 - 0 - 8
31	1 q: seiter	0 - 0 - 4
	1 q: seiter	0 - 0 - 4
	1 q: bir	0 - 0 - 6
Juny 9	gelent [lent]	1 - 0 - 0
	1 b: Wein	0 - 1 - 2
	1 b: Wein	0 - 1 - 2
10	1 q: bir	0 - 0 - 6
	1 gill tram	0 - 0 - 3
		1-12-3
	mit Joh: **Wentel Kretsch** abgerechnet d: 24: October 1764 bleibt Er schuldig [Settled with Joh. Wentel Kretsch 24 October 1764. He still owes]	3 - 0 - 0
1765		
Aprill 19	4 1/2 q: seiter 2 gill Rom un Vor Essen	0 - 2 - 10
Juny 24	verzehrt	0 - 2 - 0
July 8	Vor Essen un 1 q: seiter	0 - 0 - 7
24	4 1/2 q: seiter un vor 2 mann Essen un 1 q: bir un 2 gill Rom	0 - 3 - 8
	Vergessen Worden das nicht verrechnet ist [Forgotten which was not settled up]	0 -18- 8
1767		
February 24	Verzehrt	0 - 1 - 6
Juny 15	Verzehrt	0 - 0 - 8
October 12	ist schultig vor Kost und Trincken [owes for food and drink]	2 - 7 -10
Decem: 25	1 q: bir 1 1/2 gill Rom un Essen	0 - 2 - 0
1769	**Wendel Kretsch**	
January 16	Verzehrt	0 - 3 - 6
Mertz 6	1/2 b: m: wein 1 b: seiter	0 - 1 - 2
May 22	Verzehrt	0 - 1 - 9

No 188		
1764	**Wilhelm Besh**	
Mertz 9	1 b: Wein	0 - 1 - 2
	2 b: M: Wein	0 - 4 - 0
	1 Rom schling	0 - 0 - 6
	1/2 b: Wein	0 - 0 - 7
12	1/2 lb alspeis 1/2 lb Peffer 1 b: seitereol	0 - 1 - 4
13	1 q: seiter	0 - 0 - 8
	1 gill Rom 1/4 lb imber	0 - 0 - 9
19	1 schling 1/2 b: M: Wein 1 b: M: Wein	0 - 3 - 6
	vor Wein	0 - 0 - 6
	gelent Bey dem Hornung [lent at Horning's]	0 - 2 - 0
	1/2 beck haber	0 - 0 - 6
	1 q: bir	0 - 0 - 6
	1 schling	0 - 0 - 6
	1 gaul gelent [1 horse lent]	0 - 2 - 6
26	1 q: Br: Wein	0 - 1 - 2

Aprill 6	1 b: seitereol	0 - 0 - 4
April 6	1 q: bir	0 - 0 - 6
12	1 q: Rom 1 q: seiter 1 q: bir 2 q: haber	0 - 2 - 3
13	2 q: seiter	0 - 0 - 8
20	1 1/2 q: seiter	0 - 0 - 6
	1 b: Wein	0 - 1 - 2
25	2 q: bir 1 b: seiter	0 - 1 - 2
	3 q: bir 1 b: Wein 1 q: haber	0 - 2 - 10
30	1 b: Br: wein	0 - 0 - 7
May 1	1 1/2 q: bir	0 - 0 - 9
1	2 q: seiter	0 - 0 - 8
4	1 b: Wein 1 q: seiter	0 - 1 - 6
7	Bleibt shuldig vor die Bender Wegen Keller [Still owes for the hinges on Keller's account]	1 - 0 - 6
	2 b: wein	0 - 2 - 4
	1 gill Rom	0 - 0 - 9
15	3 q: seiter	0 - 1 - 0
17	2 q: seiter	0 - 0 - 8
22	1 q: bir	0 - 0 - 6
29	Credit	0 - 4 - 6
31	2 q: seitereol	0 - 0 - 8
	4 q: seiter	0 - 1 - 4

No 189

Wilhelm Besch

1764		
Juny 9	2 q: seiter	0 - 0 - 8
	1 q: seitereol	0 - 0 - 8
14	4 q: seiter	0 - 1 - 4
	2 q: haber	0 - 0 - 3
	1 Wein schling	0 - 0 - 9
	1 q: seiter	0 - 0 - 4
July 5	2 q: seiter	0 - 0 - 8
	1/2 lb hut zucker	0 - 0 - 9
27	2 q: Rom	0 - 2 - 4
	gelehnt an geld [lent in money]	0 - 0 - 7
	2 q: seiter	0 - 0 - 8
	2 1/2 q: Rom	0 - 2 - 11
9	2 q: seiter	0 - 0 - 8
12	3 q: seiter	0 - 1 - 0
December 18	Bezahlt an geld [paid in money]	1 - 0 - 0
Aug 10	1 bol. bunsch	0 - 1 - 0
Sep: 10	2 Rom schling	0 - 1 - 0
28	1 b: M: Wein	0 - 2 - 0
Octo 15	1/2 b: M: wein	0 - 1 - 0
	3 1/2 q: seiter	0 - 1 - 2
24	1 schling	0 - 0 - 6
	Abgerechnet mit Wilhelm Besch den 19t February 1765 bleibt Er schuldig [Settled with Wilhelm Besch 19 Feb. 1765. He still owes]	7 - 0 - 0
Mertz 27	2 q: seiter	0 - 0 - 8
Aprill 4	1 q: seiter	0 - 0 - 4
	Bezahlt an geld [paid in money]	0 - 7 - 6
May 1	1 b: Wein	0 - 1 - 2
	3 1/2 q: seiter 1 Peif	0 - 1 - 3
13	1 b: seiter 1 peif	0 - 0 - 3

Juny 1	1/2 b: wein 1 R: schling	0 - 1 - 1
4	2 b: m: wein	0 - 4 - 0
8	3 q: seiter	0 - 1 - 0
24	3 q: seiter 1 b: br: wein	0 - 1 - 6
25	2 q: seiter	0 - 0 - 8
	4 q: seiter 1 weck	0 - 1 - 5
July 8	Verzehrt	0 - 1 - 5

No 190

1764 **Michael Reger**

April 20	1 b: seitereol	0 - 0 - 4
26	1 q: Tram	0 - 1 - 2
28	2 q: seiter 1 gill Tram 1 Weck	0 - 1 - 0
May 1	1 1/2 gill Rom	0 - 0 - 6
	4 lb Pech	0 - 1 - 4
	1 1/2 b: Wein	0 - 1 - 9
7	1 q: bir 1 gill tram	0 - 0 - 9
22	2 q: Br: wein 2 q: seiter 1/2 lb Pulver	0 - 3 - 8
	5 q: bir und vor Essen vor ihn vor sein sohn und vor schramm [for him, for his son, and for Schramm]	0 - 4 - 0
28	1 q: Br: wein	0 - 1 - 0
	1 b: seiter	0 - 0 - 2
	1 q: seiter 1 q: bir	0 - 0 - 10
29	2 q: tram 1 q: bir	0 - 2 - 10
31	1 q: bir	0 - 0 - 6
	1 gill Rom	0 - 0 - 4
Juny 6	1 q: bir	0 - 0 - 6
10	1 bol Mim	0 - 1 - 0
	4 q: bir	0 - 2 - 0
	1 b: seiter	0 - 0 - 2
	1 q: seiter	0 - 0 - 4
10	1/2 gill Rom	0 - 0 - 2
	ist schuldig vor [owes for] ein sentz	0 - 3 - 0
Sept. 7	1 gill Rom	0 - 0 - 4
Nov: 3	1 gill Rom 1b: seitereol	0 - 0 - 8
1765		
d. 1. Hornung	Michael Reger Bleybt schuldig in der abrechnung [Michael Reger still owes in the settlement]	1 - 4 - 8
	gelehnt an geld [lent in money]	0 - 9 - 0
	Bezahlt an geld [paid in money]	0 - 6 - 4
4	2 gill Rom	0 - 0 - 8
Mertz 18	Verzehrt	0 - 4 - 3
April 13	1 q: bir	0 - 0 - 6
May 9	2 gill Rom 2 q: seiter 2 weck	0 - 1 - 6
27	3 q: bir	0 - 1 - 6

No 191

1764 **Antony Stiegel**

Mertz 6	2 bol Mim	0 - 2 - 0
	3 q: haber	0 - 0 - 6
9	1 q: bir	0 - 0 - 6

Juny	1 q: bir 3 q: haber	0 - 0 - 11
14	1 bol Mim	0 - 1 - 0
20	1/2 bo: mimm	0 - 0 - 6
July 2	3 sicheln un 1 bo: mim	0 -10- 0
19	1/2 bo: mimm	0 - 0 - 6
27	1 bol. Mim	0 - 1 - 0
31	2 q: bir	0 - 1 - 0
	gelent an geld [lent in money]	0 - 0 - 6
August 10	1 q: bir	0 - 0 - 6
Septem 15	1 bol Leims bunsch	0 - 1 - 6
November 10	1/2 bol. Mim	0 - 0 - 6
1767	**Antony Stigel**	
Feruary 7	1 b: Bir	0 - 0 - 3
26	1 b: seiteröl	0 - 0 - 4
Mertz 9	Vor holtz führen [for carting wood]	0 - 5 - 0
12	1 gill Rom	0 - 0 - 4
Augst 1	1 b: seiteröl	0 - 0 - 4
Decem: 3	1 q: seiter	0 - 0 - 4
1768		
February 6	1 q: Bir	0 - 0 - 6
26	1 q: seiter	0 - 0 - 4
Mertz 19	1 q: seiter	0 - 0 - 4
Aprill 20	1 q: seiter	0 - 0 - 4
May	1 q: seiter	0 - 0 - 4
	1 q: seiter	0 - 0 - 4
5	1 b: seiteröl	0 - 0 - 4
	1 gill Rom	0 - 0 - 4
31	1 gill Rom	0 - 0 - 4
Juny 3	1 q: seiter	0 - 0 - 4
	1 q: seiter	0 - 0 - 4
11	2 q: seiter	0 - 0 - 8
Augst 4	1 bol. Mim	0 - 1 - 0
	Credit Vor 1 haut 33 lb:	0 - 8 - 9
1769 Merz 3	1 q: seiter	0 - 0 - 4
6	1/2 b: mim	0 - 0 - 6
20	1 b: seiteröl	0 - 0 - 4
25	Vor stroh	0 - 3 - 0

[The two right hand columns of this page are torn and partially illegible.]

No 192		
1764	**Andreas Rücker**	
April 20	1 1/2 q: seitereol	0 - 1 -
	2 q: seiter	0 - 0 -
28	2 q: seiter	0 - 0 -
30	1 1/2 q: seiter	0 - 0 -
May 29	1 1/2 q: seitereol	0 - 1 -
29	1 b: seiter 1 Weck	0 - 0 -
Juny	1 q: bir	0 - 0 -
9	1 q: seiter	0 - 0 -
14	1 q: seiter	0 - 0 -
	1 q: seitereol 1 q: bir	0 - 1 -
28	1 b: seiteröl	0 - 0 -
Aug	1 q: seitereol 1 Weck [?] yd bendel	0 - 1 -
16	1 q: seitereol	0 - -
25	1 q: seitereol	0 - -
	Vor Indego	0 - -

Sep: 3	1 bol Leims bunsch 2 Weck	0 - -
4	3 b: seitereol	0 - -
	1/2 b: Wein 1 Wein schling 1 b: seol	0 - -
	1 q: seitereol 2 Weck 1/2 gill Rom	0 - 1 -
Octo 15	1 b: seiter 2 Weck	0 - 0 -
	3 b seitereol	0 - 0 -
	3 1/2 seiter	0 - 1 -
1765	**Andreas Rücker**	
Juny 13	1 b: seiteröl	0 - 0 -
July 9	3 q: seiter	0 - 1 -
10	1 1/2 q: seiter	0 - 0 -
	gelehnt [lent]	0 - -
	Credit	0 - 0 -
Sebt 13	1 q: seiteröl un Essen	0 - -
Octo 10	1 b seiteröl	0 - 0 -
16	1 q 1/2 b: seiteröl	0 - -
	Verzehrt	0 - 0 -
25	Verzehrt	
Nov 2	1 q: seiteröl	0 - -

No 193		
1764	**Henry Wm. Stiegel**	
Aprill 12	Vor Zehen Tag lohner haven zweӱ mahl gessen un 1 q: Rom gehabt [For ten day laborers who ate twice a day and had 1 q. rum]	0 -11- 2
	wieder Zehen Mann gessen [again, ten men ate]	0 - 6 - 0
	7 geil beym Heu un 1/2 buschel Haber [7 horses at hay and 1/2 bushel oats]	0 - 6 - 0
May 15	1 1/2 q: Rom sein Mohler [his painter]	0 - 2 - 3
17	1 b: Rom sein Mohler [his painter}	0 - 0 - 9
26	sein Mohler [his painter] 1 q: Rom	0 - 1 - 4
31	2 b: Mimm	0 - 2 - 0
Juny 9	sein Knecht [his servant boy] vor heu	0 - 1 - 6
	10 Haxxet wasser zu dem Thorn geführt [10 hogsheads of water carted to the Thorn]	0 - 7 - 6
14	1/2 buschel haber	0 - 1 - 6
	1 bole mimm	0 - 1 - 0
	Vor heu	0 - 1 - 6
Sept 28	1 Boll. Mim	0 - 1 - 0
	sein franck 4 Bole senckery 4 q: Haber	0 - 6 - 8
29	2 b: M: wein 2 bol: Mim 1 beck Haber Vor heu 3 geul der greier Melcher stock verzehrt [The auctioneer Melcher Stock consumed]	0 - 9 - 0
Mertz 30	vor Latten von Michael Müller zu füllen [for lath ?]	0 - 2 - 6
1765	**Henrich Wm. Stigel**	
[ ] y 13	1 q: 1/2 b: Rom das Pohre geholt [which Pohre fetched]	0 - 1 - 5
	1 1/2 b: Rom das Bohren geholt [which Bohren fetched]	0 - 0 - 11
sebt 13	10 geil Bey heu buschel haber un 1 beck haber 2 bol: mim 1 b: bir	0 -10- 0
Juny 5	sein Mauren [his mason] 1 q: Br: wein	0 - 1 - 0
1766		
ember 23	35 hundert Ertz geführt	0 -14- 0
April 25	1 q: 1/2 b: M: wein un 3 bol mim	0 - 8 - 0
July 23	2 bol Bunsch 1 b: m: wein	0 - 5 - 0
1768		
Mertz 14	2 q: seiter 3 q: haber sein Kutscher [his coachman]	0 - 1- 2

No 194		
1764	**Weitzel Schuhmacher in Lancaster** [shoemaker in Lancaster]	
May 7	Verzehrt	0 - 4 - 10
1765	**Georg Lautenschleger**	
March 6	6 1/4 lb: fleisch	0 - 2 - 1
8	1 1/2 b: wein	0 - 1 - 9
17	2 q: thron	0 - 2 - 0
Aprill 19	1 gill Rom	0 - 0 - 4
1765	**George Lautenschleger**	
Nov: 24	5 scheiben glas	0 - 2 - 11
1766 Jan. 28	1 lb: Pulver	0 - 3 - 6
Febrary 20	1 b: seiteröl	0 - 0 - 4
Augst 2	2 q: seiter	0 - 0 - 8
	1 q: seiter	0 - 0 - 4
1768		
January 1	1 q: seiter	0 - 0 - 4
May 1	1 hut	0 - 7 - 0
1770	**George Lautenschleger**	
May 7	gerechnet Bleibt schultig [settled. Still owes]	0 - 9 - 7

No 195		
1764	**Balthaser Schadt**	
May 7	1 buschel haber gelehnt [lent]	
22	1/2 lb: seiffen un vor neths	0 - 0 - 8
1765	**Baltzer Schadt**	
May 1	gelehnt an geld [lent in money]	2 - 1 - 0
	gelehnt an geld [lent in money]	0 - 1 - 0
1765	**Baltzer Schad**	
Novem: 29	Bleibt schuldig in der abrechnung [still owes in the settlement]	0 - 3 - 4
1765	**Adam Baer**	
April 10	vor Kirsch Bäum	0 - 3 - 0
1768	**Jacob Bauler**	
Aprill 2	1 b: wein 2 man Essen 1 q: bir 2 gill tram	0 - 3 - 11
1769	**Jacob Beuler**	
February 2	bleibt schuldig in der abrechnung [still owes in the settlement]	0 - 6 - 7
1771		
May 29	Verzehrt	0 - 3 - 10
1764	**des Mausen Mad** [Maus's maid]	
October 24	Vor Cattun	0 - 2 - 6

No 196		
1764	**Caspar Schweitzer**	
Juny 24	1 q: seiter	0 - 0 - 4
July 3	1 q: seiter	0 - 0 - 4

12	1 R: schling 2 q: seiter	0 - 1 - 2
27	4 q: seiter	0 - 1 - 4
	gelent in Läncaster [lent in Lancaster}	0 -16- 0
Sep: 21	1 b: seitereol	0 - 0 - 4
26	1 b: Ditto	0 - 0 - 4
October 4	1 b: Ditto	0 - 0 - 4
24	1 q: seiter	0 - 0 - 4
	2 Wein schling	0 - 1 - 6
March 16	der Heinerich Käyler vor Kohl brennen [Heinerich Kaÿler for making charcoal]	1 - 9 - 0
November 6	2 seuger	0 - 3 - 0
	1 feil	
Decem: 3	3 lb: Bley	0 - 1 - 6
1765		
Jan 1	4 q: seiter	0 - 1 - 4
14	1 b: Rom 1 gill rom	0 - 0 - 10
29	1 b Rom	0 - 0 - 6
Febr. 4	2 q: seiter 1 schling 1 q: Bir	0 - 1 - 8
	1 b: Rom	0 - 0 - 6
9	1 q: seiter	0 - 0 - 4
20	1 1/2 q: seitr 1 b: Rom	0 - 1 - 0
	1 q: Rom	0 - 1 - 0
	2 q 1/2 b: Rom	0 - 2 - 3
	1 1/2 q: Rom	0 - 0 - 9
	1 q: Rom	0 - 1 - 0
29	1 1/2 b: Rom	0 - 0 - 9
	1 b: Rom	0 - 0 - 6
Mertz 6	3 q: seiter	0 - 1 - 0
17	1 buch Babir	0 - 1 - 6
	1 b: Rom	0 - 0 - 6
	1/2 gill Rom 1 b: m: wein 1 weck	0 - 2 - 3
18	5 lb: negel gelehnt	
April 10	1/2 gill Rom	0 - 0 - 2
19	1 q: rom	0 - 1 - 0
		3 -14- 4
		4 - 7 - 6

No 197
1764

Jacob Shaub, Satler

September 3	1 q: bir 1 Neb leims bunsch	0 - 1 - 3
	1 Neb Ditto	0 - 0 - 9
	1 bol leims bunsch	0 - 1 - 6
19	1 b: m: Wein	0 - 2 - 0
26	1 bol Leims bunsch	0 - 1 - 6
Octo 15	1/2 b: Mathery wein	0 - 1 - 0
19	1 Wein schling	0 - 0 - 9
	1 q: seiter	0 - 0 - 4
24	1 b: Wein 1 q: seiter	0 - 1 - 6
	1 gill Rom	0 - 0 - 3
November 6	2 Rom schling un 1 Peif	0 - 1 - 0
10	4 1/2 q: seiter 1 gill Rom	0 - 1 - 10
21	18 schnallen	
	1 gill Br: wein 1 gill Rom 1 b: seiter	0 - 0 - 9
26	1 1/2 gill Tram 1 weck	0 - 0 - 6
30	1 gill Br: wein	0 - 0 - 3

December 6	1 q: seiter	0 - 0 - 4
12	1 lb: Tuback 1 Peif 1 q: seiter	0 - 0 - 10
	1 1/2 gill Rom	0 - 0 - 6
14	1 w: schling	0 - 0 - 9
19	2 q: seiter 2 Peiffen	0 - 0 - 10
28	1 gill Rom	0 - 0 - 4
31	1 gill Rom	0 - 0 - 4
1765		
January 4	1 b: seiter	0 - 0 - 2
	1 1/2 q: seiter	0 - 0 - 6
21	1/2 gill Rom 1 q: seiteröl	0 - 0 - 10
29	1 gill Br: wein 1 q: seiteröl 1 q: seiter 1/2 gill Rom	0 - 1 - 5
	2 q: seiter	0 - 0 - 8
	2 1/2 yd. gorden 5 schnallen	
	1 q: seiter	0 - 0 - 4
Hornung 1	1 q: seiter	0 - 0 - 4
4	1 q: seiter	0 - 0 - 4
5	1 gill Br: wein	0 - 0 - 3
Fe: 9	2 q: seiter	0 - 0 - 8
	1 b: M: wein 1 b: seiter	0 - 2 - 2
13	1/2 Dutzent Cramben	0 - 0 - 7
17	2 gill Br: wein	0 - 0 - 6
20	2 gill Tram 1 q: seiter	0 - 0 - 10
29	3 q: seiter	0 - 1 - 0
	1 Par schnallen	0 - 0 - 9

No 198

Gotten Stiegels Haffengiesser [pot pourer]

July 23	Vor Trincken	0 - 2 - 2
Aug. 10	1 Bol bunsch	0 - 1 - 0
18	1/2 b: Wein 1 bol Mim 1 Rom schling 1 Wein schling	0 - 4 - 3
Sep: 4	3 bol 1: bunsch	0 - 4 - 6
Oct. 24	1 b: wein	0 - 1 - 2
November 19	2 bol: senckery	0 - 3 - 0
Decem: 14	1 q: bir 2 gill Rom	0 - 1 - 2

1765

Gottes Stigels Heffengiesser

Agst 26	1 bol mim 1 1/2 seiter un 2 q: bir un Essen	0 - 3 - 2
	6 q: seiter un 2 q: bir un 2 Mal gessen	0 - 5 - 6
Octo: 25	3 q: seiteröl	0 - 2 - 0
Decem: 25	1 q: seiteröl un 1 R: schling un 2 gill Rom	0 - 1 - 10
	7 b: M: wein 1 1/2 gill Rom	0 -14- 6

1765

Michael Neff alte [Sr.]

Mertz 4	1 yd: 1/2 yd: bay 1 1/2 dutzend Knöp 1 strang Camel Garn	0 -15- 1

Michael Neff alt [Sr.]

Decem: 15	1 catecismus	0 - 2 - 6

No 199

Dewald Miller

July 27	1 q: Rom	0 - 1 - 0
Nov: 3	1 q: Rom	0 - 1 - 0
6	2 q: Thron	0 - 2 - 0

15	1 q: seiter	0 - 0 - 4
	1 b. seiter	0 - 0 - 2
1765		
January 4	2 q: Thron	0 - 2 - 0
Sebt 2	3 lb: Negel	0 - 3 - 0
1766 Febar 20	Bleibt schultig vor Rend [owes on rent]	0 - 1 - 9
January 6	1 b: seitereol	0 - 0 - 4
Feburary 14	ist schultig vor spilen [owes on gambling]	0 - 1 - 11
1767		
February 24	1 lb: Pulver	0 - 3 - 6
Septem: 19	8 b: M: wein	0 -16- 0
January 2 1769	Dewald Miller bleibt schuldig in rechnung [Dewald Miller owes in the settlement]	0 - 9 - 4

1766	**Jacob Dumman** in der statt [in the city]	
Aprill 7	1 q: Tar	0 - 0 - 6
July 11	4 q: Rom	0 - 3 - 6
Sebt 1	1 q: Thron	0 - 1 - 0
15	gelehnt an geld [lent in money]	2 - 2 - 0
October 3	Vor Catun un floret	0 - 2 - 3
	Abgerechnet mit Jacob Duman d: 5 tn: Metz 1768 Bleibt schultig [Settled with Jacob Duman 5 March 1768. Still owes]	1 -10- 0
Mertz 14	gelehnt [lent]	0 - 2 - 9
Aprill 26	gelehnt [lent]	3 -10- 0
April 10 1769	Jacob Duman bleibt shuldig in Rechn [Jacob Duman still owes in settlement]	2 - 0 - 0

No 200		
1764	**Phillip Wohlbein**	
July 27	1 Wein schling	0 - 0 - 9
Sep: 10	1 lb schrot	0 - 0 - 7
Nov. 6	1/2 lb Caffe	0 - 0 - 9
	2 seuger	0 - 3 - 0
Decem: 6	1/4 lb: Pulver	0 - 0 - 11
1765		
January 1	1 Colender	0 - 0 - 8

1765	**Adam Weiand**	
Mertz 4	4 q: Thron	0 - 4 - 0
13	2 yd: seuget 1 schnub tuch un Neths	0 - 8 - 9
April 10	1 Par schnallen un spellen	0 - 1 - 6
1767	**Adam Weiand**	
Janary 7	Vor schab gut	2 -11- 0
	1 feil das Vergessen [which was forgotten]	0 - 1 - 6
	bezalt an seiner schult [paid on his debt]	1 -10- 0
Mertz 27	1 hut 1 Par strümb	0 -13- 0
1767	**Adam Weyand**	
October 25	1 b: wein das vergessen [which was forgotten]	0 - 1 - 2
1769	**Adam Weyand**	
Juny 20	1 q: Bir	0 - 0 - 6

No 201

1764	**Henrich Keÿler**	
July 27	1 q: seitereol	0 - 0 - 8
Aug: 9	1 b: Rom 1 b: seitereol	0 - 0 - 10
10	1 Neb bunsch	0 - 0 - 6
	Credit vor 6 Tag arbeit am Keller [Credit for 6 days work on the cellar]	0 -15- 0
18	1 q: bir 1 Rom schling	0 - 1 - 0
23	1 sentz 1 gill Tram	0 - 5 - 4
25	1 b: bir	0 - 0 - 3
29	1 par schnallen 1 Rom schling	0 - 2 - 0
	1 bol leims bunsch 1 q: bir	0 - 2 - 0
Septem: 10	1 b: wein 1 q: bir 1 schling	0 - 2 - 2
19	1 b: Rom	0 - 0 - 6
	3 beck Weitzen 1 Wein schling 1 q: Rom	0 - 4 - 9
24	1/2 b: wein 1 Rom schling	0 - 1 - 1
Octo 8	1/2 bol bunsch	0 - 0 - 6
11	2 q: seiter 1 gill gatsel	0 - 1 - 0
15	1/2 b: M: Wein 1 b: Rom	0 - 1 - 6
	1/2 b: wein 1 q: seiter	0 - 0 - 11
19	1 q: seiter	0 - 0 - 4
Nov: 3	1 q: seiter	0 - 0 - 4
	Bezahlt an geld [paid in money]	2 -12- 6
1765	Abgerechnet mit Henrich Keÿler den 16 ten Mertz Bleÿbt er [Settled with Henrich Keyler 16 March. He owes].	
20	1 hut un 1 Par strümp	0 -13- 0
27	1 q: Thron 1 b: Rom	0 - 1 - 6
30	gelehnt an geld [lent in money]	0 - 7 - 6
	1 b: wein 1 b: Rom	0 - 1 - 8
Aprill 4	1 b: wein	0 - 1 - 2
	1 q: Rom 1 q: seiteröl	0 - 1 - 8
19	1 b: Br: wein	0 - 0 - 6
May 6	1 gaul in die Mühl [1 horse to the mill]	0 - 0 - 6
9	1 b: Br: wein	0 - 0 - 6
Juny 12	1 q Thron un 1 Nestel	0 - 1 - 2
Augst 7	1 b: Rom un 1 lb: Zucker	0 - 1 - 1

No 202

1764	**Johannes Endres** alte [Sr.]	
August 29	1/2 lb Peffer	0 - 1 - 8
Sep: 24	Vor ihn bezalt an Jacob Hetzel [Paid for him to Jacob Hetzel]	0 - 4 - 6
Octo 8	4 q: Thron	0 - 4 - 0
1765	**Johannes Endres** alte [sr.]	
Aprill 6	1 b: M: wein 2 q: seiter	0 - 2 - 8
Juny 1	2 lb: zucker	0 - 1 - 8
July 9	1/2 b: wein	0 - 0 - 7
1766 Febr 5	1 q: Rom	0 - 1 - 2
1766	**Johannes Endres** alte [sr.}	
Juny 5	1 b: wein	0 - 1 - 2
1767		
January 13	1 q: wein 1 bottel 1 stober	0 - 3 - 2
	1 Berrel Brandewein	
Augst 24	1/2 b: wein 1 1/2 q: Br: wein	0 - 1 - 0

1768	Bezahlt [paid] vor Br: wein	3 - 0 - 0
October 8	Bezahlt [paid]	1 - 0 - 0
1769		
Mertz 13	1 Ram Haffen	0 - 1 - 6

No 203

1764	**Stiegels Gärtner der klein Frantzos** [Stiegel's gardner, the little Frenchman]	
Aug 25	1 bole bunsch 1 q: bir	0 - 1 - 6
Sep: 4	1 bole leims bunsch	0 - 1 - 6
	2 bole mim	0 - 2 - 0
November 19	1 bole senckery	0 - 1 - 6
	1 bole Bunsch	0 - 1 - 0
1768		
Novem: 9	**John Hemmig**	
	1 fass	0 - 3 - 0
1765	**Thorst Thomas** in der Statt [in the city]	
Mertz 20	1 botel Baumöl	0 - 4 - 0
1766	**Jacob Duman** bei der statt [near the city]	
Mertz 3	2 1/2 Dutzend Knöp	0 - 2 - 1
1768	**Jacob Duman** bei der Statt [near the city]	
Janu: 23	1 q: bir	0 - 0 - 6
Febru: 12	1 q: tar	0 - 0 - 6

No 204

1764	**Phillip Wolffersberger**	
Sept 3	1 Wein schling	0 - 0 - 9
15	1 q: Rom	0 - 1 - 0
October 8	1 q: Br: Wein	0 - 1 - 0
19	2 gallen Tram	0 - 8 - 0
	2 lb Reiss	0 - 0 - 9
	1 par strümpff das sein knecht geholt [which his servant boy fetched]	0 - 7 - 0
31	1 q: Br: Wein	0 - 1 - 0
	1 Psalter	0 - 2 - 4
	1 lb: Caffe 1 lb Zucker 1 lb Pech	0 - 2 - 8
1765	**Phillip Wolffersperger**	
Febru 20	1 b: Wein 3 weck	0 - 1 - 8
Mertz 17	1 q: Wein	0 - 2 - 4
Aprill 10	1 hut 1 lb: Zucker	0 - 0 - 10
1765	**Philip Wolfersperger**	
Octo 19	1/2 lb: Pulver	0 - 1 - 9
Nov: 18	1 b: M: wein	0 - 2 - 0
1766		
Janr 21	1/2 buch Babir	0 - 0 - 9
1766	**Philip Wolfersperger**	
Mertz 17	1 q: Br: wein	0 - 1 - 0
18	2 fisch	0 - 0 - 6

Juny 12	1 q: Br: wein	0 - 1 - 0
July 7	1 w: schling	0 - 0 - 9
1767	**Philipp Wolfersporger**	
Mertz 9	1 hut	0 - 7 - 0
May 28	1 q: Bir	0 - 0 - 6

No 205

1764	**Johannes Riel** und Andreas Riel	
October 11	1 q: Thron	0 - 1 - 0
31	1 q: Rom	0 - 1 - 0
1764	**Johannes Riel** und Andreas	
November 26	1 Brodt	0 - 0 - 8
Decem: 19	1 1/2 yd Blau Tuch 1 strang Camel garn	0 -16- 10
1765		
January 4	vor holtz	0 - 6 - 0
Mertz 4	1 q: Rom	0 - 1 - 0
	credit vor to mak riel	0 - 5 - 6
1765	**Johannes Rul an Andereas Rul**	
Sebt 30	3 q: seiter	0 - 1 - 0
	1 gill Rom	0 - 0 - 4
	3 q: thron	0 - 3 - 0
1766		
Mertz 7	2 q: seiter	0 - 0 - 8
	1 q: Bir	0 - 0 - 6
	1 q: Bir	0 - 0 - 6
10	6 Buschel Weitzen	1 - 6 - 0
20	1 q: Bir	0 - 0 - 6
24	1 lb: Zucker	0 - 0 - 10
27	8 lb: fleisch	0 - 2 - 0

1765	**Michael Meÿer** Gatshel brenner [Gatshel distiller]	
Augst 17	gelehnt Vor Keÿler vor butter [lent from Keyler for butter]	0 - 4 - 0
No: 23	Verzehrt	0 -18- 6

No 206

1764	**Leonhart Kurtz**	
October 15	1 q: Thron	0 - 1 - 0
	1/4 lb alspeis	0 - 0 - 7
1769 metz 20	Bauer man Bleibt schultig in rechnung [Bauerman still owes in the settlement]	0 - 4 - 5

1765	**Valedin Dinjes**	
Apill 13	1 q: Thron	0 - 1 - 0

1766	**Nicolaus Remmen**	
Mertz 10	1 Namen Buch	0 - 0 - 8
Maj 20	1 q: seiteröl	0 - 0 - 8
1767		
Augst 29	1 hut	0 - 7 - 6
Sebtem: 15	1 b: wein	0 - 1 - 2

1768		
Apr: 23	1 lb: Zucker 1/4 lb: alspeis	0 - 1 - 3
May 16	1 lb: Zucker	0 - 0 - 10
	2 Buschel saltz	0 - 4 - 0
July 20	1 sichel	0 - 3 - 0
Augst 17	vor Endego	0 - 0 - 6
	Credit	0 - 7 - 6
	Credit	0 - 5 - 0
	Credit	0 - 5 - 0

No 207		
1764	**Henrich Hensching**	
Nov: 3	1 Hut	0 - 7 - 6
1765		
April 19	44 lb: Negel	2 - 4 - 0
	Bezahlt an geld [paid in money]	0 -15- 0
Juny 8	Bezahlt an geld [paid in money]	1 - 4 - 0
	1 w: schling	0 - 0 - 9
1765	**Henrich Hensching**	
Decem: 25	4 lb: Negel 1 w: schling 3 q: haber 1 gill anis	0 - 5 - 8
	Bezahlt an geld [paid in money]	0 - 2 - 6
	Aus dem Alten Buch folio no: 5 [From the old book, page 5]	0 - 1 - 7
1767	**Henrich Hensching**	
January 12	1 hut	0 - 7 - 6
1765	**Spangler**	
May 1	1 lb: Cafee 1 lb: Zucker 1 feil	0 - 4 - 0
13	1 lb: schrot	0 - 0 - 7
Juny 8	1 q: seiter	0 - 0 - 4
24	1 feil	0 - 1 - 8

No 208		
1765	**Thomas Weller**	
Mertz 4	Gelehnt an geld [lent in money]	3 - 0 - 0
	1 lb: Tuback	0 - 0 - 5
27	2 1/2 yd: Druget	0 - 8 - 9
	1 kap	0 - 3 - 0
July 28	1 b: Rom	0 - 0 - 6
Sebt 13	1 b: Rom	0 - 0 - 6
Octo 25	1 b: Rom	0 - 0 - 6
1767	**Friedrich Stumb**	
October 29	6 b: m: wein	0 -12- 0
1765	**Claus**	
May 1	b: seiter	0 - 0 - 2
6	1 sens 1 sichel	0 - 7 - 1
	Abgerechnet mit Nicolaus Cesinger d: 30ten 1765 October Bleibt er schuldig [Settled with Nicolaus Cesinger 30 October 1765. He still owes]	0 - 1 - 0

1765 Nov: 1	2 bogen Babir	0 - 0 - 2
	1/4 yd: Catun un 2 yd: floret	0 - 1 - 9
23	1 q: seiter	0 - 0 - 4
	1 1/2 q: thron	0 - 1 - 6
29	1/2 lb: Peffer un 1 B: seiter	0 - 2 - 2
Decem: 13	1 q: Rom	0 - 1 - 0
1766		
January 15	1 lb: Lichter	0 - 0 - 9
	1 b: Bir un 3 bogen Babir	0 - 0 - 6
20	1 1/2 b: bir	0 - 0 - 9
	1 bogen Babir	0 - 0 - 1

No 209

1764

Johannes Lausser

November 30	1 buch Babir	0 - 1 - 6
Decem: 19	vor Catun 3 yd: floret vor Nodeln 1 b: seiteröl	0 - 5 - 11
20	1 b: seiteröl 1/2 b: wein	0 - 1 - 0
28	1 Muscatamus 1 b: rom	0 - 1 - 1
	1/2 b: M: wein	0 - 1 - 0
1765		
January 10	1 b: Rom	0 - 0 - 6
19	1 b: seiteröl	0 - 0 - 4
21	1 q: Rom 1 bottel Baumöl	0 - 5 - 6
29	1 q: Rom	0 - 1 - 0
Hornung 1	1/2 Buschel Weitzen	0 - 2 - 0
4	1 q: seiteröl	0 - 0 - 8
9	1 q: Rom	0 - 1 - 0
20	1 q: seiter	0 - 0 - 4
	1 hut	0 - 7 - 6
	1 schnub Tuch	0 - 1 - 6
Merz 18	1 b: wein	0 - 1 - 2
Aprill 10	1 b: seiteröl 1 q: Rom	0 - 1 - 4
13	1/2 b: M: wein	0 - 1 - 0
19	2 q: seiter	0 - 0 - 8
	sein geschwey Vor Rossenwein	0 - 0 - 6
		1 -15- 6
	vor holtz	0 - 4 - 1
	Abgerechnet mit Johannes Lausser d. 27 May 1765 Bleibt er schuldig [Settled with Johannes Lausser 27 May 1765. He still owes]	0 - 7 - 7
July 11	1 q: wein	0 - 2 - 4
Sebt 2	1 gaul in die mühl [1 horse to the mill]	0 - 0 - 6
6	2 q: Rom	0 - 2 - 0
12	1 q: Rom	0 - 1 - 0
Octo 7	1 q: Thron	0 - 1 - 0
10	1 q: Rom	0 - 1 - 0
29	1 q: Thron un 1 lb: zucker	0 - 1 - 10
30	2 lb: Zucker	0 - 1 - 8
Decem: 7	Vor gewirtz un schabgut	0 -11- 2
12	2 q: Thron	0 - 2 - 0
15	1 yd: Catun un 4 yd: floret	0 - 6 - 6
1766 Jan: 28	Vor stroh	0 - 2 - 0

No 210

1764	**Jacob Shenck**	
December d. 20	3 b: M: wein	0 - 6 - 0
	1 b: wein	0 - 1 - 2
1765		
January 4	1/4 lb: alspeis 1 lb. Bley 1 q: Br: wein 3 Peiffen	0 - 2 - 3
Febr. 4	1 q: thron 1 q: tram 1 lb: Zucker 1/2 lb: Caffe 1 q: seiter un 1 b: Wein	0 - 5 - 1
Mertz 30	Bezahlt an geld [paid in money]	0 - 2 - 6
May 9	1 q: Br: wein	0 - 1 - 0
	1 q: Br: wein	0 - 1 - 0
13	1 b: seiter	0 - 0 - 2
Juny 1	1/2 b: Wein	0 - 0 - 7
	1 q: br: wein 1 q: seiter	0 - 1 - 4
July 2	1 q: seiter	0 - 0 - 4
	1 q: seiter	0 - 0 - 4
Sebt 2	1 q: seiter	0 - 0 - 4
1766	Abgerechnet mit Jacob Schenck d: 24 t. November 1766 Bleibt schultig[Settled with Jacob Schenck 24 November 1766. Still owes]	0 - 4 - 9
	Jacob Schenck	
Septembr 5	1 bottel mit stober un 1 hut das vergessen [which was forgotten]	0 - 8 - 4
1767		
January 1	1 q: seiter	0 - 0 - 4
5	1 w: schling	0 - 0 - 9
July 6	1 sichel	0 - 2 - 8
1768	**Jacob Schenck**	
February 6	1/2 b: wein	0 - 0 - 7
12	2 q: seiter	0 - 0 - 8

No 211

1765	**Christoph Tribschuch**	
January 1	7 q: m: wein 7 bole Mim vor mann essen [for a man eating]	1 -16- 4
February 20	2 q: seiter 1/2 gill Rom	0 - 0 - 10
1771	**Peter Leineweber**	
April 25	2 q: Bir	0 - 1 - 0
1765	**Panne Schmitt**	
Nov: 6	Verzehrt	0 - 1 - 0
1766		
Febrary 16	Verzehrt	0 - 1 - 4
Augst 20	Verzehrt	0 - 2 - 9
Decem: 10	Verzehrt	0 - 0 - 10
12	2 q: seiter un 1 gill Rom	0 - 0 - 10
	Credit	0 - 2 - 6
1767		
February 17	Verzehrt	0 - 1 - 1
1765	**Johannes Hummerum** im Schwam [at the Swamp -- near Reinholds?]	
Aprill 19	1 b: Wein	0 - 1 - 2

1765	**Peter Leineweber**	
	3 w: schling un 1 1/2 b: Bir	0 - 3 - 6
	1 Messer	0 - 1 - 4
1766		
Febrary	1 q: seiter un Vor bir	0 - 0 - 6
1	2 b: wein	0 - 2 - 4
27	1 q bir un 1 w: schling	0 - 1 - 3

No 212		
1765	**Jacob Shaub**	
Mertz 8	2 gill Rom 1 b: seiter	0 - 0 - 10
17	1 1/2 gill Rom	0 - 0 - 6
20	2 q: seiter 1/2 gill Rom	0 - 0 - 10
27	1 q: seiter	0 - 0 - 4
30	1 q: seiter	0 - 0 - 4
Aprill 4	1 q: seiter	0 - 0 - 4
6	1 q: seiter	0 - 0 - 4
10	1 gill Rom 3 b: seiteröl	0 - 1 - 4
	1 q: seiter	0 - 0 - 4
May 1	1 b: M: wein	0 - 2 - 0
6	1 gill Rom	0 - 0 - 4
13	1/2 gill Rom	0 - 0 - 2
19	1 strang seiten 1 b: seiter	0 - 1 - 0
28	1 hut	0 - 4 - 6
	Vor Essen	0 - 0 - 8
	1 1/2 q: bir	0 - 0 - 9
	1 q: bir	0 - 0 - 6
Juny 4	1 1/2 q: seiter 1/2 gill Rom	0 - 0 - 8
8	1 1/2 q: seiter 1 b: Bir	0 - 0 - 9
	1 q: bir 1 b: seiter	0 - 0 - 8
13	1 q: seiter 1/2 gill Rom 1 gaul in die Mühl [1 horse to the mill]	0 - 1 - 0
18	1 q: seiter	0 - 0 - 4
24	1 Neb Leims Bunsch	0 - 0 - 9
July 8	2 q: seiter	0 - 0 - 8
9	1 q: bir 5 q: seiter	0 - 2 - 2
25	1 b: seiter	0 - 0 - 2
28	1 q: seiter	0 - 0 - 4
Augst 7	2 q: br: wein 2 q: bir 1 q: seiter	0 - 3 - 4
13	1 q: bir 1 q: seiter	0 - 0 - 10
15	1 q: seiter	0 - 0 - 4
17	2 1/2 q: seiter	0 - 0 - 10
	1 q: seiter	0 - 0 - 4
23	3 1/2 q: seiter	0 - 1 - 2
29	2 q: seiter un 1/2 gill rom un Essen	0 - 1 - 2
	1 b: seiteröl 2 q: seiter	0 - 1 - 0
	1 R: schling	0 - 0 - 6
Sebtem: 2	1 1/2 gill Br: wein	0 - 0 - 5
6	1 q: seiter un 1 q: bir	0 - 0 - 10
	1 q: seiter	0 - 0 - 4
13	3 q: seiter	0 - 1 - 0
	1 1/2 q: seiter	0 - 0 - 6
20	1 q: seiter un 1/2 gill Rom	0 - 0 - 6

No 213		
1765	**Jacob Müller**	
Febr: 20	1 q: Thron	0 - 1 - 0
Mertz 20	1 b: wein	0 - 1 - 2
July 1765	**Jacob Miller**	
26	1 q: Rom	0 - 1 - 0
28	1 q: Rom un 1 lb: Negel	0 - 2 - 0
	1 lb: Zucker	0 - 0 - 10
Sebt 12	2 lb: Negel	0 - 2 - 0
30	1 q: Thron	0 - 1 - 0
Octo: 2	1 lb: Negel	0 - 1 - 0
19	1/4 lb: Peffer 1 q: Rom 1/2 lb: negel	0 - 2 - 6
No: 2	1 q: thron	0 - 1 - 0
1766 Febar 20	1 b: seiteröl	0 - 0 - 4
Augst 2	1 q: seiter	0 - 0 - 4
1767 Mertz 14	1 lb: Pulver	0 - 3 - 6
27	1 lb: Pulver	0 - 3 - 6
Augst 25	1 Mantelbiss	0 - 5 - 0
Novem: 22	Vor Kreiten	0 - 0 - 9
	1/2 b: wein	0 - 0 - 7
1768		
February 20	Vor 1 gaul in die Mühl [For 1 horse to the mill]	0 - 0 - 6
Mertz 26	1 hut	0 - 7 - 6
Aprill 16	1 q: Mallasis	0 - 0 - 10
1769 Mertz 7	Jacob Miler Bleibt shultig in der rechnung [Jacob Miler still owes in the settlement] und muss noch 1 par stiffel machen [and still has to make 1 pair of boots]	0 - 2 - 4
Juny 7	Jacob Miller Bleibt schultig in der rechnung [Jacob Miller owes in the settlement]	0 -15- 5
1770	**Jacob Miller**	
February 13	bleibt schultig in der abrechnung [owes in the settlement]	0 - 7 - 6
1771	**Jacob Miller**	
Juny 15	Bleibt schuldig in der abrechnung [owes in the settlement]	0 -11- 6

No 214		
1765	**Johannes Wolfersberger**	
Mertz 6	1 q: bir 1 b: seiteröl	0 - 0 - 10
8	1/2 b: M: wein	0 - 1 - 0
April 13	gelehnt an geld Vor Parren [lent in money for the pastor]	4 - 0 - 0
19	1/2 b: M: wein 1 q: Rom	0 - 2 - 0
	gelehnt an geld Vor Parren [lent in money for the pastor]	0 -15- 0
	Von der schutenmetsch von Michael Reyer [For the shooting match at Michael Reyer's]	0 - 7 - 0
Juny 12	1 q: bir	0 - 0 - 6
Octo: 23	Verzehrt	0 - 1 - 7
24	2 b: M: wein	0 - 4 - 0
	1 Nagel Boren un 1 fisch	0 - 0 - 9
	1/2 lb: negel vor schul Hauss [for the schoolhouse]	0 - 0 - 6
Novem: 16	1 Par schnallen	0 - 2 - 0
20	1 Catecismus	0 - 2 - 6
29	3 lb: Negel	0 - 3 - 0
Decem: 19	2 hüt un yd; floret un 1/4 Imber un 1/4 lb alspeis un 1 R: schling	0 -10- 6

May 19	2 q: Bir 1 gill Rom	0 - 1 - 4
24	1 w: schling	0 - 0 - 9
Sebtem: 16	ist schultig vor schulgeld [owes for tuition]	1 - 0 - 0
27	1 Munstück	0 - 0 - 6
	Aberechnet mit John wolfersperger den 7tn: October 1767 bleibt er schultig	10 -0- 0
	Johannes Wellffer Perger	
	[Settled with John Wolffersperger 7 October 1767. He still owes]	

No 215

1765	**Peter Bore**	
Mertz 8	1 b: Wein	0 - 1 - 2
Aprill 4	1 q: Thron	0 - 1 - 0
10	1 lb: Zucker	0 - 0 - 10
19	1 gill Rom 1 q: seiter	0 - 0 - 8
1765	Abgerechnet mit Peter Bohre d: 9: May 1765 bleibt er schuldig [Settled with Peter Bohre 9 May 1765. He still owes]	0 -16- 6
May 21	1 q: seiteröl 1/2 gill Rom	0 - 0 - 10
	Abgerechnet mit Peter Bore d: 30ten October 1765 Bleibt er schultig [Settlement with Peter Bore, 30 October 1765. He still owes]	0 -17- 9
1765	**Peter Bohre**	
Novem: 18	1 q: seiter un 1 fisch gessen	0 - 0 - 7
1766		
Mertz 17	1 q: seiter 1 gill Rom	0 - 0 - 8
Aprill 5	1 q: seiter	0 - 0 - 4
May 2	1 q: seiter	0 - 0 - 4
Augst 26	1 wetzstein 3 q: seiter un 1 gill Rom 1 Peif	0 - 3 - 4
Sebtem 29	1 q: Br: wein	0 - 1 - 0
October 18	1 gill Rom	0 - 0 - 2
20	1/2 gill Rom	0 - 0 - 4
Novem: 24	2 q: Rom	0 - 2 - 0
	gelehnt an geld [lent in money]	0 - 5 - 0
	1/2 b: m: wein	0 - 1 - 0
January 17	Vor wein	0 - 0 - 8
Aprill 2	2 q: seiter	0 - 0 - 8
Juny 13	3 q: seiter un 1 fisch	0 - 1 - 2
	1/2 gill rom	0 - 0 - 2
July 16	3 q: seiter	0 - 1 - 0
Augst 1	1 q: seiter	0 - 0 - 4
7	2 q: seiter	0 - 0 - 8
15	1/2 b: wein 1 lb: zucker	0 - 1 - 4
Septem:	gelehnt [lent]	0 - 0 - 6
21	2 q: seiter 1 gill Rom	0 - 1 - 0

No 216

1765	**Caspar Schwitzer**	
25 Juny	Bleibt Schuldig in der abrechnung [Owes in the settlement]	1 -12- 2
	Bezahl an geld [paid in money]	0 - 7 - 6
	Bezahlt an geld [paid in money]	0 - 4 - 6
27	1 q: bir un 1 q: seiter	0 - 0 - 10

July 8	1 q: seiter	0 - 0 - 4
9	4 q: seiter	0 - 1 - 4
10	1 q: seiter un 1 b: seiteröl	0 - 0 - 8
	Vor Buch Weitzen	0 - 1 - 0
	1/2 lb: zucker	0 - 0 - 5
15	2q: seiter	0 - 0 - 8
25	1 q: seiter	0 - 0 - 4
28	1 lb: schrot	0 - 0 - 8
Augst 15	4 q: seiter	0 - 1 - 4
23	1 q: seiter 3 q: haber	0 - 1 - 0
Sebt 6	1 b: m: wein un 1 q: seiter	0 - 2 - 4
13	2 q: seiter un 1 gill Rom	0 - 1 - 0
16	3 q: seiter un 2 gill rom	0 - 1 - 8
	1/2 gill Rom	0 - 0 - 2
23	1 b: Rom	0 - 0 - 6
27	1 b: M: wein un 2 q: seiter	0 - 2 - 8
30	4 q: seiter	0 - 1 - 4
	2 buschel Weitzen	0 - 8 - 0
Octo 10	3 q: seiter	0 - 1 - 0
19	2 q: seiteröl un 1/2 gill Rom	0 - 1 - 6
	1 q: seiter	0 - 0 - 4
	5 q: seiter	0 - 1 - 8
25	2 b: wein	0 - 2 - 4
	1 q: seiter	0 - 0 - 4
	2 q: seiter	0 - 0 - 8
29	1 q: seiter	0 - 0 - 4
30	3 q: seiter	0 - 1 - 0
	1 q: seiter	0 - 0 - 4
Novem: 6	2 q: seiter	0 - 0 - 8
10	1 lb: schrot 1/2 gill Rom	0 - 0 - 9
	2 1/2 q: seiter	0 - 0 - 10

No 217

May 1765	**Henrich Leineweber**	
19	4 q: bir 1 gill Rom	0 - 2 - 4
	1 gras sichel	0 - 1 - 2
21	1 q: bir	0 - 0 - 6
Juny 1	1 q: seiter 1 q: Rom	0 - 1 - 4
	1 q: bir	0 - 0 - 6
4	1 q: Rom	0 - 1 - 0
	1 sentz 1 wetzstein	0 - 7 - 0
	1 q: Rom	0 - 1 - 0
12	1 q: bir 1/2 gill Rom 1 q: Rom	0 - 1 - 8
	1 q: Rom	0 - 1 - 0
13	1 q: Rom	0 - 1 - 0
18	1 b: M: wein	0 - 2 - 0
24	1 lb: Zucker	0 - 0 - 10
July 2	1 q: Rom 1 gill Rom	0 - 1 - 4
8	1 q: Rom 1 gill Rom	0 - 1 - 4
	1 q: seiter	0 - 0 - 4
	3 q: seiter	0 - 1 - 0
9	2 q: Rom	0 - 2 - 0
13	2 q: Rom	0 - 2 - 0
15	1 q: seiter	0 - 0 - 4
	1 q: bir	0 - 0 - 6
	1 q: seiter	0 - 0 - 4

24	1 q: bir	0 - 0 - 6
25	1 q: seiter 1 q: bir 1 gill Rom	0 - 1 - 2
	1 q: bir	0 - 0 - 6
	2 q: seiter 1 Neb leims busch	0 - 1 - 5
Augst 7	4 q: seiter	0 - 1 - 4
13	1 q: bir 1 q: Rom 3 q: bir	0 - 3 - 0
15	2 q: bir	0 - 1 - 0
	1 q: Rom	0 - 1 - 0
17	1 q: seiteröl	0 - 0 - 8
26	1 bottel un 1 q: Rom	0 - 1 - 9
29	2 q: seiter	0 - 0 - 8
Sebtember 2	1 b: Rom	0 - 0 - 6
	2 q: seiter un 1 gill Rom	0 - 1 - 0
12	1 q: Rom un 1 q: Thron	0 - 2 - 0
23	1 q: Rom	0 - 1 - 0
	1 b: wein un 1 b: seiter	0 - 1 - 4
Octo 1	1 bol: mim	0 - 1 - 0
7	2 q: Rom	0 - 2 - 0
8	2 q: Rom	0 - 8 - 0
10	1 Par strümb un 1 Licht un Vor Endego	0 - 9 - 0

No 218

1765	**Willhelm Besch**	
July 15	2 q: seiter	0 - 0 - 8
Augst 11	2 q: bir 1 Rom schling	0 - 1 - 6
13	2 q: seiter	0 - 0 - 8
	1 b: Br: wein	0 - 0 - 6
17	1 b: seiteröl 1 1/2 q: br: wein	0 - 1 - 0
	4 q: seiter	0 - 1 - 4
	2 q: seiter 1/2 gill Rom	0 - 0 - 10
	1 q: seiteröl	0 - 0 - 8
July 28	2 q: seiteröl un 1 q: rom	0 - 2 - 4
	1 q: bir	0 - 0 - 6
	1 1/2 b: seiter un 1 lb: Br: wein	0 - 1 - 8
Seb: 6	1 q: Thron	0 - 1 - 0
23	1 q: Tram un 3 q: seiter	0 - 2 - 0
Octo 23	2 q: seiteröl	0 - 1 - 4
	1/2 gill rom un 1 b: seiter	0 - 0 - 4
	gelehnt an geld [lent in money]	0 - 1 - 0
	1/2 gill rom	0 - 0 - 2
	1/2 gill rom	0 - 0 - 2
	1 b: seiteröl 1 gill Rom 1 b: seiter	0 - 0 - 10
25	4 q: seiter	0 - 1 - 4
	2 buschel Weitzen	0 - 8 - 0
No. 2	1 gill Rom un 1 b: Br: wein 3 q: seiter	0 - 1 - 10
Decem: 7	1 q: seiter	0 - 0 - 4
15	1 q: seiter	0 - 0 - 4
29	1 q: Thron un 1 q: seiter	0 - 1 - 4
Jan: 1766 15	1 q: Thron	0 - 1 - 0
22	2 q: seiter	0 - 0 - 8
	1 q: seiter	0 - 0 - 4
28	2 1/2 q: Thron	0 - 1 - 6
Febrary 1	2 q: seiter	0 - 0 - 8
3	2 q: seiter	0 - 0 - 8
5	1 q: seiter	0 - 0 - 4
	1 Calender	0 - 0 - 8

11	1 q: seiter	0 - 0 - 4
16	1 q: seiter	0 - 0 - 4
20	1 q: seiter	0 - 0 - 4
27	1 q: seiter	0 - 0 - 4
Mertz 3	1 q: Thron	0 - 1 - 0

No 219		
1765	**Jacob Fahler**	
May 19	1 Par strümb	0 - 6 - 6
Juny 13	gelehnt an geld [lent in money]	0 - 2 - 6
July 28	gelehnt an geld [lent in money]	0 - 9 - 0
Augst 13	1 hut	1 - 8 - 0
Oct 1	gelehnt an geld [lent in money]	1 - 0 - 0
	gelehnt an geld in Germanton[lent in money in Germantown]	0 - 1 - 6
19	1 Par strümb	0 - 5 - 6
No: 2	1 Par schnallen	0 - 2 - 0
Decem: 7	3 yd: Blau Tuch	2 -17- 0
	3 yd: shallun	0 - 9 - 0
	Vor Neths	0 - 1 - 0
	3 streng Camel garn	0 - 1 - 0
	3/4 yd: schechter	0 - 1 - 8
	3 streng seiten	0 - 2 - 6
	1/4 yd hasenbrick	0 - 0 - 6
	1 Dutzent Knöp	0 - 0 - 10
	1 Hirsch fell	1 - 0 - 0
13	3 1/2 yd: fein Tuch 2 yd: schalun un 3/4 yd: Hassen Brick un 2 streng neths	1 - 1 - 10
19	1 Par hassen schnallen	0 - 0 - 9
25	gelehnt an geld [lent in money]	0 - 5 - 6
	1 b: M: wein	0 - 2 - 0
29	gelehnt an geld [lent in money]	0 - 8 - 6
1756 Jan 5	1 q: bir	0 - 0 - 6
	1 q: bir	0 - 0 - 6
23	5 3/4 yd: Leinen tuch	0 -17- 3
	Von Berned Jacob Bleibt schuldig [Owes from Berned Jacob]	1 - 4 - 1
	Abgerechnet mit Jacob Fehler d: 21 ten Febrary 1766 bleib ich ihm schultig [Settled with Jacob Fehler 21 February 1766. I owe him]	1 - 6 - 2
1766	**Jacob Fehler**	
27	1 q: bir	0 - 0 - 6
Maj 19	1 q: bir	0 - 0 - 6

No 220		
1765	**Carl Muckenfuss**	
May 28	1 q: Essig	0 - 0 - 3
Juny 8	1 q: Essig	0 - 0 - 2
18	1 q: Essig	0 - 0 - 2
July 10	1 q: Essig	0 - 0 - 2
24	gelehnt an geld [lent in money]	
	1 q: Rom un 1 Namon	0 - 1 - 9
Augst 17	1 q: Essig	0 - 0 - 2

Sebt 12	Vor Nodeln un 1 q: Essig	0 - 0 - 3
	Abgerechnet mit Carl Muckenfuss den 10 February 1766 Bleibt er schuldig [Settled with Carl Muckenfuss 10 February 1766. He still owes]	0 - 7 - 7
12	1 q: bir	0 - 0 - 6
14	Vor ein Kam un 1 nestel un 1 q: bir	0 - 3 - 2
April 10	1 b: seiter	0 - 0 - 2
May 1	2 q: Essig	0 - 0 - 4
2	1 b: Br: wein	0 - 0 - 6
9	1 q: Essig	0 - 0 - 2
29	12 q: Waser seitter	0 - 1 - 0
Juny 23	2 q: saltz	
Augst 2	1 q: Bir 2 q: seiter	0 - 1 - 2
	1 gill Rom	0 - 0 - 4
	1 1/2 yd: Kelsch	0 - 3 - 5
26	2 q: Wasser seiter	0 - 0 - 2
Sebtem: 20	Vor Imber	0 - 0 - 8
29	1 q: Rom un 1 lb: zucker	0 - 1 - 10
October 7	1 gill Baumöl	0 - 0 - 8
14	1 lb: zucker	0 - 0 - 10
27	1 q: Rom	0 - 1 - 0
Decem: 8	1/4 lb. Imber	0 - 0 - 6
19	1 strang neths	0 - 0 - 2
	1 bottel un 2 Nestel	0 - 1 - 0
31	1 q: Br: wein	0 - 0 - 9
	Credit von Adam Speck	0 -12- 8

No 221

1765

Michael Reger

Juny 8	1 b: bir 1/2 gill Rom	0 - 0 - 5
July 28	1 q: bir	0 - 0 - 6
Augst 15	2 q: Rom un 1 bottel un 1 brill un 1 1/2 q: bir un 1 R: schling un 3 weck	0 - 5 - 9
Sebt 16	1 q: seiter	0 - 0 - 4
30	1 Rom schling un 2 gill Rom	0 - 1 - 2
Octo: 7	1 Catecismus 1 /4 lb: Pulver 1 gill Rom	0 - 3 - 0
16	1 lb: Pulver 2 gill rom un 1 q: seiter	0 - 4 - 6
	1/2 gill Rom	0 - 0 - 2
25	3 Nagel Born 1 1/2 q: seiter 1/2 gill Rom	0 - 3 - 1
Novem 10	1 q: seiter un 1/2 gill rom	0 - 0 - 6
23	1 lb: Pulver un 3 lb: Bley	0 - 5 - 0
1766		
January 5	2 q: seiter un 1 feil	0 - 2 - 8
30	1/2 gill Rom	0 - 0 - 2
Feberary 25	1 gill Rom	0 - 0 - 4
27	1 q: Bir	0 - 0 - 6
Mertz 3	1 q: seiter	0 - 0 - 4
Maj 9	Verzehrt	0 - 1 - 10
Novem: 3	2 b: m: wein un 2 gill rom	0 - 4 - 8
1767		
January 19	2 1/2 gill rom	0 - 0 - 10
31	1 q: seiter 1 gill rom	0 - 0 - 8
February 14	1 gill rom	0 - 0 - 4
May 20	1 lb: Pulver 5 q: Br: wein 2 gill Br: wein	0 - 7 - 9

1767	**Henrich Keyler**	
Sebtem: 7	3 w: schling 1 q: seiter 1 lb: Tuback	0 - 3 - 0
1768	**Peter Keyler**	
Juny 14	1 gill Rom	0 - 0 - 4

No 222

1765	**Jacob Seltzer** Vor die Kirch [for the [Lutheran] church]	
July 24	3 lb: Negel	0 - 3 - 0
25	1 haxet seiter	1 -18- 0
	1 q: bir	0 - 0 - 6
26	2 lb: negel	0 - 2 - 0
	1 b: m: wein	0 - 2 - 0
27	2 bol: Leims Bunsch	0 - 3 - 0
	2 lb: Negel	0 - 2 - 0
Sebtem 23	3lb: negel	0 - 3 - 0
24	3 lb: negel	0 - 3 - 0
26	2 lb: negel	0 - 2 - 0
Octo: 2	1 lb: negel	0 - 1 - 0
3	1 q: seiter	0 - 0 - 4
	2 lb: negel	0 - 2 - 0
10	2 lb: negel	0 - 2 - 0
19	1 lb: negel	0 - 1 - 0
	1/2 lb: negel	0 - 0 - 6
29	1/2 lb: negel	0 - 0 - 6
	1 lb: negel un 1/2 lb: Pulver	0 - 2 - 9
Novem: 10	2 lb: negel	0 - 2 - 0
		3 - 7 - 4
1767		
Augst 24	2 Dutzent scheiben	0 -12- 0
1768	**Ludwig Schellmann**	
October 20	1 Bottel	0 - 0 - 9
1770	**Ludwig Schellmann**	
October 17	gerechnet Bleibt nichts [Settled, owes nothing]	

No 223

1765	**Henrich Keÿler**	
Augst 13	1 q: seiter un 1 b: Bir	0 - 0 - 7
15	1 bottel un 1 q: Rom un 2 q: seiter	0 - 2 - 6
	3 q: seiter	0 - 1 - 0
17	1 bogen babir un 1 b: Bir	0 - 0 - 4
23	1 q: seiter un 1 gill Rom	0 - 2 - 0
Sebt 2	1 b: seiter un 1 w: schling	0 - 1 - 1
6	1 q: seiter	0 - 0 - 4
23	2 q: seiter	0 - 0 - 8
30	1 bottel un 2 q: seiter	0 - 1 - 5
	1 q: seiter 1 b: Rom un 1 gill Rom	0 - 1 - 2
Octo. 16	3 q: seiter 1 b: seiteröl 1 gill Rom 1 b: Rom	0 - 2 - 0
17	1 gill Rom 1 b: seiteröl	0 - 0 - 8
19	2 q: seiteröl un 1 q: seiter un 1 gill Rom	0 - 2 - 0
25	2 1/2 q: seiteröl 1 q: seiter	0 - 2 - 0

Novem 2	2 q: seiter	0 - 0 - 8
6	2 q: seiter	0 - 0 - 8
10	1 q: Rom 3 q: seiter	0 - 2 - 0
	4 q: seiter	0 - 1 - 4
18	4 q: seiter un 1 fisch	0 - 1 - 7
20	1 Namen Buch	0 - 0 - 9
	3 q: seiter	0 - 1 - 0
24	1 q: seiter	0 - 0 - 4
	1 q: seiter un 1 lb: Zucker	0 - 1 - 2
Decem: 12	1 q: seiter	0 - 0 - 4
25	1 q: seiter	0 - 0 - 4
1766		
January 1	1 q: Bir un 2 gill rom	0 - 1 - 2
10	2 q: seiter 1 gill rom un 1 q: Br: wein	0 - 2 - 0
15	2 buschel Weitzen un 1/2 gill Rom	0 - 8 - 2
21	1 q: seiter	0 - 0 - 4
	Abgerechnet mit Henrich Keÿler den 13 ten February 1766 Bleibt er nichts [Settled with Henrich Keyler 13 February 1766. He owes nothing]	
Mertz 7	1 q: seiter un 1 b: bir	0 - 0 - 7
8	2 q: seiter 1/2 lb Zucker	0 - 1 - 1

No 224

1765

Jacob Shaub

Sebt: 23	1 Rom schling	0 - 0 - 6
	1 gill annis un 1 q: seiter	0 - 0 - 10
Octo. 2	2 q: seiter	0 - 0 - 8
10	2 q: seiter	0 - 0 - 8
16	1 Par strümp	0 - 5 - 3
23	1 b: seiter	0 - 0 - 2
	1 q: seiter	0 - 0 - 4
25	1 q: seiter 1/2 gill rom	0 - 0 - 6
	1 b: seiteröl un 1 b: seiter	0 - 0 - 6
	2 q: seiter	0 - 0 - 8
29	1 gill br: wein 1 b: seiter	0 - 0 - 5
30	1 gill annis un 1 q: seiter	0 - 0 - 9
No: 2	1 q: seiter	0 - 0 - 4
	1 b: wein 1 1/2 q: seiter 1 fisch	0 - 1 - 11
6	1 Namen Buch	0 - 0 - 9
	50 Negel	0 - 0 - 6
	1 fisch	0 - 0 - 3
	1 gaul ins steitzen [1 horse to Steitzen=Lebanon]	0 - 1 - 0
10	1 q: seiter	0 - 0 - 4
18	5 q: seiter un 2 r: schling	0 - 2 - 8
20	1 q: seiter	0 - 0 - 4
23	1 q: seiter	0 - 0 - 4
	1 1/2 un 1/2 4 yd: halb Tuch	0 - 5 - 7
Decem 12	2 q: seiter un 2 Peiffen	0 - 0 - 10
13	1 gill Br: wein un 1 fisch	0 - 0 - 6
15	1 q: seiter	0 - 0 - 4
25	1 q: bir	0 - 0 - 6
	2 q: seiter	0 - 0 - 8
	1 q: seiter	0 - 0 - 4
29	1 q: seiter	0 - 0 - 4

1766		
Jann: 1	1 q: bir un 2 q: seiter	0 - 1 - 2
	1/2 lb Zucker	0 - 0 - 5
8	1 q: bir un 1 q: seiter	0 - 0 - 10
	2 1/2 lb: un schlich	0 - 1 - 5
	1 b: seiter	0 - 0 - 2

No 225

1765	**Henrich Leinewewer**	
October 23	Verzehrt	0 - 1 - 7
25	1 b: wein	0 - 1 - 2
	2 lb: Zucker un 2 yd: floret un vor spellen	0 - 2 - 6
	1 b: m: wein 1 gill Rom	0 - 2 - 4
	2 q: seiter	0 - 0 - 8
30	2 gallen Rom	0 - 8 - 0
	1/2 Tag holtz gefuhrt [carted wood 1/2 day]	0 - 4 - 0
	2 lb: Reiss 4 q: seiter	0 - 1 - 10
Novem 2	1 lb: Negel 1 q seiter un 1 fisch	0 - 1 - 7
8	2 q: seiter	0 - 0 - 8
10	2 q: seiter un 1 q: Rom	0 - 1 - 8
	Vor schab gut	5 - 3 - 10
	2 feilen	0 - 2 - 5
	2 q: Rom	0 - 2 - 0
12	1 bole mim	0 - 1 - 0
16	1 q: Rom	0 - 1 - 2
18	2 q: Thron un 1/2 4 lb: Baumwolle das ewig geholt [which Ewig fetched]	0 - 2 - 8
20	1 q: Br: wein	0 - 1 - 0
	1 q: Br: wein	0 - 1 - 0
29	2 lb: Zucker 1/2 Cafe	0 - 2 - 5
Decem 7	1 q: seiter	0 - 0 - 4
12	2 q: Thron	0 - 2 - 0
13	1 q: Br: wein	0 - 1 - 10
15	ist schuldig von Wegen Charles Davis die Suma [owes on account of Charles Davis the sum]	1 -18- 10
23	1 q: Br: wein	0 - 1 - 0
25	1 w: schling	0 - 0 - 9
1766		
January 1	1 q: Thron	0 - 1 - 0
8	1 q: Br: wein	0 - 1 - 0
	2 lb: Pulver	0 - 7 - 0
	1 w: schling un 1 b: seiteröl	0 - 1 - 1
10	1 q: Br: wein	
	1 q: Br: wein vor Camelgarn	0 - 1 - 7
	1 Dutzet un 4 Knöp	0 - 2 - 8
20	1 q: seiter un 1 b: Br: wein	0 - 0 - 10
21	1 q: Br: wein	0 - 1 - 0

No 226

1765	**Berned Jacob**	
Sebtem: 12	1/2 gill gatschal un 1 Namen Buch	0 - 1 - 0
20	1 b: annis	0 - 1 - 0
	1 lb: negel	0 - 1 - 0

23	1 b: annis	0 - 1 - 0
	1 q: annis	0 - 2 - 0
Octo: 10	1 q: seiter	0 - 0 - 4
25	1/2 gill annis	0 - 0 - 3
	1 b: annis	0 - 1 - 0
Nov: 16	1/2 gill annis	0 - 0 - 3
18	1/2 gill annis	0 - 0 - 3
29	1 b: annis	0 - 1 - 0
1766		
January 8	1 q: Thron	0 - 1 - 0
	Abgerechnet mit Berned Jacob d. 18t: February 1766 Bleibt er schuldig [Settled with Berned Jacob 18 February 1766. He still owes.]	1 - 9 - 9
	Bezahl an geld [paid in money]	0 - 4 - 0
February 25	1/2 b: m: wein un 1 1/2 q: bir	0 - 1 - 9
Mertz 8	1 q: Thron	0 - 1 - 0
10	4 q: seiter 1 b: Bir 1/2 gill annis	0 - 1- 10
	credit	1 -10- 0
Aprill 5	Vor Baum Vor den Brunnen [for trees for the fountain]	1 - 1 - 0
20	2 fisch	0 - 0 - 6
24	1 b: Bir	0 - 0 - 3
Maj 1	3 q: Milch	0 - 0 - 9
17	1 b: Baumöl 1/2 b: annis 1 q: 1/2 b: M: wein	0 - 7 - 6
19	1/2 gill annis	0 - 0 - 3
23	1 q: M: wein	0 - 4 - 0
Juny 4	1 m: w: schling un 1 q: Br: wein	0 - 2 - 2
12	Vor stock 1 strohut	0 - 3 - 0
	1 q: Br: wein	0 - 1 - 0
23	1 q: Bir	0 - 0 - 6
July 1	Vor Bleiel 6 sicheln	0 -19- 10
5	1/2 gill annis	0 - 0 - 3

No 227

Jacob Lautermilch

1765		
October 10	Vor Pulver un Bleÿ	0 - 6 - 10
25	1 lb: Pulver	0 - 3 - 6
No: 2	1 Par strümb	0 - 6 - 0
12	1/2 lb: Pulver un 1 lb: Bleÿ	0 - 2 - 3
20	1/2 gill Rom	0 - 0 - 2
23	1 lb: Pulver un lb: Bleÿ	0 - 4 - 0
1766		
January 15	1 lb: Bleÿ 1/2 b: Rom	0 - 1 - 0
21	1 gill Rom	0 - 0 - 4
Februa: 15	1 b: m: wein un M: w: schling un 1 w: schling	0 - 3 - 11
	1 glas Verbrochen [1 glass broken]	0 - 3 - 6
27	2 Dutzet un 2 grose Knöp	0 - 2 - 0
Aprill 20	1 b: wein un 3 wein schling	0 - 3 - 5
Juny 19	1 sentz Vor Ditz [for Ditz]	0 - 4 - 0
July 5	1 Par strümb 1 q: Rom un 1 bottel 1 stober	0 - 9 - 4
1767		
Feberu 14	ist schultig vor schissen [owes for shooting]	0 - 7 - 10
28	ist schultig vor schissen [owes for shooting]	0 - 5 - 0
	Abgerechnet mit Jacob Lautermilch d. 1ten Juny 1767 bleibt schutig [Settled with Jacob Lautermilch 1 June 1767. Still owes]	1 - 3 - 6
		2 - 4 - 0
		1 - 7 - 10

1768	**Jacob Lautermilch**	
Aprill 9	1/2 b: wein	0 - 0 - 7
1768	**Jacob Lautermilch**	
Sebtem: 12	1 w: schling	0 - 0 - 9
1769 Apr: 3	2 gill gatchal	0 - 0 - 10
July 4	1 w: schling	0 - 0 - 9
October 17	1 q: Rom	0 - 1 - 0
Decem: 20	1 gill Rom	0 - 0 - 4
	1 R: Schling	0 - 0 - 6
23	1 gill Rom	0 - 0 - 4
1770		
Mertz 1	1 b: Br: wein	0 - 0 - 5

No 228		
1765	**Peter Druckenmiller**	
Octo: 16	2 1/2 q: Rom un 1 bottel	0 - 3 - 10
Juny 23	1 sentz un 1 wetzstein	0 - 6 - 0
1767	**Peter Druckenmiller**	
February 28	ist schultig vor schiesen [owes for shooting]	0 - 4 - 0
1765	**Glatz**	
December 12	hat Credit Vor hüt	3 - 0 - 0
1767		
Febrary 23	Hat Credit Vor hüt	4 - 0 - 0
	1 fuchs balg	0 - 2 - 6
1769	**Georg Gärtner Docter**	
April 8	2 b: wein	0 - 2- 9
	8 mal Essen	

No 229		
1765	**Johann Theodor Hofius**	
October 23	1 1/2 gill Rom un 1 1/2 b: wein	0 - 2 - 3
25	geleht an geld [lent in money]	0 -10- 0
	1/2 b: m: wein	0 - 1 - 0
	1/2 yd: schalun un 8 streng neths 1/4 schechter	0 - 4 - 9
28	1 buch Babir	0 - 1 - 6
No: 2	1/2 b: wein 1/2 gill Rom	0 - 0 - 9
6	1/2 gill Rom 1 b: seiter 1/2 b: wein	0 - 0 - 11
	1/2 b: wein	0 - 0 - 7
10	Vor schab gut	1 - 7 - 7
	1/2 b: wein 1/2 gill Rom	0 - 0 - 9
12	1 Par schnallen un 1/2 b: wein	0 - 2 - 7
	1 gill Rom	0 - 0 - 4
23	1/2 b: wein 1/2 gill Rom	0 - 0 - 9
	4 gill Rom	0 - 1 - 4
Decem 7	1 1/2 q: seiter	0 - 0 - 6
13	1 seiten halls Tuch	0 - 8 - 0
	1 b: seiter	0 - 0 - 2
	1/2 b: wein	0 - 0 - 7
	1 b: seiter	0 - 0 - 2

15	1 lb schnub Tuback	0 - 1 - 4
	1 yd: Bäy un [blotched] Dutzent knöp un 1/4 hassenbrick un neths	0 -13- 7
	6 b: seiter	0 - 1 - 0
19	2 b: seiter	0 - 0 - 4
	1/2 b: wein	0 - 0 - 7
25	4 b: seiter	0 - 0 - 8
	3 b: Bir	0 - 0 - 9
29	1 buch Babir	0 - 1 - 6
	2 b: Bir	0 - 0 - 6
	2 b: Bir	0 - 0 - 6
	1 b: Bir 1 gill Rom 2 q: Br: wein	0 - 2 - 6
	6 b: Bir	0 - 1 - 6
	1/2 gill Rom	0 - 0 - 2
		4 - 9 - 5

Lumb [rag] is written across this page twice.

No 230
1766 **Johann Theodor Hofius** ist ein Lumb dass ist gewiss dass ist gewiss wahr [is a rag, this is most certainly true]

January 1	1/2 b: wein	0 - 0 - 7
	2 b: Bir	0 - 0 - 6
	1 b: Bir	0 - 0 - 3
5	4 b: Bir	0 - 1 - 0
	1/2 b: wein	0 - 0 - 7
	2 q: Br: wein	0 - 2 - 0
	3 b: Bir	0 - 0 - 9
	3 b: Bir	0 - 0 - 9
8	3 b: Bir	0 - 0 - 9
10	3 b: Bir	0 - 0 - 9
15	6 b: Bir	0 - 1 - 6
20	1 lb: schnub Tuback	0 - 1 - 4
	2 b: Bir	0 - 0 - 6
	1 q: Br: wein	0 - 1 - 0
21	2 b: Bir	0 - 0 - 6
	1 b: Bir	0 - 0 - 3
	1 b: Bir	0 - 0 - 3
	1 b: Bir un 1 b: seiter	0 - 0 - 5
22	1 q: Br: wein	0 - 1 - 0
24	3 b: Bir	0 - 0 - 9
	4 q: Bir	0 - 2 - 0
28	4 b: Bir	0 - 1 - 0
	2 b: Bir	0 - 0 - 6
30	3 b: Bir	0 - 0 - 9
	3 b: Bir	0 - 0 - 9
Febr: 1	1 b: Bir	0 - 0 - 3
	4 b: Bir	0 - 1 - 0
3	4 b: Bir	0 - 1 - 0
5	3 b: Bir	0 - 0 - 9
	2 b: Bir	0 - 0 - 6

8	3 b: Bir	0 - 0 - 9
	1 q: Br: wein	0 - 1 - 0
	4 b: Bir	0 - 1 - 0
	2 b: Bir	0 - 0 - 6
	2 b: Bir	0 - 0 - 6
	5 b: Bir	0 - 1 - 3
	1 q: br: wein	0 - 1 - 0
		1 - 8 - 11

[Lumb, rag, is written across this page in large letters]

No 231

Casper Schwitzer

1765		
November 12	3 q: seiter	0 - 1 - 0
16	2 q: seiter	0 - 0 - 8
18	2 q: seiter	0 - 0 - 8
20	1 q: seiter	0 - 0 - 4
29	4 q: seiter	0 - 1 - 4
	3 q: seiter	0 - 1 - 0
Decem: 12	1 q: seiter	0 - 0 - 4
	1 b: m: wein 1/2 gill Rom 1 q: seiter	0 - 2 - 6
14	1 gill Rom	0 - 0 - 4
1766		
January 5	2 q: seiter	0 - 0 - 8
	2 q: seiter 1 q: br: wein	0 - 1 - 8
8	2 q: seiter	0 - 0 - 8
	1/2 lb: Weisen zucker	0 - 0 - 9
	Bezahlt an geld [paid in money]	0 - 4 - 0
28	1 q: seiter	0 - 0 - 4
Febrary 3	2 q: seiter	0 - 0 - 8
	1 b: M: wein	0 - 2 - 0
14	2 q: seiter 1 q: bir	0 - 1 - 2
16	1 q: seiter	0 - 0 - 4
	2 gill Rom	0 - 0 - 8
	2 buschel Weitzen 2 q: seiter	0 - 8 - 10
20	2 q: seiter	0 - 0 - 8
	1 q: seiter	0 - 0 - 4
	Abgerechnet mit Casper Schwitzer d: 11ten Aprill 1766 Bleibt er schultig [Settled with Casper Schwitzer 11 April 1766. He owes]	4 -18- 11
	abrechnet mit Casper Schwitzer d: 24 September 1766 bleibt nichts [Settled with Casper Schwitzer 24 September 1766. Owes nothing]	
1767		
January	den 26tn Bleibt Caspar Schweyter schuldig auf Rechnung [The 26th Caspar Schweyter owes at the settlement]	2 - 0 - 7

No 232

Anderes Rücker

1765		
Novem: 18	1 q: seiter	0 - 0 - 4
23	1/4 lb: Peffer un 1 q: seiter	0 - 1 - 4
	Abgerechnet mit Andereas Rücker d: 1 November 1766 Bleibt er schuldig [Settled with Andereas Rücker 1 November 1766. He still owes]	0 -12- 4
1767	2 q: seiter	0 - 0 - 6
January 13	1 q: Bir 1 q: seiter 1 gill Rom	0 - 1 - 2
Aprill 20	2 q: seiter	0 - 0 - 8
25	1 b: seiteröl	0 - 0 - 4

Juny 1	1 hut un 1 yd: Baumwollen zeug	0 - 9 - 9
	darauf Bezahlt [paid thereon]	0 - 3 - 0
Sebtem: 21	1 q: seiteröl un 1 Peif	0 - 0 - 9
Octo: 25	3 b: seiteröl	0 - 1 - 0
Novem: 10	1 hut 1 q: seiter 1/2 gill Rom	0 - 6 - 6
13	2 q: seiter	0 - 0 - 8
	1 w: schling	0 - 0 - 9
18	1 gill Rom 1 weck	0 - 0 - 5
Decem: 21	1 q: seiter	0 - 0 - 4
1768		
January 2	1/2 yd: Cattun 3 yd: floret 1 w: schling 1 gill Rom	
	2 q: seiter	0 - 4 - 10
9	1 q: seiter 1 weck	0 - 0 - 5
23	1 buschel Weitzen	0 - 5 - 0
	7 q: seiter 1 gill Rom	0 - 2 - 8
February 8	1 b: seiteröl	0 - 0 - 4
20	2 q: seiter	0 - 0 - 8
Mertz 21	2 q: seiter	0 - 0 - 8
28	2 q: seiter 1 q: seiteröl 1 gill Br: wein 1 weck	0 - 1 - 8
Aprill 9	5 q: seiter 1 q: seiteröl	0 - 2 - 4
16	2 q: seiter 1 b: seiteröl	0 - 1 - 0
	Credit vor Kreben machen 5 tag	
20	4 q: seiter	0 - 1 - 4
	2 q: seiter	0 - 0 - 8
23	1 1/2 Centner heu 3 q: seiter	0 - 4 - 9
	1 q: seiter	0 - 0 - 4
	1 q: seiter	0 - 0 - 4
May 18	1/2 gill Rom	0 - 0 - 2
	2 q: seiter	0 - 0 - 8

No 233

Michael Müller

1765		
Nov: 23	1 dutzend Knöp	0 - 0 - 10
1766		
January 10	5 lb: hut Zucker	0 - 7 - 6
	5 lb: Zucker	0 - 4 - 2
	50 Zigel gelehnt Vor Berned Jacob [50 tiles lent for Berned Jacob]	
June 4	4 1/2 q: Rom	0 - 5 - 3
July 7	2 1/2 yd: Kelsch	0 - 8 - 9
	d. 25 December 1767 hab ich mid Michel Miller zusammen gerechnedt bleibt keiner dem andern nichts mer schultig 1767 [25 December 1767 I settled together with Michel Miller. Neither owes the other anything]	
1767		
January	4 dutzent knöp das bergessen [which was forgotten]	0 - 8 - 0
22	1 bottel	0 - 0 - 9

No 234

George Conrad

1765		
Nov: 23	gelehnt an geld[lent in money]	0 -12- 0
Decem: 15	1 Bottel	0 - 0 - 9

1766		
Jan: 20	1 q: Br: wein	0 - 1 - 0
26	1 feil	0 - 0 - 10
Febr: 1	1/4 lb: Weisen Zucker	0 - 0 - 5
	1/2 gill Baumöl	0 - 0 - 4
	bezahlt im voll d. 25 Mertz 1766 [paid in full 25 March 1766]	
1766	**George Conrad**	
Mertz 29	2 schnub tücher	0 - 2 - 6
	5 lb fleisch	0 - 1 - 3
Aprill 14	1 gill Baumöl	0 - 0 - 8
20	1 b: wein	0 - 1 - 2
May 19	2 q: br: wein	0 - 1 - 0
Juny 5	2 buschel Weitzen 12 q: Rom 2 lb: zucker	1 - 3 - 10
Sebtem: 15	2 buschel Weitzen	0 - 8 - 8
16	1 sens 3 Par Henter Knöp un 2 lb: zucker	0 - 6 - 8
		2 - 5 - 9
1766		
May 12	Abgerechnet mit **Martin Schuty** d: 12 May 1766 Bleibt er schultig [Settled with Martin Schuty 12 May 1766. He still owes]	4 - 7 - 3
	Bezahlt an geld [paid in money]	1 - 6 - 0
	abgerechnet mit Martin Schuty d: 1 tn: November 1766 bleibt er schultig [Settled with Martin Schuty 1 November 1766. He still owes]	5 - 4 - 3
1767		
Mertz 5	Martin Schuty Bleibt in der rechnung [still owes in the settlement]	0 - 7 - 0
20	6 q: Rom 1/2 lb: Pulver	0 - 7 - 9
July 20	2 q: Rom	0 - 2 - 0
Sebtem: 4	2 q: Rom	0 - 2 - 0
1768		
Aprill 6	6 q: Rom	0 - 6 - 0
1769		
Novem: 4	Martin Schuty Bleibt schultig in rechnung [Martin Schuty remains owing at the settlement]	0 -19- 1

No 235		
1765	**Michael Meyer**	
Novem: 24	1/2 lb: Pulver	0 - 1 - 9
1766		
January 10	1/2 lb: Pulver	0 - 1 - 9
1766	**Michael Meyer**	
Aprill 14	1 b: wein	0 - 1 - 2
16	1 w: schling	0 - 0 - 9
1767 Febr: 28	ist schultig vor schisen [owes for shooting]	0 - 6 - 0
1769 Aprill 20	1 b: wein 1 gill gatshal	0 - 1 - 7
May 15	1 b: wein	0 - 1 - 2

1765	**John Lautermilch** junor	
Decem: 25	1/4 lb: Pulver	0 - 0 - 11
1766		
May 2	1 w: schling	0 - 0 - 9

No 236

1765	**Johannes Lauser**	
Decem: 19	1 q: Br: wein	0 - 1 - 0
	1 yd: Catun	0 - 5 - 0
	92 lb: Rindfleisch	0 -15- 4
29	1 q: Br: wein	0 - 1 - 0
1766		
January 1	1 lb Zucker un 1 Par schnallen	0 - 1 - 3
5	4 lb: Zucker un 2 q: Thron	0 - 5 - 4
	1 q: Rom	0 - 1 - 2
21	1 Negel Boren un 1 b: wein	0 - 1 - 10
	1 q: Br: wein 1/2 b: wein	0 - 1 - 7
Feb: 5	1 b: Wein	0 - 1 - 2
14	2 lb: Zucker un 4 yd: floret	0 - 2 - 8
21	gelehnt an geld Vor Tax [lent in money for tax]	0 - 4 - 0
25	7 lb: zucker	0 - 5 - 10
Mertz 3	1 b: Br: wein	0 - 0 - 6
	Abgerechnet mit John Lauser d: 19ten May 1766 Bleibt er schultig [Settled with John Lauser 19 May 1766. He still owes]	1 - 2 - 4
May 23	Vor Wellen	0 - 5 - 0
Octo: 10	1 q: Rom	0 - 1 - 0
25	1 gill Baumöhl	0 - 0 - 8
27	1 b: Rom	0 - 0 - 6
28	1 b: Rom	0 - 0 - 6
	Abgerechnet mit John Lauser d: 14ten July 1767 bleibt nichts [Settled with John Lauser 14 July 1767. No balance]	
1768		
Novem 6	1 q: Rom	0 - 1 - 0
	John Lausser gerechnet d: 4 ten Juny 1770. Bleibt nichts [John Lauser settled 4 June 1770. No balance]	

No 237

1765	**Jacob Brecht**	
Decem: 13	1/4 lb: Peffer 1/4 lb: alspeis	0 - 1 - 7
19	1 lb: Zucker	0 - 0 - 10
25	1 q: Thron	0 - 1 - 0
29	1 lb: Zucker	0 - 0 - 10
1766		
January 8	1 b: Br: wein	0 - 0 - 6
10	1 lb: Zucker	0 - 0 - 10
20	2 q: Thron	0 - 2 - 0
21	2 yd: Kelsch un 1 lb: Zucker	0 - 5 - 4
26	1 b: Br: wein	0 - 0 - 6
28	Vor holtz führen [for carting wood]	0 - 2 - 0
30	1 lb: Zucker	0 - 0 - 10
February 3	1 b: Br: wein	0 - 0 - 6
8	1 lb: Zucker	0 - 0 - 10
16	1 lb: Zucker	0 - 0 - 10
20	1 b: seiteröl	0 - 0 - 4
25	gelehnt an geld [lent in money]	0 - 7 - 6
27	1 lb: Zucker	0 - 0 - 10
	Abgerechnet mit Jacob Brecht d: 17ten Mertz 1766 bleibt nichts [Settled with Jacob Brecht 17 March 1766. No balance.]	

Mertz 18	1 lb: Zucker	0 - 0 - 10
20	1 q: Thron un 2 fisch	0 - 1 - 4
Aprill 7	1 q: Br: wein	0 - 1 - 0
10	1 q: Rom	0 - 1 - 2
14	1 b: Rom	0 - 0 - 7
20	1 b: Br: wein	0 - 0 - 6
	6 q: flags samen gelehnt [lent]	
24	1 hut	0 - 7 - 6
May 17	1 Kelsch	0 - 2 - 3
20	2 1/4 yd: Kelsch	0 - 7 - 10
Juny 4	gelehnt [lent]	0 - 0 - 9
12	1 lb: Zucker	0 - 0 - 10
July 1	1 lb: Zucker	0 - 0 - 10
5	Vor schab gut	0 - 8 - 9

No 238

1766	**Bethesen sein Fuhr Leit** [Bethesen's drivers]	
January 8	Verzehrt auf zweÿ mahl [ate twice]	0 - 6 - 1
15	6 q: seiter un 1 b: Rom un 1 gill Rom	0 - 3 - 1
20	3 q: seiter un 1 q: Bir	0 - 1 - 6
21	Friedrich 4 q: seiter un 1/2 b: Rom	0 - 1 - 10
22	Krum 4 q: seiter	0 - 1 - 4
23	Friedrich 1 q: seiter un 1 q: Bir un 1/2 b: Rom	0 - 1 - 4
24	Krum 3 q: seiter 2 gill Rom	0 - 1 - 8
	Friedrich 3 q: bir 1/2 bol Rom	0 - 2 - 0
Forbr 10tn	Krum ein peint und 1 shil Rom	0 - 1 - 0
	Krum 2 mal gessen [ate twice] 1 q: seiter 1/2 gill Rom	0 - 1 - 6
	Krum 1 q: Rom	0 - 1 - 4
24	Krum 2 q: seiter 1 b: Rom	0 - 1 - 4
Novem 27	Krum 1 1/2 b: Rom 1 q: seiter 1 gill Rom	0 - 1 - 7
Decem: 2	Krum 1 q: Rom un 3 q: seiter	0 - 2 - 2
Decem: 8	Krum 3 1/2 q: seiter 1/2 b: Rom	0 - 1 - 8
10ten fo	Zacharis ein Rom	0 - 0 - 4
	1 b: Rom	0 - 0 - 7
		1 - 9 - 5

1766	**Nicholaus Cesinger**	
January 26	1 lb: Zucker	0 - 0 - 10
febrary 11	1 q: Thron	0 - 1 - 0
1766		
Julyus 3	Nicholaus Cesinger Bleibt schuldig in der abrechnung [Nicholaus Cesinger still owes in settlement]	0 -12- 8
1766	Abgerechnet mit Nicholaus Cesinger d: 9 October 1766 Bleibt er schultig [Settled with Nicholaus Cesinger 9 October 1766. He owes]	1 - 3 - 0
	Bezahlt an geld [Paid in money]	0 -12- 0
Novem: 10	1 gill gatschal 1 q: seiter	0 - 0 - 8
	1 q: Rom 2 q: seiter	0 - 1 - 6
16	Verzehrt	0 - 2 - 6
	1 b: seiter	0 - 0 - 4
17	1 kam	0 - 0 - 6
	1 q: Bir un 1 q: seiter	0 - 0 - 9

No 239

	Abgerechnet mit **Jacob Shaub** den 14 February 1766 Bleibt er Schuldig [Settled with Jacob Shaub 14 February 1766. He still owes]	13 -9- 7

1766		
february 5	2 gill Br: wein	0 - 0 - 6
8	1 gill Br: wein	0 - 0 - 3
	1 q: seiter	0 - 0 - 4
21	1 Namen Buch	0 - 0 - 8
25	2 gill Br: wein	0 - 0 - 6
	1 b: m: wein 1 q: bir	0 - 2 - 6
27	Vor fensterglas das er Verbrochen [for window glass which he broke]	0 - 2 - 6
Mertz 3	1 gill Rom	0 - 0 - 4
7	1 q: seiter	0 - 0 - 4
	1 q: seiter	0 - 0 - 4
17	1 b: Bir	0 - 0 - 3
20	2 q: seiter	0 - 0 - 8
24	1 b: Bir un 1 gill Br: wein	0 - 0 - 6
	2 gill Br: wein un 1 q: Br: wein	0 - 1 - 6
	hat Credit Vor Leder [Has credit for leather]	0 - 9 - 3
29	Vor Kelsch	0 - 3 - 1
	1 q: seiter un 1 gill Rom	0 - 0 - 8
31	1 gill annis un 1 q: seiter	0 - 0 - 9
Aprill 10	1 gill Br: wein	0 - 0 - 3
14	2 q: seiter	0 - 0 - 8
24	Vor Essen un 1 b: seiter	0 - 0 - 9
May 17	3 q: seiter	0 - 1 - 0
	1 1/4 yd: Kelsch un 1 gill Br: wein	0 - 3 - 1
23	Vor Hassen Brick	0 - 1 - 6
24	1/2 gill Rom	0 - 0 - 2
Juny 5	2 q: seiter	0 - 0 - 8
July 16	1 q: seiter	0 - 0 - 4
5	1 q: seiter	0 - 0 - 4
7	2 q: seiter	0 - 0 - 8
	1 gill Br: wein	0 - 0 - 3
	1 q: seiter	0 - 0 - 4
		14-15-3

No 240

1766	**Henrich Leineweber**	
January 22	1 b: Br: wein	0 - 0 - 6
30	5 gill Rom	0 - 1 - 6
february 3	gelehnt an geld [lent in money]	0 - 7 - 6
5	4 q: M: wein 4 q: bir	0 -18- 0
11	1 q: Br: wein	0 - 1 - 0
	2 R: schling	0 - 1 - 0
	Henrich Leinenweber bezahlt den 25tn Mertz [Henrich Leinenweber paid March 25]	0 - 7 - 6
	1 q: Bir	0 - 0 - 6
	1 q: Rom	0 - 1 - 2
	1 q: Bir	0 - 0 - 6
27	15 1/4 lb: fleisch	0 - 3 - 10
Aprill 5	gelehnt an geld [lent in money]	2 -10- 0
10	1 q: Rom	0 - 1 - 2
16	1 hut das Peter geholt [which Peter fetched]	0 - 7 - 6
	Vor Bendel	0 - 0 - 4
May 1	1 q: Br: wein	0 - 1 - 0
	Abgerechnet mit Henrich Leineweber d: 11 December 1766. Bleibt er schultig [Settled with Henrich Leineweber 11 December 1766. He still owes]	3 - 9 - 6 20-12-0

1766	**Henrich Leineweber**	
Decem: 29	1/2 b: M: wein	0 - 1 - 0
	2 q: Thron	0 - 2 - 6
1767		
April 2	1 b: m: wein 1 q: bir	0 - 2 - 6
July 20	ist schultig Vor Wagen Leitern hab ich Bezahlt an Wagner [owes for hay wagon racks. I paid to Wagner]	0 -16- 0
Augst 1	3 b: m: wein	0 - 6 - 0
	Vor schreiben un Essen	0 - 1 - 4
Octo: 29	1 1/2 yd: Blo Tuch	0 -18- 0
1768		
January 6	1 1/4 yd: Blotuch un 1 strang Camelgarn	0 -15- 4
April 6	2 gill Rom 1 b: bir 1 q: seiter Essen den gaul bey heu	0 - 2 - 6
9	1 q: bir	0 - 0 - 6
July 7	1/2 gill Rom	0 - 0 - 2
1769		
Augst 21	6 q: Haber 2 gill Rom	0 - 1 - 8
October 28	Verzehrt	0 - 0 - 10
	1 gill Rom	0 - 0 - 4
1771		
May 4	1 q: seiter	0 - 0 - 9

[There is considerable doodling on this page, including twice the name Henrich Schaffer which is written in the same handwriting as all but a few entries in this account book.]

No 241		
1766	**Johannes Lausser**	
febrary 5	1 b: wein	0 - 1 - 2
14	2 lb: Zucker un 4 yd: floret	0 - 2 - 8

1766	**Nicholaus Cesinger**	
ferbu 15	1 lb: Zucker	0 - 0 - 10

1766	**Johannes Mohr**	
Mertz 20	1 yd: Catun	0 - 5 - 3
31	1/2 b: Br: wein	0 - 0 - 4
Aprill 18	1 b: wein 1 q: Tar un 1 b: Thron	0 - 2 - 2
Juny 4	1/2 b: m: wein	0 - 1 - 0
Sebtem: 3	1 gill Rom	0 - 0 - 4
1767	**Johannes Mohr**	
Mertz 2	1 b: m: wein	0 - 2 - 0
May 25	1 b: m: wein	0 - 2 - 0
Decem: 15	Verzehrt Bey Jury [eaten by the jury]	0 - 3 - 0
1768		
Sebt 27	1 b: m: wein	0 - 2 - 0
Novem: 21	1 gill Rom	0 - 0 - 4
1766	**Gottfried Röhrer** und **Nicholaus Kintzer** un **Henrich Leineweber**	
Mertz 24	12 1/2 q: M: wein un 2 q: Bir	2 -11- 0
	darauf hatt Gottried Röhrer und Nicholaus Kintzer Bezahlt [Gottfried Röhrer and Nicholaus Kintzer paid thereon]	0 -15- 0

No 242

1766	**Henrich Peffer**	
febrary 5	1 q: Bir	0 - 0 - 6
14	Vor Catun	0 - 2 - 9
15	1 q: Bir	0 - 0 - 6
21	1 q: Bir	0 - 0 - 6
	5 Berrel bir auf steitzen gefuhrt[driven to Steitzen=Lebanon]	0 -10- 0
25	1 b: Bir	0 - 0 - 3
	abgerechnet mit Henrich Peffer Alt D: 5 Julius 1766 Bleibt schuldig [Settled with Henrich Peffer, Sr., 5 July 1766. Still owes]	1 - 9 - 1
	abgerechnet mit Henrich Peffer d 31 December 1766 Bleibt ich ihm schultig [Settled with Henrich Peffer 31 December 1766. I still owe him]	0 - 5 - 0
1767		
January 5	1 glas Verbrochen [1 glass broken] 1 b: m: wein	0 - 2 - 8
6	1 spruch Catecismus	0 - 2 - 6
13	50 Letli [?] negel	0 - 0 - 6
17	gelehnt an geld [lent in money]	0 -10- 0
	Abgerechnet mit Henrich Peffer d: 6ten February 1768 in Voll und ein Barril bir aus der Peif an ihm schon bezahlt [Settled with Henrich Peffer 6 February 1768 in full and one barrel beer from the tap already paid him]	
february 8	1 q: Bir	0 - 0 - 6
20	1 b: mim	0 - 1 - 0
Mertz 21	1 gill Br: wein	0 - 0 - 3
26	1 b: m: wein	0 - 2 - 0
1769 Mertz 28	Henrich Peffer gerechnet Bleibt keiner dem andern nichts schultig [Henrich Peffer settled neither owes the other anything.]	
Aprill 3	Vor Jury 5 q: Bir 5 man Essen	0 - 5 - 6
8	7 b: wein 1 q: Bir Vor Lauck und seltzer	0 - 8 - 8
Maj 15	1 b: wein	0 - 1 - 2
Juny 29	1/2 lb: negel	0 - 0 - 6

No 243

1766	**Johannes Schaffer**	
febrary 8	gelehnt an geld [lent in money]	0 -10- 0
21	gelehnt an geld Vor Tax [lent in money for tax]	<u>0 - 5 - 0</u>
	Bezahlt an geld [paid in money]	0 - 7 - 6
1766	**John Schaeffer**	
May 19	1 hut	0 - 6 - 6
1768	**John Schaffer**	
Novem: 7	Bleibt schultig in der Rechnung [Still owes in settlement]	0 -15- 0
1769	**John Schaffer**	
Febr 9	Vor soleder	0 -16- 4
14	1/2 haut obeleder	0 -10- 10
	Credit Vor 1 kalbs Haut 8 1/2 lb:	0 - 2 - 10

No 244	**Johann Theodor Hofius**	
febrary 14	2 b: Bir	0 - 0 - 6
	1 hut	1 -10- 0
15	1 q: Br: wein un 2 b: Bir	0 - 1 - 6
16	1 b: m: wein un 4 b: Bir	0 - 3 - 0
	2 b: Bir	0 - 0 - 6
17	2 q: Bir un 1 q: Br: wein	0 - 2 - 0
20	3 1/2 q: Bir	0 - 1 - 9
21	3 q: Bir un 1 q: Br: wein	0 - 2 - 6
	1 q: Br: wein	0 - 1 - 0
25	3 b: Bir	0 - 0 - 9
	3 b: Bir	0 - 0 - 9
27	3 q: Bir	0 - 1 - 6
	3 1/2 q: Bir	0 - 1 - 9
	2 q: bir	0 - 1 - 0
Mertz 3	3 b: Bir	0 - 0 - 9
	1 q: Bir	0 - 0 - 6
	3 b: Bir	0 - 0 - 9
7	3 q: Bir un 1 q: Br: wein	0 - 2 - 6
8	1 q: bir	0 - 0 - 6
	1 q: Bir	0 - 0 - 6
10	2 q: Bir un 1 q: Br: wein	0 - 2 - 0
15	3 q: Bir	0 - 1 - 6
17	1 q: Bir	0 - 0 - 6
18	2 q: Bir un 1 q: Br: wein	0 - 2 - 0
	1 q: Bir	0 - 0 - 6
20	1 q: Bir	0 - 0 - 6
	3 q: Bir	0 - 1 - 6
	1 q: bir	0 - 0 - 6
24	2 b bir	0 - 0 - 6
27	2 q: bir	0 - 1 - 0
	2 b: Bir	0 - 0 - 6
29	1 q: bir	0 - 0 - 6
	2 b: Bir	0 - 0 - 6
	2 q: bir	0 - 1 - 0
Aprill 2	3 q: Bir	0 - 1 - 6
	2 b: Bir	0 - 0 - 6
5	1 q: Br: wein un 3 b: Bir	0 - 1 - 9
7	hat Credit Von Shwengel sein schulgeld [has credit from Schwengel's tuition]	1 - 2 - 0
	hat Credit von Crebil sein schulgeld [has credit from Crebil's tuition]	1 - 0 - 0
	hat Credit von Mohr sein schulgeld [has credit from Mohr's tuition]	0 - 2 - 0

No 245		
1766	**Adam Bollender**	
Mertz 3	1/2 lb Zucker	0 - 0 - 5
1767		
January 5	1/2 yd: Hassen Brick 4 streng neths	0 - 1 - 6
May 25	3 hüt	0 -12- 0
1769	**Adam Bollender**	
Novem: 2	gerechnet Bleibt schultig [Settled. Still owes]	0 -13- 2
1769	**Adam Bollender**	
October 9	1 gill Baumöl sein geschweÿ	0 - 0 - 8
Decem: 4	1: seiter	0 - 0 - 4
1771 Sebt: 21	1 gill Rom	0 - 0 - 4

No 246

1766	**Wilhelm Besch**	
Mertz 29	1 b: Br: wein un 2 q: seiter	0 - 1 - 2
31	1 q: seiter	0 - 0 - 4
Aprill 5	1 q: seiter un 1 b: Br: wein	0 - 0 - 10
	2 q: seiter	0 - 0 - 8
20	2 q: seiter	0 - 0 - 8
24	1 q: seiteröl	0 - 0 - 8
25	2 q: seiter	0 - 0 - 8
May 2	1 b: wein 1 1/2 q: Br: wein 1 b: Bir	0 - 2 - 11
	1 q: seiter	0 - 0 - 4
	1 b: Br: wein un 1 q: seiter	0 - 0 - 10
9	1 b: Bir	0 - 0 - 3
	2 q: seiter	0 - 0 - 8
17	2 q: seiter	0 - 0 - 8
19	Verzehrt	0 - 0 - 5
24	1 q: Thron	0 - 1 - 0
29	3 q: seiter	0 - 1 - 0
	2 q: seiter	0 - 0 - 8
Juny 4	1 q: seiter	0 - 0 - 4
19	2 q: seiter	0 - 0 - 8
July 7	2 q: seiter	0 - 0 - 8
	4 q: seiter	0 - 1 - 4
	1 Beck Buchweitzen	0 - 0 - 9
11	2 q: seiter	0 - 0 - 8
	3 q: seiter un 1 Peif	0 - 1 - 1
20	2 q: seiter	0 - 0 - 8
25	1 q: seiter	0 - 0 - 4
30	2 q: seiter	0 - 0 - 8
	Bezahlt an geld [paid in money]	1 - 0 - 0
	1 b: wein	0 - 1 - 2
	2 q: seiter	0 - 0 - 8
Augst 11	1 q: seiteröl	0 - 0 - 8
15	1 b: seiteröl 1 q: Br: wein un 1 munstück	0 - 1 - 8
20	1 q: seiteröl	0 - 0 - 8

No 247

1766	**Johann Theotor Hofius**	
Aprill 8	2 b: Bir	0 - 0 - 6
	2 b: Bir	0 - 0 - 6
9	1/2 gill Rom	0 - 0 - 2
1766	**Johann Theotor Hofius**	
	2 b: Bir	0 - 0 - 6
Sebtm: 20	1 q: Br: wein 1/2 lb: Zucker 1 gill Rom	0 - 1 - 3
	2 b: Bir	0 - 0 - 6
25	1 q: Rom	0 - 1 - 0
	1 1/2 b: wein	0 - 1 - 9
	1 gill Rom 1 b: seiter	0 - 0 - 6
29	1/2 b: wein 1 gill Rom 1 b: seiter	0 - 1 - 1
October 3	1 b: seiter 1/2 gill Rom	0 - 0 - 4
	1 gill rom	0 - 0 - 4
7	1/2 b: wein 1/2 gill Rom un 1 q: seiter	0 - 1 - 1
8	2 q: seiter	0 - 0 - 8
10	3 q: seiter	0 - 1 - 0
14	3 b: seiter un 1/2 lb: zucker	0 - 0 - 11
18	3 b: seiter	0 - 0 - 6

20	1 q: seiter un 1 gill Rom	0 - 0 - 8
25	2 q: seiter un 1 q: Rom	0 - 1 - 8
	1 q: Bir un 1 q: seiter	0 - 0 - 10
27	1 b: seiter	0 - 0 - 2
28	1 b: seiter	0 - 0 - 2
Novem: 2	1 q: Rom	0 - 1 - 0
15	4 q: seiter 1/2 gill Rom	0 - 1 - 2
16	2 q: seiter	0 - 0 - 6
	2 q: seiter	0 - 0 - 6
Decem: 2	1 q: seiter	0 - 0 - 4
	1 q: seiter	0 - 0 - 4
6	1 q: seiter	0 - 0 - 4
8	2 1/2 q: seiter un 1 q: Br: wein	0 - 1 - 10
10	1 q: seiter	0 - 0 - 4
12	1 1/2 q: seiter	0 - 0 - 6
15	2 streng neths 1/2 gill Rom	0 - 0 - 6
		1 - 2 - 3

No 248

Jacob Schaub

1766		
July 20	1 q: seiter	0 - 0 - 4
25	1/2/4 Peffer 1/2/4 alspeis 1/2/4 Imber	0 - 1 - 1
28	1 b: seiter	0 - 0 - 2
Augst 2	3 q: seiter	0 - 1 - 0
	1 gill Rom	0 - 0 - 4
	2 q: Bir	0 - 1 - 0
	Hat Credit Von wegen Conrad Kirschner [Has credit from the account of Conrad Kirschner]	0 - 4 - 0
16	1 b: seiter	0 - 0 - 2
25	1 gill Br: wein 1 b: Bir	0 - 0 - 6
	2 q: seiter	0 - 0 - 8
26	1 gill Br: wein	0 - 0 - 3
Sebt: 1	1 q: seiter	0 - 0 - 4
	2 q: seiter	0 - 0 - 8
	1 Muschcatennuss un 1 gill Br: wein	0 - 0 - 6
6	1 b: M: wein	0 - 2 - 0
10	2 q: seiter	0 - 0 - 8
	1 hut	0 - 4 - 0
	1 b: Br: wein	0 - 0 - 6
	1 1/2 1: seiter	0 - 0 - 6
15	1 q: seiter	0 - 0 - 4
	ist schultig Vor schulgeld [owes for tuition]	0 -12- 0
25	1 q: seiter	0 - 0 - 4
27	1 q: seiter	0 - 0 - 4
	1 gill Rom	0 - 0 - 4
29	1 gill annis 1/2 b: M: wein	0 - 1 - 5
Octo: 3	1 b: Br: wein	0 - 0 - 6
8	1 1/2 yd: hasen Brick 1 q: seiter	0 - 3 - 1
	3 q: seiter	0 - 0 - 9
14	2 q: seiter	0 - 0 - 6
18	1 hut 1/2 gill Rom	0 - 7 - 8
	1 lb: zucker	0 - 0 - 10
		2 - 2 - 9

No 249

1766	**Conrad Kerschner**	
Aprill 5	3 q: M: wein	0 -12- 0
18	2 b: Bir 1 fisch	0 - 0 - 9
	4 q: Waser seiter	0 - 0 - 4
24	1 b: Bir	0 - 0 - 3
	Abgerechnet mit Conrad Kirschner d: 2 tn: December 1766. Bleibt er schuldig [Settled with Conrad Kirschner 2 December 1766. He still owes]	3 - 5 - 0
	2 q: tar 1 b: Thron	0 - 1 - 6
	1 b: wein	0 - 1 - 2
	1 gill gatchal	0 - 0 - 5
Decem: 3	2 fisch	0 - 0 - 6
	1 1/2 b: wein	0 - 1 - 9
10	gelehnt an geld [lent in money]	0 - 5 - 0
19	1/2 gill Rom un 1 q: Bir	0 - 0 - 8
23	1 q: Bir un 1 q: Rom	0 - 1 - 6
	1 q: Bir	0 - 0 - 6
1767		
January 1	1 b: seiteröl 1/2 gill Rom	0 - 0 - 6
	2 buschel Weitzen	0 - 9 - 6
17	1 b: wein	0 - 1 - 2
22	1 q: Rom 1 b: wein 1/2 gill Rom	0 - 1 - 5
29	1 b: Bir	0 - 0 - 3
february 7	1 gill gatshal	0 - 0 - 5
11	1 b: bir	0 - 0 - 3
14	1 q: seiter 2 fisch	0 - 0 - 8
17	1 q: m: wein	0 - 4 - 0
Mertz 2	1 gill schimber	0 - 0 - 5
9	1 q: Rom	0 - 1 - 0
23	1 q: Tar 1 lb: Pulver	0 - 1 - 0
Aprill 2	1 q: tar	0 - 0 - 6
10	1 q: Tar	0 - 0 - 6
	1 q: Rom	0 - 1 - 0
11	1 q: bir	0 - 0 - 6

No 250

1766	**Andereas Müller**	
Novem 17	Abgerechnet d: 17 November 1766. Bleibt nichts [Settled 17 November 1766. Owes nothing]	
Decem: 19	Vor Endego	0 - 9 - 6
1769	**Andereas Miller**	
febru 21	gelehnt an geld [lent in money]	4 - 0 - 0
	Bezahlt [paid]	3 - 0 - 0
Juny 1	1/4 stroh	0 - 2 - 0
9	20 lb fleisch	0 - 8 - 4
July 17	2 halss tücher	0 - 8 - 0
	wieder Vor 1 halss tuch	0 - 0 - 6
	1 lb: seiffen	0 - 0 - 10
1771	**Andereas Miller**	
October 19	gerechnet Bleibt Schuldig [settled. Still owes]	6 - 15 - 3

No 251

1766	**Berned Jacob**	
July 11	3 gill aniss un 1 q: Br: wein	0 - 2 - 0
Augst 2	6 1/2 b: M: wein 1/2 gill annis	0 -13- 3
4	1 b: M: wein	0 - 2 - 0
11	1 1/2 b: M: wein un 1 bo: senckery	0 - 4 - 6
15	1 b: annis 1 b: Rom	0 - 1 - 6
	1 gill annis	0 - 0 - 5
16	1/2 gill annis	0 - 0 - 3
25	1 q: seiter	0 - 0 - 4
29	1/2 gill annis	0 - 0 - 3
Sebt: 3	1/2 gill Rom	0 - 0 - 2
5	1/2 B: annis 1 lb: Zucker	0 - 1 - 4
20	1 q: Rom	0 - 1 - 0
	4 q: seiter	0 - 1 - 0
	2 q: Rom	0 - 2 - 0
25	1 q: Rom 1 b: m: wein 1 gill annis	0 - 3 - 5
27	1 q: Rom	0 - 1 - 0
29	1 q: Rom	0 - 1 - 0
Octo: 3	1/2 b: annis	0 - 0 - 6
7	1 q: Rom	0 - 1 - 0
	1 q: Rom	0 - 1 - 0
20	1 q: Rom	0 - 1 - 0
25	1 q: Rom	0 - 1 - 0
28	1 q: Rom 1 q: seiter	0 - 1 - 3
	1 1/2 b: m: wein	0 - 3 - 0
15	1 q: Rom 2 q: seiter	0 - 1 - 6
Decem 6	1/2 b: m: wein	0 - 1 - 0
1767		
January 7	hat Credit Von Willem Miller	0 - 7 - 6
February 28	ist schultig Vor schissen [owes for shooting]	0 - 4 - 0
	2 q: M: wein	0 - 8 - 0
	1 q: seiter 1/2 gill Rom	0 - 0 - 6
	1 1/2 gill Rom	0 - 0 - 6
	1 b: Bir	0 - 0 - 3
	1/2 gill Rom	0 - 0 - 2

No 252

1766	**John Bright**	
May 2	4 1/2 1/2 4 lb: Hut Zucker	
	1 q: M: wein gelehnt [lent]	
	3 1/4 1/2 4 lb: hut Zucker	
Juny 16	2 q: M: wein gelehnt [lent]	
July 1	2 Mal heu von Jacob Schend gefuhr [twice carting hay from Jacob Schend]	0 -10- 0
14	1 3/4 lb: hut Zucker gelehnt [lent]	
Augst 15	2 buschel weitzen gelehnt [lent]	
25	2 q: Rom gelehnt [lent]	
Sebt 7	1/2 b: Baumöl	0 - 1 - 0
16	ist schultig vor schulgeld [owes for tuition]	0 -10- 0
Decem: 2	2 yd: Hasen Brick	0 - 3 - 0

23	1 b: Thron	0 - 0 - 7
	Abgerechnet mit John Brecht d: 7tn: December 1767 bleibt er schuldig [Settled with John Brecht, 7 December 1767. He still owes]	ii- 9 - 3
	Credit Von Wegen Georg Weis [Credit on account of George Weis]	3 -11- 0
	ist schultig vor heu [owes for hay]	2 - 0 - 0
Decem: 10	1/2 b: m: wein	0 - 1 - 0
1768 Mertz 28	2 hut zucker gelehnt [lent]	
May 16	gelehnt [lent]	10 -0- 0
	Vor fuhrlohn vor Philadelphia [For driver's fee from Philadelphia]	1 - 4 - 0
	Vor dem kercher Bezahlt [Paid for Kercher]	0 - 5 - 6
Augst 29	2 lb: Zucker	0 - 1 - 6
	7 1/2 jd: Zeug Vor 1 Rock un futter-tuch	
1771	**John Bright**	
January 30	gerechnet Bleibt schultig [settled. Still owes]	161-4-5
	8 q: W: Rom 1 q: Rom 3 q: W: Rom	

No 253		
1766	**Adam Speck**	
May 24	1 stroh hut	0 - 3 - 0
Juny 19	3 gallen Wasser seiter	0 - 1 - 0
July 20	1 lb: Zucker	0 - 0 - 10
30	3 gallen Waser seiter	0 - 1 - 0
Augst 6	1 b: seiter	0 - 0 - 2
	1 b: seiter	0 - 0 - 2
	1 q: seiter	0 - 0 - 4
18	2 q: seiter	0 - 0 - 8
20	1 gill Rom	0 - 0 - 4
29	1/4 lb: Pulver un 2 flinten stein	0 - 1 - 2
Sebtem: 10	1 q: seiter	0 - 0 - 4
	Abgerechnet mit Adam Speck d: 8 tn: January 1768 bleibt er schultig [Settled with Adam Speck 8 January 1768. He still owes]	0 - 3 - 0
1769	**Adam Speck**	
Novem; 14	Bleibt schuldig in der Abrechnung [Still owes in the settlement]	0 - 5 - 4
20	3 gallen seiter 1 q: Rom	0 - 4 - 0
Decem: 20	1/2 Beck saltz	0 - 0 - 8
1770		
January 28	1/2 b: wein 1/2 4 lb: Thee 1 lb: Zucker	0 - 2 - 0
Aprill 18	1 q: seiter	0 - 0 - 4
May 12	1 q: seiter	0 - 0 - 4
1771		
July 6	2 q: Essig 2 q: seiter 1 lb: Reiss	0 - 1 - 5

No 254		
1766	**Henrich Peffer** Alte [Sr.]	
December 31	Abgerechnet d: 31 December 1766 Bleibt schuldig [Settled 31 December 1766. Still owes]	0 -11- 7
	Dato empfangen Vor Zehrung [Same day. Received for provisions]	0 - 1 - 3

1767		
Janary 17	3 q: Bir 1 Rom schling	0 - 2 - 0
	3 q: seiter 1 1/2 gill Rom	0 - 1 - 6
	1 q: seiter 1 gill Rom	0 - 0 - 8
19	1 b: wein 1 q: seiter	0 - 1 - 6
	1 b: M: wein 2 q: bir 2 gill Rom	0 - 3 - 8
February 2	2 Rom schling	0 - 1 - 0
20	1 q: seiter	0 - 0 - 4
Mertz 14	Credit	0 - 0 - 6
Aprill 11	1 q: Br: wein	0 - 0 - 9
25	1 q: Br: wein	0 - 0 - 9
May 1	1 q: Br: wein	0 - 0 - 9
	1 q: Br: wein	0 - 0 - 9
9	1 q: Br: wein	0 - 0 - 9
17	1 q: Br: wein	0 - 0 - 9
12	1 q: Br: wein	0 - 0 - 9
25	1 q: Br: wein	0 - 0 - 9
Juny 13	1 q: Br: wein	0 - 0 - 9
15	1 q: Br: wein	0 - 0 - 9
22	1 q: Br: wein	0 - 0 - 9
July 3	1 q: Br: wein	0 - 0 - 9
6	1 q: Br: wein	0 - 0 - 9
9	1 q: Br: wein	0 - 0 - 9
10	1 q: Br: wein	0 - 0 - 9
16	1 q: Br: wein	0 - 0 - 9
23	1 q: Br: wein	0 - 0 - 9
	1 q: Br: wein	0 - 0 - 9
25	1 q: Br: wein	0 - 0 - 9
	1 q: Br: wein	0 - 0 - 10
Augst 1	1 q: Br: wein	0 - 0 - 10
5	1 b: m: wein 1 R: schling	0 - 2 - 6
15	1 q: wein	0 - 2 - 4

No 255

1766	**Casper Löb**	
May 24	2 q: seiter	0 - 0 - 6
29	gelehnt an geld [lent in money]	1 - 5 - 0
	1 stroh hut	0 - 2 - 6
	Vor floret	0 - 0 - 10
July 18	gelehnt an geld [lent in money]	0 -10- 0
	gelehnt an geld [lent in money]	0 - 7 - 6
	Abgerechnet mit Casper Löb d: 14tn November 1767 Bleibt nichts [Settled with Casper Löb 14 November 1767. Owes nothing]	
	den 20 ten gerechnet 1768 bleibt schultig [20th settled 1768. Owes nothing]	0 - 2 - 0
	abgerechnet mit Casper Löb d: 10ten Augst 1768 Bleibt nichts [Settled with Casper Löb 10 August 1768. Owes nothing]	

1766	**Anengel Löb**	
May 29	1 seiten halss tuch	0 - 8 - 0
Sebtm: 27	gelehnt an geld [lent in money]	0 - 9 - 4
	1 1/4 1/2 4 yd Catun	0 - 6 - 11
October 14	2 nester	0 - 0 - 4
1767		
May 20	3 1/2 yd: gestrefelt zeug	0 -13- 5

July 4	Vor schab gut	1 - 5 - 0
Sebtm: 4	3 1/2 yd: weiss Tuch 1 1/2 yd: floret 1 halss Tuch	0 -17- 4
Decem: 8	gelehnt [lent]	0 - 3 - 6
1770		
January 9	Bleibt nichts [owes nothing]	

No 256

1766	**Michael Meiser**	
May 29	1 stroh hut 2 1/2 yd floret 1 b: seiteröl	0 - 4 - 2
Sebtem: 7	1 sentz 1 gill Br: wein un 2 Peiffen	0 - 5 - 5
October 8	1 gill Br: wein	0 - 0 - 3
	1 gill Br: wein	0 - 0 - 3
Novem: 10	1 q: seiteröl	0 - 0 - 8
15	1/2 b: Br: wein	0 - 0 - 4
17	1 gill Br: wein	0 - 0 - 3
Decem: 10	1 b: seiteröl un 1 Peif	0 - 0 - 5
1767		
January 19	2 q: seiter	0 - 0 - 8
29	1 gill Br: wein	0 - 0 - 3
	1 gill Br: wein	0 - 0 - 3
31	1 gill Br: wein	0 - 0 - 3
Mertz 5	1 q: Bir un 1 q: seiter	0 - 0 - 10
7	1 gill Br: wein	0 - 0 - 3
	1 q: seiter	0 - 0 - 4

No 257

1766	**Berned Weber**	
Juny 5	3 yd: wollen Tuch 2 yd Kelsch 1 b: seiter	0 -16- 2
	Abgerechnet mit Berned Weber d: 12ten Augst 1767. Bleibt nichts [Settled with Berned Weber 12 August 1767. Owes nothing]	

1767	**Adam auf dem Hammer** [at the forge]	
January 29	1 q: seiteröl	0 - 0 - 8
31	3 q: seiteröl	0 - 2 - 0
	3 q: seiter	0 - 1 - 0

1767	**Peter Dolmeyer** auf den Hamer [at the forge]	
January 31	1 q: seiteröl	0 - 0 - 8

1767	**Jacob Helder** auf der Fornes	
January 31	1 1/2 q: seiteröl	0 - 1 - 0

1768	**George Ditrich**	
Seb: 27	7 b: m: wein	0 -14- 0
	2 glasser Verbrochen [2 glasses broken]	0 - 2 - 0
	1 gaul Bey heu 3 q: Haber	0 - 1 - 2
1770	**Georg Ditrich**	
Mertz 1	Bleibt schultig in Rechnung [Still owes in account]	0 - 7 - 7

No 258

1766	**Gotes Stigels Heffengisser** [Stiegel's pot pourer]	
July 1	2 gill Rom	0 - 0 - 8
11	1 bo: senckery 3 q: seiter 2 q: Bir un Essen	0 - 4 - 0
	2 1/2 q: seiter un 1 gill Rom un 1 b: m: wein	0 - 3 - 2

[some entries have been cut out at this point]

1767	**Henrich Besch** in Lancaster	
February 24	Verzehrt	0 - 4 - 6
1767	**Tollmeyer Serves Tochtermann** [Tollmeyer, Serves = Zerbe's son-in-law]	
July 10	Verzehrt	0 - 1 - 11
Octo: 5	1 bol senckery	0 - 1 - 6
1768	**die Jury Von steitzen Weg** [The jury from the road to Lebanon]	
January 23	Verzehrt	1 - 0 - 3

No 259

1766	**Philip Kiesecker**	
July 7	1 yd: floret	0 - 0 - 4

[some entries have been cut out at this point]

1767	**Phillipp Kiesecker**	
Sebtem: 27	1/2 gill Rom	0 - 0 - 2
	sein Tochter 1 yd: floret	0 - 0 - 3
Novem 18	1 q: seiter 1 gill Rom	0 - 0 - 8
20	1/2 gill Rom	0 - 0 - 2
1768		
Aprill 20	vor wein	0 - 2 - 4
1770	**Philip Kiesecker**	
January 9	Bleibt schultig in der Abrechnung mit dem Band [Still owes in settlement with the bond]	1 -13- 0

No 260

1766	**Henrich Meiser**	
July 7	1 lb: Zucker	0 - 0 - 10
Augst 26	1 q: Rom un 1 Bottel	0 - 1 - 10
Septem: 29	2 lb: zucker un 1 q: wein	0 - 4 - 0
October 14	1 q: wein un 1 q: westindien Rom	0 - 3 - 10
1767		
february 17	1 q: bir 1 lb: Zucker	0 - 1 - 4
Augst 15	1b: Zucker	0 - 0 - 10
	1 b: wein	0 - 1 - 2
29	2 lb: Zucker	0 - 1 - 8
Sebtem: 12	1 lb: Roth holtz 1 b: Rom 1 lb: schrot	0 - 1 - 10
14	1 lb: Toback	0 - 0 - 5
		0 -17- 9
		10
		0 -18- 7

No 261

1766	**Jacob Brecht** Telor [tailor]	
July 28	1 q: seiter	0 - 0 - 4
Augst 2	1 b: Bir	0 - 0 - 3
20	2 q: Thron	0 - 2 - 0
	1 b: Rom	0 - 0 - 6
25	1 b: Rom	0 - 0 - 6
Sebt 20	1 lb: Zucker 1 q: Br: wein	0 - 1 - 10
October 14	1 q: wein un 1 lb: Zucker	0 - 3 - 2
28	1 q: Rom un 1 Peif	0 - 1 - 1
Novem: 16	1 lb: Zucker un 1 b: Rom	0 - 1 - 4
	2 q: Thron	0 - 2 - 6
1767		
Janary 6	1/4 lb: Pulver	0 - 0 - 11
1768	**Jacob Brecht**	
Augst 4	1 b: Rom	0 - 0 - 6
Sebt 12	2 q: Thron	0 - 2 - 0
Novem: 9	3/4 lb: Kriten	0 - 0 - 3

No 262

1766	**Wihlem Besch**	
Augst 29	2 q: seiter un 1 b: seiteröl	0 - 1 - 0
Sebt 1	2 q: seiter	0 - 0 - 8
3	1 q: Br: wein 2 q: seiter un 1 gill Rom	0 - 2 - 0
	1 q: Br: wein 1 q: seiter	0 - 1 - 4
6	1 q: seiter	0 - 0 - 4
15	1 q: seiter	0 - 0 - 4
25	1 q: seiter	0 - 0 - 4
Octo: 7	1 R: schling	0 - 0 - 6
8	1 q: seiter	0 - 0 - 4
	2 q: seiter	0 - 0 - 8
18	2 q: seiter	0 - 0 - 6
20	1 q: seiter	0 - 0 - 3
25	3 q: seiter	0 - 0 - 9
Novem: 1	1 q: seiter	0 - 0 - 3
	2 gill Br: wein	0 - 0 - 6
	1/2 b: wein 1/2 gill Rom 2 q: seiter 1 fisch	0 - 1 - 6
24	3 q: seiter	0 - 0 - 9
27	3 q: seiter un 1/2 gill Rom	0 - 0 - 11
Decem: 10	1/2 buch Babir	0 - 0 - 8
12	3 q: seiter	0 - 1 - 0
19	1 q: seiter un 1 gill Rom	0 - 0 - 8
	2 q: seiter	0 - 0 - 8
29	2 q: 1/2 b: Br: wein 1 q: seiter	0 - 2 - 1
	gelehnt an geld Kisecker [lent in money Kisecker]	0 - 1 - 0
1767		
January 24	2 q: seiter	0 - 0 - 8
febru: 5	1 q: seiter	0 - 0 - 4
24	1 q: seiter	0 - 0 - 4
Mertz 7	1 q: seiter	0 - 0 - 4
12	1 q: seiter 2 Leb Kuchen	0 - 0 - 6
14	1 q: seiter	0 - 0 - 4
27	3 q: seiter	0 - 1 - 0

No 263		
1766	**Bastian Keller**	
Ausgt 15	1 b: m: wein	0 - 2 - 0
1766	**Frantzos**	
Novem: 10	1 b: wein	0 - 1 - 2
1766	**Docter Land**	
Augst 15	2 1/2 b: m: wein	0 - 5 - 0
1766	**Abraham Ernn**	
Augst 23	Vor feilen	0 -16- 0

No 264		
1766	**Frantz Schmitt**	
August 16	1 gill annis	0 - 0 - 5
Novem: 10	1 b: m: wein	0 - 2 - 0
1768		
Mertz 26	1 q: Rom	0 - 1 - 0
1769	**Frantz Schmitt**	
Juny the 19tn:	gerechnet Bleibt schuldig in der Rechnung [Settled. Still owes in the accounting]	0 - 1 - 9
1769	**Frantz Schmitt**	
Decem: 4	Credit in Rechnung [Credit on account]	0 - 5 - 6
5	1 q: Thron	0 - 1 - 0
20	1 q: Thron	0 - 1 - 0
1770		
January 8	1 q: Thron	0 - 1 - 0
28	1 q: Thron	0 - 1 - 0
Aprill 6	1 q: Thron	0 - 1 - 0
July 4	1/2 buschel Buchweitzen	
Sebt: 19	1 q: Thron	0 - 1 - 0
1771 Janu: 7	1/2 4 lb: Peffer	0 - 0 - 7
25	1 b: Rom	0 - 0 - 6
1773	**Frantz Schmitt**	
Augst 16	gerechnet Hat Credit [Settled. Has credit]	0 -18- 7

No 265		
1766	**Jacob Schaub**	
Octo 20	1 streng seiten un 1/2 dutzent Knöp	0 - 1 - 5
	1 yd: schechter 1 b: Br: wein	0 - 3 - 6
	2 q: seiter 3 1/2 Dutzent Knöp	0 - 4 - 6
25	1 b: Br: wein 1 Par Hossen schnallen 3 q: seiter	0 - 2 - 0
	4 q: seiter	0 - 1 - 0
27	1 gill Rom 1 b: seiter 1 Peif	0 - 0 - 7
	1 gill Br: wein	0 - 0 - 3
28	1 b: Rom 1 1/2 q: seiter	0 - 0 - 11
	1/2 4 alspeis 1/2 4 Imber	0 - 0 - 7
Novem: 1	1/2 b: M: wein	0 - 1 - 0
	1/2 b: M: wein 1/2 beck Haber	0 - 1 - 8

Decem 8	1 q: seiter	0 - 0 - 4
15	2 q: seiter	0 - 0 - 6
19	2 q: seiter	0 - 0 - 8
	1/2 gill Rom	0 - 0 - 2
28	1 q: seiter	0 - 0 - 4
29	1/2 gill Rom 1 q: seiter 1 gill Rom	0 - 0 - 10
1767		
January 1	1 q: seiter	0 - 0 - 4
6	2 q: seiter	0 - 0 - 8
February 27	Credit vor sattler geschirr [Credit for saddler's equipment]	3 - 0 - 0
	Abgerechnet mit Jacob Schaub d: 27tn: November 1767 Bleibt er schultig [Settled with Jacob Schaub 27 November 1767. He still owes]	12-10-8
	[signature] Jacob Schaub	
1768		
July 4	Jacob Schaub bleibt schuldig in der Rechnung [Jacob Schaub still owes at settlement]	16- 8 - 7
7	1 b: seiter 1 tram	0 - 0 - 6
	1/2 gill Rom	0 - 0 - 2
Sebt 3	frau q: seiter	0 - 0 - 4
1769 Merz 25	vor stroh	0 - 2 - 6

No 266

1766

Michael Hack

Sebtember 1	1 q: M: wein un 1 lb: Weisen Zucker	0 - 5 - 3
6	1 q: M: wein 1 q: Rom Vom Besten 1/2 lb: alspeis	0 - 6 - 3
October 10	1 q: Rom	0 - 1 - 0
1767		
Janary 1	2 1/4 yd: Halbtuch 1 b: wein	0 - 4 - 0
february 14	415 lb: Eissen	5 - 7 - 0
May 1	gelehnt an geld [lent in money]	1 - 1 - 0
July 4	3 sichlen	0 - 9 - 7
Augst 1	3/4 yd: Blautuch	0 - 6 - 9
October 15	2 1/2 yd: Blotuch	1 -18- 0
1768		
January 2	1 b: m: wein	0 - 2 - 0
febru: 26	2 hüt 1 Dutzent Knöp	0 -14- 10
Aprill 2	2 q: mallassis	0 - 1 - 8
May 8	1 b: m: wein	0 - 2 - 0
Sebt 12	2 q: Rom das Michael Weber geholt [which Michael Weber fetched]	0 - 2 - 0
Novem 6	ist schultig vor negel Von schweitzer [owes for nails from Schweitzer]	0 -11- 0
Decem 19	ist schuldig Von Claus [owes from Claus]	0 - 2 - 7
1769 feb: 21	1/4 lb: Peffer	0 - 1 - 0
Mertz 22	2 hüt	0 - 6 - 0
1771 May 1	gelehnt [lent]	1 - 0 - 0
	gelehnt [lent]	60 -0- 0

No 267

1766

Balzer Derter

Septem 6	1 q: Thron	0 - 1 - 0

October 14	3 yd: Kelsch	0 -10- 6
1767		
May 1	1 b: Thron	0 - 0 - 6
6	1 b Thron	0 - 0 - 6

No 268

1766	**Georg Ulrich**	
Septem: 15	2 q: Rom	0 - 2 - 0
October 8	3 q: Rom	0 - 3 - 0
Novem: 3	1 q: Rom	0 - 1 - 0
1767		
fbruary 7	1 q: Br: wein	0 - 0 - 9
Mertz 14	1 q: Rom	0 - 1 - 0
20	1 q: Bir	0 - 0 - 6
Aprill 17	1 b: Bir	0 - 0 - 3
1770	Georg Ulrich gerechnet [Georg Ulrich settled]	
Novem 20	Bleibt No Rest [Owes nothing]	
1771		
Aprill 4	1 q: seiter	0 - 0 - 4

No 269

1766	**Georg Conrad**	
Sebtem: 16	1 lb: Pulver un fingerhut	0 - 3 - 5
1768	**Danel Clerck** Junior	
January 6	1 q: seiter	0 - 0 - 4
	als 1 q: Rom 1 b: seiter	0 - 1 - 4
1769		
Juny 20	1 sichel	0 - 3 - 0
	Credit	0 - 2 - 6

No 270

1767	**Johann Theodor Hofius**	
Janary 1	1 q: seiter	0 - 0 - 4
6	1 q: seiter	0 - 0 - 4
	Abgerechnet mit Johann Theodor Hofius d: 18tn: Mertz 1767 Bleibt [Settled with Johann Theodor Hofius 18 March 1767. Remains]	
1767	**Henrich Simon**	
November d: 10tn:	1 Neb Mim 4 q: haber	0 - 1 - 2
1768		
february 6	1 q: Bir	0 - 0 - 6
20	2 q: seiter 3 q: Haber	0 - 1 - 2
Mertz 4	1 q: seiter	0 - 0 - 4
Aprill 6	6 q: haber 1 q: seiter	0 - 1 - 4
May 6	1 bol: mim	0 - 1 - 0
Juny 24	1 b: m: wein	0 - 2 - 0

1769		
Juny 11	1 b: wein 6 q: Haber 1 gill Rom	0 - 2 - 6
Novem 20	1/2 b: M: wein 1/2 b: wein	0 - 1 - 7
1770 Mertz 28	1 q: Rom das sein Fuhrleit [which his drivers]	0 - 1 - 0
		12 - 7
	Credit	0 - 4 - 9

1767	**Peter Rihm**	
february 11	2 bottlen	0 - 1 - 6
1768		
Octo: 29	1 bol mim	0 - 1 - 0
	1/2 b: Baumöl 1 q: wein	0 - 3 - 4
1769 May 5	15 lb: Negel 1 q. Tar	0 -15- 5
22	Bezahlt [paid]	1 - 5 - 0

No 271		
1766	**Pilip Wisnand**	
Septem: 25	1 gill Rom	0 - 0 - 4
1767		
January 25	1 q: Bir	0 - 0 - 6
1767	**Michael Egold**	
July 9	1 sichel	0 - 3 - 2
		2 - 4
1771	**Michael Egolf**	
Merz 11	gerechnet Bleibt Schultig [Settled. Still owes]	0 - 4 - 0
1771	**Michael Egolf**	
Augst 12	gerechnet Bleibt nichts [Settled. Owes nothing]	

No 272		
1766	**Peter Wolfersperger**	
October 7	1 q: Rom un 1 q: wein	0 - 3 - 4
1767	**Peter Wolfersparger**	
february 7	1 b: wein	0 - 1 - 2
Aprill 17	1/2 b: m: wein	0 - 1 - 0
1768	**Peter Wolfersperger**	
January 1	1 b: m: wein	0 - 2 - 0

No 273		
1766	**Andereas un Johannes Rul**	
October 10	1 gill Rom	0 - 0 - 4
Novem 15	2 q: seiter	0 - 0 - 8
17	1 q: seiter	0 - 0 - 4
27	1 gill Rom	0 - 0 - 4
Juny d: 17 1769	John Riel un Andereas Riel sind Bezahlt auf den Brunnen [John Riel and Andereas Riel were paid for the fountain]	2 - 3 - 0

1770	**John Riel**	
Oct: 28	1 lb: schrot	0 - 0 - 6
1771		
Augst 21	1 gill Rom	0 - 0 - 2
1768	**Billy Hay**	
Decem 22	2 b: m: wein 2 Mal Essen 5 gill Rom un 1 q: seiter den Gaul by heu 10 q: haber	0 -10- 3
1769		
January 2	1 b: m: wein 2 gill tram 2 mal Essen heu 8 q haber	0 - 6 - 4
february 6	2 b: m: wein un Essen 3 q: haber	0 - 5 - 2
Mertz 22	2 b: M: wein 3 q: Haber un Essen	0 - 5 - 2
	Credit	0 -15- 0

No 274		
1767	**Johannes Lautermilch** Junge [Jr.]	
february 14	ist schulltig vor schissen [owes for shooting]	0 -11- 0
28	ist schultig vor schisen [owes for shooting]	0 - 8 - 0
1767	**Johannes Lautermilch** Junge [Jr.}	
Juny 1	Bleibt schuldig in der Abrechnung [Still owes in settlement]	0 - 7 - 6
1767	**John Lautermilch**	
Dem: 8	1 w: schling	0 - 0 - 9
1770		
July 4	1 q: Tar	0 - 0 - 5

No 275		
1767	**Hanickel Maurer**	
february 14	ist schultig Vor schisen un spilen [owes for shooting and gambling]	0 - 5 - 9
28	ist schultig Vor schisen un spilen [owes for shooting and gambling]	0 - 3 - 0
Augst 24	1 b: wein	0 - 1 - 2
1768	**Andereas Rücker**	
July 2	2 q: seiter 1 Peif	0 - 0 - 9
15	1 beck saltz 2 1/2 q: seiter 1 b: Rom	0 - 2 - 8
Augst 1	4 q: seiter	0 - 1 - 4
29	bleibt schultig Vor Thron [owes for Thron]	0 - 0 - 5
Sebt 3	1 b: Rom	0 - 0 - 6
12	2 1/2 q: seiteröl	0 - 1 - 8
18	5 b: seiteröl	0 - 1 - 8
	1 q: seiteröl 1 gaul ins steitzen [1 horse to Steitzen = Lebanon]	0 - 2 - 2
27	1 b: seiteröl 2 q: seiter	0 - 1 - 0
October 3	1 b; seiteröl 1 b: Thron	0 - 0 - 10
8	1 gill Rom	0 - 0 - 4
19	1 b: seiteröl 1/2 gill Rom	0 - 0 - 6

29	2 1/2 q: seiteröl	0 - 1 - 8
Decem: 1	1 b: seiteröl	0 - 0 - 4
	1 1/2 q: seiteröl	0 - 1 - 0
22	1 b: seiteröl	0 - 0 - 4
27	1 b: seiteröl	0 - 0 - 4
1769		
January 2	1 b: seiteröl 1 q: seiter	0 - 0 - 8
16	1 1/2 q: seiteröl	0 - 1 - 0
febr 6	1 q: seiter	0 - 0 - 4
14	3 q: seiter	0 - 1 - 0
Mertz 3	3 q: seiter	0 - 1 - 0
13	2 q: seiter	0 - 0 - 8
	1 1/2 q: seiteröl 2 q: seiter	0 - 1 - 8
22	2 q: seiter 1 gill Rom 1 fisch	0 - 1 - 3
25	1 1/2 q: seiter	0 - 0 - 6
Aprill 3	2 q: seiter	0 - 0 - 8
8	2 q: seiter 2 fisch	0 - 1 - 2

No 276

1767	**Benedictem Lang**	
february 14	ist schultig vor spilen [owes for gambling]	0 - 2 - 3
1769	**Benedictem Lang**	
Augst 1	Bleibt Schultig Vor Leder [owes for leather]	0 - 4 - 6
1771		
May 8	1 w: schling	0 - 0 - 9
1767	**Jacob Becker**	
October 25	8 scheiben glas 3 b: m: wein	0 -11- 0
29	6 scheiben glas	0 - 3 - 6
1768		
Mertz 11	4 1/2 b: m: wein 1 q: seiter	0 - 9 - 4
Aprill 23	2 q: bir 1 R: schling un 1 q: seiter	0 - 1 - 10
	Credit	0 -15- 0
	1 b: wein	0 - 1 - 2
Augst 1	2 b: wein 2 q: seiter	0 - 3 - 0
Sebt 12	1 1/2 b: m: wein	0 - 3 - 0
18	1 1/2 b: wein 1/2 gill Rom	0 - 0 - 9
Decem 19	2 b: m: wein 1 gill rom 4 q haber	0 - 5 - 0
1769		
January 2	4 b: m: wein 1 glas verbrochen [1 glass broken]	0 - 9 - 0
Dec: 30	3 gill Rom	0 - 1 - 0
1770		
Mertz 28	3 1/2 b: wein	0 - 4 - 1
	2 q: seiter 2 gill Rom	0 - 1 - 4
1771		
January 1	1 gill Rom	0 - 0 - 4
12	4 b: m: wein 1 q: seiter	0 - 8 - 4
1771	**Jacob Becker**	
Aprill 25	gerechnet Bleibt Schultig [Settled. Still owes]	1 -19- 9

No 277

1767	**Jacob Neff** meiers Tochtermann [Meier's son-in-law]	
February 28	ist schulitg Vor schissen [owes for shooting]	0 - 5 - 0

1768	**Samuel Gag**	
February 1	3 q: M: wein 1 gill Rom	0 -12- 4
May 1	1 b: m: wein	0 - 2 - 0
1769 Juny 7	3 gallen Br: wein	0 - 9 - 0
1770		
July 6	Vor wein	0 - 0 - 10

No 278

1767	**Gyhann**	
february 28	ist schultig vor schiesen [owes for shooting]	0 - 7 - 0
1768	**Andereas Besch**	
July 15	1 w: schling	0 - 0 - 9
Decem 1	Vor schab gut	1 -18- 10
1769		
Juny 9	1 b: wein 1 q: seiter	0 - 1 - 6
July 4	1 q: seiter	0 - 0 - 4
	1 w: schling	0 - 0 - 9
Augst 1	2 w: schling	0 - 1 - 6
	1 Par schnallen	0 - 1 - 4
Decer: 4	1 q: seiter	0 - 0 - 4
	1 q: Br: wein	0 - 0 - 10
6	1 q: seiter	0 - 0 - 4
30	1 w: schling 3 b: wein	0 - 4 - 6
Maj 3	1 q: seiter	0 - 0 - 4
1771 feb: 25	1 b: seiteröl	0 - 0 - 4
July 25	1 q: seiter	0 - 0 - 4
Sebt 7	1/2 gill Rom	0 - 0 - 2
	1 q: thron	0 - 1 - 0
1772	**Andereas Besch**	
february	gerechnet bleibt nichts [Settled. Owes nothing]	
1766	**John Kohr**	
otober 28	breibt [sic] schultig Vor Eisen [Still owes for iron]	1 - 0 - 0

No 279

1767	**Jacob Gass**	
february 28	ist schultig Vor schiesen un spilen [owes for shooting and gambling]	0 -11- 0
	1 q: seiter	0 - 0 - 3
July 16	1 Neb Leims Bunsch	0 - 0 - 9

No 280

1766	**John Miller**	
Decem: 15	1 q: Bir	0 - 0 - 6
23	1 b: wein	0 - 1 - 2
27	1 q: Bir	0 - 0 - 6
1767		
february 28	ist schultig vor Blay [owes for lead]	0 - 1 - 7

1767	**John Miller**	
Sebtem: 4	1 b: M: wein	0 - 2 - 0

1767	**Philipp Wohlwein**	
Augs 15	1 q: seiter 3 mann Essen	0 - 1 - 4

Abgerechnet mit Philip Wohlwein d: 25tn: february 1769 bleibt keyner dem andern nichts mehr schultig auf ale inweis bis Datto [Settled with Philip Wohlwein 25 February 1769. Neither owes the other anything more on all invoices until today]

[signature:] Philib Wohlwein

zeuge [witness]
Frantz Schmidt

No 281

1766	**Andereas Bäyer** Kieffer Brander [cooper brander?]	
Novem: 1	gelehnt an geld [lent in money]	0 -13- 6
Decem: 10	2 q: Thron	0 - 2 - 6
1767		
January 3	1 A: b: C: Buch	0 - 0 - 8
17	1 q: Thron	0 - 1 - 3
Juny 8	2 q: Essig	0 - 0 - 4
July 9	1/2 buschel Buchweitzen	0 - 1 - 6
Sebtem: 14	1 lb: Tuback	0 - 0 - 5
October 15	1 b: wein 2 q: seiter	0 - 1 - 10
27	bleibt schultig Vor [still owes for] Hassen Brick	0 - 0 - 4
1768		
May 1	1/2 lb: Tuback	0 - 0 - 3
18	1 1/2 lb: Tuback	0 - 0 - 7
Juny 11	1 lb: Tuback	0 - 0 - 5
October 8	2 Peiffen	0 - 0 - 2
1769		
January 2	1 q: Rom 1 q: wein	0 - 2 - 2
	1 q: Rom 1 q: wein	0 - 2 - 2
february 1	1 b: Rom	0 - 0 - 6
	1 q: Rom	0 - 1 - 0
14	1 q: Rom	0 - 1 - 0
18	Credit Vor 1 Kabs Haut	0 - 1 - 6
21	1 q: Rom	0 - 1 - 0
Mertz 3	1 q: Rom	0 - 1 - 0
6	gelehnt [lent]	0 - 2 - 6
Oct 2	1 q: Rom	0 - 1 - 0
1770 May 24	1 q: seiter	0 - 0 - 4

No 282

1766	**Johannes Knauer**	
Novem: 24	1 q: seiter	0 - 0 - 4
	42 fuss Bort	
1767		
Decem: 15	2 q: seiter	0 - 0 - 8
1768		
January 25	1 1/2 q: seiter	0 - 0 - 6

1769		
October 2	**John Ungar**	
	gerechnet Bleibt schultig [Settled. Still owes]	1 -19- 1
17	1 gallen Br: wein	0 - 3 - 4
28	2 b: wein 2 man Essen	0 - 3 - 8
1770		
October 18	3 gill Rom	0 - 1 - 0

No 283		
1766	**Nickolaus Cesinger**	
Novem: 17	1 b: Bir	0 - 0 - 3
24	1 q: Bir un 2 q: Thron	0 - 1 - 9
December 6	1 q: seiter 1/2 gill gatschal	0 - 0 - 6
	gelehnt an geld [lent in money]	0 - 4 - 0
	1 1/2 q: seiter	0 - 0 - 6
	1 gill Rom	0 - 0 - 4
8	1 b: m: wein un 1 gill Rom	0 - 2 - 4
10	1 b: seiter	0 - 0 - 2
15	1 q: seiter 1/2 gill gatschel	0 - 0 - 7
19	1 q: Thron	0 - 1 - 3
23	1 b: m: wein un 1 q: seiter	0 - 2 - 4
1767		
January 5	1 b: seiter	0 - 0 - 2
	Abgerechnet mit Nickolaus Cesinger d: 24ten: July 1767 Bleibt er schultig [Settled with Nickolaus Cesinger 24 July 1767. He still owes]	2 - 3 - 1
	Nickolaus his X mark	Cesinger
	Credit von Casper Löb	0 - 4 - 9
Sebtem: 15	1/2 gill Rom	0 - 0 - 2
October 27	1 b: M: wein	0 - 2 - 0
	1 q: seiter	0 - 0 - 4
29	1 q: Rom	0 - 1 - 0
Nov 10	1 b: M: wein 1 M: w: schling	0 - 3 - 2
13	1/2 b: m: wein 1 q: seiter	0 - 1 - 4
22	1 q: Rom	0 - 1 - 0
	1/2 b: M: wein	0 - 1 - 0
Decem: 25	1 1/2 q: bir	0 - 0 - 9
	1 q: seiter	0 - 0 - 4
1768		
January 2	1 q: bir	0 - 0 - 6
	1 b: bir	0 - 0 - 3
6	1 q: seiter	0 - 0 - 4
9	1 R: schling	0 - 0 - 6
	1 b: bir	0 - 0 - 3
11	1 q: rom	0 - 1 - 0

No 284		
1766	**Friedrich Miller** Parre [Pastor]	
Novem; 2	gelehnt an geld vor den schulmeister [lent in money for the schoolmaster]	0 - 5 - 0
Decem: 2	1 q; Thron	0 - 1 - 3
23	1 1/2 b: M: wein	0 - 1 - 0
29	1 q: Thron	0 - 1 - 3
1767		
January 5	1 b: wein	0 - 1 - 2
1767	**Friedrich Miller** Parrer [Pastor]	
Septem: 21	Bleibt in der Rechnung [owes in settlement]	0 - 0 - 3
1768		
febr: 1	1 q: m: wein 1 gill Rom	0 - 4 - 4
20	2 b: wein 3 q: haber	0 - 2 - 10
May 1	3 q; seiter	0 - 1 - 0
1769 Feb: 18	1 b; Rom 1 gill Baumöl 3 q: Haber	0 - 1 - 8
1767	**Friedrich Miller** Jung [Jr.}	
Mertz 30	1/4 1/2 4 yd: Hasen Brick	0 - 1 - 6
Augst 7	2 q: haber 1 r: schling	0 - 0 - 10

No 285		
1766	**Betens fuhrleit** [Betens drivers]	
Dember 10	2 q: seiter 1 1/2 b: Rom	0 - 1 - 8
	Zacharias Ertzgräber 1 q: Rom	0 - 1 - 4
january 29 1767	P: 3 q: seiter 1 q: Bir 1 gill Rom	0 - 1 - 10
february 2	John Krum 2 q: seiter	0 - 0 - 8
Aprill 2	John Erzgräber 1 q: Rom	0 - 1 - 4
	Krum gotfrid 1 b: seiteröl 3 q: seiter	0 - 1 - 4
	Joseph 1 q: seiter 1 b: seiteröl un 1 gill Rom	0 - 1 - 0
	Dito 1/2 b: Rom 1 q: seiter 1/2 tram	0 - 0 - 11
	Gotfried 1/2 b: Rom 2 q: seiter 1 1/2 gill Rom	0 - 1 - 7
	dito 1 bo: mim 1 q: seiter	0 - 1 - 4
1770		
January 2	1 gill Rom	0 - 0 - 4
12	4 Mann 2 Mal Essen 2 q: seiter	0 - 4 - 6
15	1 q: W: Rom	0 - 1 - 6
28	Verzehrt	0 - 2 - 0
Mertz 28	1 q: Br: wein 2 gill Rom	0 - 1 - 8
30	Bey a order Verzehrt	0 - 1 - 6
1771		
January 16	1 b: Rom	0 - 0 - 10
25	1 b: Rom	0 - 0 - 10
	1/2 b: Rom	0 - 0 - 5
febr: 25	6 q: seiter	0 - 2 - 0
1772		
January 18	1 1/2 b: Rom 1 q: seiter	0 - 1 - 7
		1 -10- 2
		1 - 9 - 5
		2 -19- 7

No 286		
1766	**Johannes Meÿer** Alte [Sr.}	
Decem: 12	2 q: tar	
1768 May 8	1 q: wein	

1767	**Panne Schmitt**	
Decem: 15	1 1/2 q: seiter 1 gill Rom	
	1 1/2 q: seiter	
1768		
febr: 16	2 q: seiter	
May 26	1 q: seiter un Essen	
July 20	1/2 gill rom	
Novem 9	2 q: seiter 1/2 gill Rom	
21	1 q: seiter 1/2 gill Rom	

No 287		
1766	**Conrad Wagner**	
December 23	1 b; wein 1/2 b: Rom	0 - 1 - 7
1767		
January 6	1 Calender 1/2 b: wein	0 - 1 - 3
Mertz 27	1 yd: Tuch 1 yd: shalun 1/2 yd: Hassen Brick un 2 streng Camelgarn un 2 dutzet Köp 2 q: bir	1 -10- 3
	Conrad Wagner	
Juny 25 1768	had Credit in der rechnung [has credit in settlement]	0 -19- 0
1769	**Conrad Wagner**	
January 16	1 1/2 gill Rom	0 - 0 - 6
1770		
febr: 18	2 gill Rom	0 - 0 - 8
1770	**Conrad Wagner**	
Aprill 16	1 q: Bir 1 gill Rom	0 - 0 - 10

No 288		
1767	**John Kapp**	
January 1	1 Calender	0 - 0 - 8
	Abgerechnet mit John Kapp d: 20tn: february 1768. bleibt nichts [Settled with John Kapp 20 February 1768. Owes nothing]	

1767	**George Trautner**	
Novem: 18	1 hut 1 halss tuch 1 bodel 1 lab Brod un 2 fesser	0 -17- 1

No 289		
1767	**Henrich Peffer** Alte [Sr.]	
Augst 25	1 gill Rom 1/2 gill Baumöl	0 - 0 - 8
October 12	1 q: Rom	0 - 1 - 0
29	1 q: Rom	0 - 1 - 0
1767	**Henrich Peffer** Alte [Sr.]	
Decem: 3	1 q: Rom 1 gill Baumöl	0 - 1 - 7
1768		
Aprill 6	1 q: Rom	0 - 1 - 0
9	1 q: Rom	0 - 1 - 0
16	1 q: Rom	0 - 1 - 0
	1 b: wein	0 - 1 - 2

20	3 q: seiter 1 b: wein	0 - 2 - 2
	1 q: Rom	0 - 1 - 0
26	1 q: Rom	0 - 1 - 0
	1 1/2 b: wein	0 - 1 - 9
May 1	1 q: Br: wein	0 - 0 - 10
	1 q: Rom	0 - 1 - 0
	1 q: Rom	0 - 1 - 0
18	1 q: Br: wein	0 - 0 - 10
20	1 q: Br: wein	0 - 0 - 10
	1 q: Ditto	0 - 0 - 10
26	1 q: Rom	0 - 1 - 0
31	1 q: Br: wein	0 - 0 - 10
	1 q: Mallassis	0 - 0 - 10
Juny 3	1 q: Dito	0 - 0 - 10
21	1 q: Dito	0 - 0 - 10
1769	**Henrich Peffer** Alt [Sr.]	
December 20	gerechnet Bleibt nichts [Settled. Owes nothing]	
23	1 q: Br: wein	0 - 0 - 10
1770		
Janary 8	1 q: Rom	0 - 1 - 0
12	1 q: Rom	0 - 1 - 0
22	1 q: Br: wein	0 - 0 - 10
31	1 q: Rom	0 - 1 - 0
Mertz 1	1 q: Rom	0 - 1 - 0

No 290		
1768	**Casper Shwitzer**	
January 25	gerechnet Bleibt er schultig [Settled. He owes]	2 -13- 0
	[signature:] Caspar Schweizter	
26	2 q: seiter	0 - 0 - 8
28	8 q: seiter	0 - 2 - 8
29	1 b: m: wein	0 - 2 - 0
febru: 1	1/2 gill Rom	0 - 0 - 2
8	1 Hirsch fell Vor Henrich Dock	1 - 0 - 0
	2 q: seiter	0 - 0 - 8
	1 q: seiter	0 - 0 - 4
12	3 q: seiter 1 M: w: schling	0 - 2 - 2
Mertz 28	1 R: schling 2 q: seiter	0 - 1 - 2
May 1	1 q: seiter	0 - 0 - 4
16	1 q: seiter	0 - 0 - 4
20	2 q: seiter	0 - 0 - 8
31	4 q: seiter 1/2 tram	0 - 1 - 6
Juny 3	5 q: seiter	0 - 1 - 8
	3 q: seiter	0 - 1 - 0
11	3 q: seiter	0 - 1 - 0
14	2 buschel Weitzen	0 -11- 4
21	1 q: seiter	0 - 0 - 4
July 7	1 q: seiter	0 - 0 - 4
11	1 q: seiter	0 - 0 - 4
	1 q: seiter	0 - 0 - 4
15	1 1/2 q: seiter	0 - 0 - 6
20	3 q: seiter	0 - 1 - 0
24	1 q: seiter	0 - 0 - 4
Augst 1	1 q: seiter	0 - 0 - 4
4	1/2 gill Rom	0 - 0 - 2
6	1 1/2 q: seiter	0 - 0 - 6
17	2 q: seiter	0 - 0 - 8

Sebt: 3	1 R: schling	0 - 0 - 6
18	2 q: seiter 1 gill Rom	0 - 0 - 10
27	5 q: seiter	0 - 1 - 8
Oct: 3	1 q: seiter	0 - 0 - 4
15	3 q: seiter	0 - 1 - 0
29	1 1/2 q: seiter	0 - 0 - 6
Nov: 6	Vor Leder	0 -12- 7
Decem: 1	1 b: m: wein	0 - 2 - 0
19	1 q: seiter	0 - 0 - 4
27	2 q: seiter	0 - 0 - 8

No 291

1768	**Berned Jacob**	
feruary 12	Bleibt schultig in der abrechnung [Still owes in settlement]	4 - 3 - 9
	14 1/2 lb: Nickerfett	0 - 7 - 3
29	1 b: Bir	0 - 0 - 3
Mertz 11	1 b: m: wein	0 - 2 - 0
19	5 R: schling	0 - 2 - 6
Aprill 9	2 q: seiter 1 R: schling	0 - 1 - 2
20	den gaul bey Heu	0 - 0 - 8
	101 lb: Heu	
	1 b: m: wein	0 - 2 - 0
May 1	1 b: Bir	0 - 0 - 3
26	1/2 lb: Zucker	0 - 0 - 5
31	4 q: Haber	0 - 0 - 8
Juny 3	1 gaul gelehnt ins Mahns [1 horse lent to - a place?]	0 - 2 - 0
21	1 q: seiter	0 - 0 - 4
July 15	1 bol Mim 1 gill Rom 1 b: Rom	0 - 1- 10
Augst 17	1 w: schling 1/2 buch Babir	0 - 1 - 4
	1/2 gill Rom	0 - 0 - 2
Sebt 3	1 q: Rom	0 - 1 - 0
October 3	1 1/2 q: seiter	0 - 0 - 6
8	1 gill Rom	0 - 0 - 4
Decem 27	1 b: Rom	0 - 0 - 6
1769		
Janary 5	1/2 b: wein 1 q: Bir	0 - 1 - 1
16	1 Neb mim	0 - 0 - 6
	68 lb fleisch	0 -17- 0
	1 gill Rom	0 - 0 - 4
23	1 b: seiter	0 - 0 - 2
february 6	1 b: m: wein 1 b: Rom	0 - 2 - 6
	1 fisch	0 - 0 - 3
Aprill 8	Vor stroh	0 - 1 - 6
May 5	1 gill Baumöl 1 b: W: Rom 1/2 4 lb: Thee 1/4 Lof Zucker	0 - 2 - 7
15	1/2 gill gatshel	0 - 0 - 2
22	1/2 gill gatshel 1 b: W: Rom	0 - 0 - 11
	6 q: Haber	0 - 1 - 0
Juny 9	1 1/2 gill Rom	0 - 0 - 6
11	1/2 gill Baumöl	0 - 0 - 4
		6 -17- 9

No 292

1767	**John Rieser**	
January 19	1 b: wein	0 - 1 - 2
1769	**John Risser**	
May 5	1 b: wein	0 - 1 - 2
22	1 Zoll stab	0 - 4 - 6
Juny 1	1 strang Camelgarn 1 strang neths	0 - 0 - 6

1767	**dem Restauner wo ein Brif Vor Borckhart**	
	[the person from Raystown who brought a letter for Borckhart]	
Juny 15	Verzehrt	0 -12- 6

No 293

1767	**Willhelm Besch**	
Aprill 8	3 q: seiter	0 - 1 - 0
	gelehnt an geld [lent in money]	0 - 6 - 0
	2 q: seiter	0 - 0 - 8
11	1 q: seiter	0 - 0 - 4
13	2 q: seiter un 1 Peif	0 - 0 - 9
20	3 q: 1 b: seiteröl	0 - 1 - 4
25	1 q: seiter	0 - 0 - 4
May 6	1 1/2 q: seiter 1 q: Bir	0 - 0 - 11
9	1 q: seiter 1 b: seiteröl	0 - 0 - 8
16	2 q: seiter	0 - 0 - 8
	ist schuldig Vor Danel Nord	0 - 0 - 6
17	3 q: seiter	0 - 1 - 0
20	3 q: seiter	0 - 1 - 0
21	3 q: seiter	0 - 1 - 0
25	3 q: seiter	0 - 1 - 0
28	2 q: seiter	0 - 0 - 8
Juny 1	2 q: seiter	0 - 0 - 8
8	1 q: Br: wein 1 q: seiter	0 - 1 - 0
15	2 q: seiter 1 weck	0 - 0 - 9
22	2 q: seiter	0 - 0 - 8
27	3 1/2 q: seiter 1/2 gill Rom	0 - 1 - 4
July 9	2 lb: Reiss	0 - 0 - 6
10	2 q: seiter 2 q: Br: wein 1 halss Tuch	0 - 5 - 3
23	2 q: seiter	0 - 0 - 8
25	1 b: seiter 1 b: Br: wein	0 - 0 - 7
Augst 1	3 b: seiteröl	0 - 1 - 0
5	1 q: seiter	0 - 0 - 4
7	2 q: Br: wein	0 - 1 - 8
15	1 q: seiter	0 - 0 - 4
	1 q: seiter 1 b: seiteröl 1 q: Br: wein	0 - 1 - 6
24	2 q: seiter	0 - 0 - 8
	1 q: seiter	0 - 0 - 4
Sebtem: 14	1 gill Br: wein 1 b: seiter	0 - 0 - 5
23	1 q: seiter 1 b: tram	0 - 0 - 9

No 294

1767	**Wilhelm Besch**	
Septem: 27	2 q: Bir Vor Parre [2 quarts of beer for the pastor]	0 - 1 - 0

October 5	1 wein Peif [?]	0 - 7 - 6
15	1 gill Rom	0 - 0 - 4
20	1 b: wein 1 q: seiter 1/2 gill Rom	0 - 1 - 8
27	1 q: seiter	0 - 0 - 4
	sein sohn [his son] 1/4 lb: Pulver 1 lb: schrot	0 - 1 - 5
	1 q: seiter 1 q: Br: wein	0 - 1 - 0
Novem: 13	2 q: seiter	0 - 0 - 8
18	gelehnt [lent]	0 - 0 - 6
Decem: 15	2 q: seiter	0 - 0 - 8
25	1 q: seiter	0 - 0 - 4
1768		
January 9	3 q: seiter	0 - 1 - 0
11	1 q: seiter	0 - 0 - 4
19	3 q: seiter	0 - 1 - 0
23	1 q: Rom 1 q: seiter	0 - 1 - 4
	2 q: seiter	0 - 0 - 8
25	Credit	0 - 7 - 6
	1 q: seiter	0 - 0 - 4
febru: 20	3 q: seiter	0 - 1 - 0
Mertz 19	1 b: mim	0 - 1 - 0
April 2	1 q: seiter	0 - 0 - 4
23	1 q: Br: wein 2 q: seiter	0 - 1 - 6
	1 q: seiter	0 - 0 - 4
	1 q: seiter	0 - 0 - 4
May 1	4 q: seiter 4 weck	0 - 1 - 8
5	1 q: seiter	0 - 0 - 4
Juny 21	1 q: seiter	0 - 0 - 4
July 2	1 q: seiter	0 - 0 - 4
20	1 q: Rom 1 q: seiter 2 weck	0 - 1 - 6
Augst: 1	3 q: seiter	0 - 1 - 0
4	1 gallen Br: wein a: 3/0	0 - 3 - 0
6	1 q: seiter	0 - 0 - 4
19	2 q: Br: wein 1 Neb mim	0 - 2 - 0
	2 q: Br: wein 1 q: Rom	0 - 2 - 6
Sebt: 27	2 q: seiter	0 - 0 - 8
	1 q: Thron	0 - 1 - 0
Octo: 3	3 q: seiter	0 - 1 - 0
	1 q: seiter	0 - 0 - 4

No 295		
1767	**Stigels fuhrleit** [Stiegel's teamsters]	
January 25	Peter Ried mit 5 geil	
	1 q: seiter 1 gill Rom	0 - 0 - 8
	der gleine Adam [little = short Adam] 3 q: seiter 1 q: Bir	0 - 1 - 6
May 16	der oxenfuhrman [The ox driver] 1 b: Rom	0 - 0 - 6

1767	**Bardel Wicker** Maurer [mason]	
Juny 27	1 q: m: wein 3 q: seiter	0 - 5 - 0
July 6	1 sichel	0 - 3 - 4
Augst 15	Vor schab gut	0 - 9 - 4
1769		
October 29	1 lb: Tuback 1/2 gill Rom	0 - 0 - 8
Novem: 5	1 lb: Tuback	0 - 0 - 6
	1 gill gatshall	0 - 0 - 5
8	1 gill gatshall	0 - 0 - 5

25	1 Par strümb	0 - 5 - 0
	1 lb: Tuback	0 - 0 - 6
	2 yd: Bay 2 dutzent Knöp	0 -12- 8
	Credit	0 - 1 - 6
1770		
Mertz 13	1 w: schling	0 - 0 - 9
28	1/2 b: m: wein	0 - 1 - 0
1771		
Juny 17	1 b: wein	0 - 1 - 4
		2 - 2 - 5

No 296		
1767	**Philipp Klein**	
	6 fisch 1 b: seiteröl das vergessen [which was forgotten]	0 - 1 - 4
Mertz 27	Bleibt schultig in der Rechnung [Still owes in the settlement]	0 - 4 - 0
May 21	1 b: wein 1 yd: Catun 2 1/2 yd: floret	0 - 7 - 0
28	1 1/2 q: Br: wein	0 - 1 - 2
July 23	1 gill Rom	0 - 0 - 4
1768	Philipp Klein Bleibt schuldig in der abrechung [sic]	1 - 4 - 6
December d: 5	[Philipp Klein still owes in the settlement]	
	1 q: seiter	0 - 0 - 4
1769		
January 16	1/2 b: wein	0 - 0 - 2
28	1 b: wein 1 weck	0 - 1 - 3
february 6	1/2 b: wein	0 - 0 - 7
9	1/2 b: wein 1 wein	0 - 0 - 8

No 297		
1767	**Phillip Peffer**	
Mertz 30	Vor schapp gut	0 -17- 0
1767	**Phillip Peffer**	
Novem: 13	1/4 lb: Pulver 1 w: schling	0 - 1 - 8
	ist schultig Vor Jacob Gass [owes for Jacob Gass]	0 -12- 0
1769	**Philipp Peffer**	
May 27	Bleibt schultig in der Rechnung [Still owes in the settlement]	5 - 3 - 3
1770	**Philipp Peffer**	
Martz 12	Bleibt schultig in der Rechnung [Still owes in the settlement]	1 - 3 - 0
13	1 b: Bir	0 - 0 - 3

No 298		
1767	**Friedrich Wolfersperger** Jung [Jr.]	
Mertz 30	1 Par strümb	0 - 6 - 6
May 28	1 w: schling	0 - 0 - 9
1767	**Friedrich Wolfersperger** Jung [Jr.]	
Sebtem: 30	1/2 b: m: wein	0 - 1 - 0

1767	**Michael Wolfersperger**	
Juny 8	1 w: schling	0 - 0 - 9
Sebtem: 27	1 b: wein	0 - 1 - 2

No 299		
1767	**Conrad Kirschner**	
Aprill 20	1 q: Bir	0 - 0 - 6
28	1 q: Tar	0 - 0 - 6
May 1	1 q: Tar	0 - 0 - 6
6	1 q: Tar	0 - 0 - 6
16	2 q: Tar	0 - 1 - 0
17	1 q: Tar	0 - 0 - 6
21	1 q: Tar	0 - 0 - 6
28	1 q: Tar 1 q: Bir	0 - 1 - 0
Juny 1	1 q: Tar	0 - 0 - 6
15	1 q: Tar 1 b: Bir	0 - 0 - 3
27	1 q: Bir	0 - 0 - 6
1767	**Henrich Krebs**	
Decem: 3	1 q: Bir 1/2 lb: Peffer un 1/4 yd: Catun 2 flintenstein	0 - 4 - 0

No 300		
1767	**Friedrich Weiser George Becker**	
	von Wegen Reger [on Reger's account]	
Aprill 28	10 b: M: wein un vor den schreiber 1/0 [and for the scribener]	1 - 1 - 0
	Georg Becker 1 q: bir	0 - 0 - 6
	Dito 2 gill Rom	0 - 0 - 8
1770		
Dec: 8	Weisser 2 gill Rom 2 q: Haber	0 - 1 - 8
1767	**Jacob Seltzer**	
October 25	1 q: Br: wein	0 - 1 - 0
1768		
Sebt 3	Vor wein	0 - 0 - 8
Novem: 6	1 Berrel fass	0 - 4 - 0

No 301		
1767	**Ulrich Reisser**	
May 25	1/2 b: Rom	0 - 0 - 5
Juny 4	1 lb Zucker	0 - 0 - 10
1768		
January 1	1 b: m: wein Bey Bel Tag	0 - 2 - 0
May 8	1/2 gill Rom	0 - 0 - 2
Augst 4	1 b: m: wein	0 - 2 - 0
1769 May 5	gelehnt [lent]	0 - 2 - 0
22	1/2 lb: Alspeis	0 - 1 - 3
Augst 8	sein Christle 1 R: schling	0 - 0 - 6
21	gelehnt Vor Tax [lent for tax]	0 - 2 - 0

1770		
Febru: 9	1/2 Buschel saltz	0 - 2 - 0
Metz 28	1 q: seiter	0 - 0 - 4
1771		
July 15	Bebe 1 q: W: Rom 1 wein schling	0 - 2 - 3
	Ditto 1 q: W: Rom	0 - 1 - 6
1772	**Ulrich Risser**	
January 18	gerechnet Bleibt no rest [Settled. Owes nothing]	

No 302

	Adam Hoffmann	
July 4	1 q: seiter	0 - 0 - 4
Augst 25	1 1/2 lb: saffen	0 - 0 - 11
Sebtem: 23	2 lb: Zucker	0 - 1 - 8
30	1 q: wein un 2 lb: Zucker	0 - 3 - 10
Juny 10tn: 1769	**Adam Hoffmann**	
	gerechnet Bleibt nichts [Settled. Owes nothing]	
Seb: 1	2 q: wein	0 - 4 - 8

No 303

1767	**Ezechial Corts** Sandhorse	
July 6	1 q: seiter 1/2 gill Rom	0 - 0 - 6
9	1 q: seiter 1/2 gill Rom	0 - 0 - 6
Augst 5	2 q: seiter 1/2 gill Rom un Essen	0 - 1 - 4
1768		
Janua: 25	5 q: seiter 1 gill Rom	0 - 2 - 0
December 9	**Ezechial Corts**	
1769	Bleibt schultig in der abrechnung [Still owes in the settlement]	0 - 1 - 5
11	1 1/2 gill Rom 1 b: Bir	0 - 0 - 9
	1 b: seiter	0 - 0 - 2
1770		
Mertz 1	3 q: seiter	0 - 1 - 0
14	1/2 gill Rom	0 - 0 - 2

1768	**Christian Bernhard**	
Decem 1	2 q: seiter	0 - 0 - 8
1769		
Mertz 20	2 q: Rom 1 b: wein	0 - 3 - 2
Aprill 8	1 q: Br: wein	0 - 0 - 9
May 22	1 q: seiter	0 - 0 - 4
Juny 29	3 q: seiter	0 - 1 - 0
Augst 1	1 q: Rom 1 q: seiter	0 - 1 - 4
5	1 q: Rom	0 - 1 - 0
12	2 q: seiter	0 - 0 - 8
26	3 q: Rom	0 - 3 - 0
Seb: 6	3 q: Rom 1 q: seiter	0 - 3 - 4
11	2 q: Rom	0 - 2 - 0
Oct: 9	3 q: Rom	0 - 1 - 0
17	1 fass	0 - 1 - 6
28	1 1/2 q: Rom	0 - 1 - 6
Dec: 30	3 q: seiter	0 - 1 - 0

1770		
febru: 9	1 q: seiter	0 - 0 - 4
18	2 q: seiter 1 q: Bir Ulrich	0 - 1 - 2
Aprill 16	2 q: seiter	0 - 0 - 8
May 24	1 b: seiteröl	0 - 0 - 4
Sebt 19	1 q: Rom	0 - 1 - 0
		1 - 5 - 9

No 304

1767	**Abraham Stumb**	
Augst 7	1 q: Br: wein	0 - 0 - 10
24	1 q: Br: wein	0 - 0 - 10
25	2 q: Br: wein	0 - 1 - 8
September 4	1 q: Br: wein	0 - 0 - 10
Decem: 8	2 lb: Reiss	0 - 0 - 7
10	1 gill Rom	0 - 0 - 4
15	1 hirschfell	1 - 2 - 6
1768		
Juny 24	1 q: Thron 1 l: wein 1 lb: Zucker	0 - 3 - 0
	1 q: Rom	0 - 1 - 0
July 20	1 bol senckery	0 - 1 - 6
1772	**Abraham Stumb**	
January 18	gerechnet Bleibt Nichts [Settled. Owes nothing]	

No 305

1767	**Michael Reger**	
Augst 29	1 w: schling	0 - 0 - 9
Decem: 15	Vor heu	0 - 1 - 0
1768		
Mertz 26	1 bo: mim 1/2 gill Rom	0 - 1 - 2
May 31	4 q: seiter	0 - 1 - 4
Juny 14	Vor Essig und seiter und Vor Walzen un tram	0 - 5 - 6
October 3	4 q: seiter 1 gill Rom	0 - 1 - 8
	2 q: seiter 1/2 gill Rom	0 - 0 - 10
1769		
January 21	2 q: wein 1 q: seiter 1 gill Rom	0 - 3 - 0
	3 lb: Pulver	0 -10- 6
28	Vor 1 hals tuch un Verzehrt	0 - 8 - 0
	2 q: seiter	0 - 0 - 8
Mertz 25	1 hut	0 - 7 - 6
Aprill 3	2 b: wein 3 q: Bir	0 - 3 - 10
Juny 20	1/2 gill Rom 4 q: haber 1 w: schling	0 - 1 - 11
	gelehnt an geld [lent in money]	1 -15- 0
29	1 Bottel 2 q: Rom	0 - 3 - 4
Augst 1	3 b: wein 2 gill Rom	0 - 4 - 2
Novem: 5	gelehnt [lent]	0 -18- 0
1770		
May 5	2 lb: Pulver 1 q: Rom	0 - 7 - 0
7	1 gill Rom	0 - 0 - 4
	2 q: seiter 1 gill Rom	0 - 1 - 0
	den gaul Bey Heu	0 - 2 - 0
Augst 9	Vor Bulver Negel und Verzehrt	0 -16- 9
	gelehnt [lent]	1 -10- 0

November 10	4 gill Rom	0 - 1 - 4
	2 gill rom 2 q: seiter 2 lb: Pulver	0 - 7 - 4
	2 gill Rom 2 q: seiter Vor Heu 4 q: Haber un Essen	0 - 5 - 4
1771		
Janua: 16	Verzehrt un Zinen geschir un Bulver un den gaul Bey Heu	2 - 7 - 6
Aprill 4	2 q: seiter 2 gill Rom	0 - 1 - 4
25	1 lb: Pulver 4 gill Rom 3 q: seiter	0 - 5 - 4
May 10	3 1/2 gill Rom 2 q: seiter 3 mal Essen	0 - 2 - 10
July 25	Vor soledar	0 - 2 - 6
	2 q: seiter 2 gill Rom	0 - 1 - 4

No 306

1767

Friedrich Taxis

Sebtember 12	1/2 Beck saltz	0 - 0 - 7
23	1 q: Rom	0 - 1 - 0
Octo: 5	1/2 b: wein	0 - 0 - 7
12	1 q: Rom	0 - 1 - 0
20	1 b: wein	0 - 1 - 2
25	1 b: wein	0 - 1 - 2
Novem: 22	1 q: Rom	0 - 1 - 0
Dec: 10	1 q: Rom	0 - 1 - 0
21	1 Calender	0 - 0 - 8
1768		
January 14	1 q: seiter	0 - 0 - 4
19	Vor Knöp	0 - 0 - 7
25	1 b: wein	0 - 1 - 2
febru: 12	Vor schab gut	1 - 8 - 6
	1 b: wein	0 - 1 - 2
	1 q: Rom	0 - 1 - 0
16	1 b: wein	0 - 1 - 2
26	1 b: wein	0 - 1 - 2
April : 2	1 lb: Zucker	0 - 0 - 10
9	1 1/2 q: Rom	0 - 1 - 6
16	1 b: Thron	0 - 0 - 6
May 16	1 q: Thron	0 - 1 - 0
Juny 3	1 1/4 yd: futertuch	0 - 3 - 9
11	1 q: seiter	0 - 0 - 4
14	1 q: Rom	0 - 1 - 0
21	1 q: Tar	0 - 0 - 6
	3 1/4 yd: Kelsch 1 sichel	0 -11- 7
Augst 17	1 q: Rom	0 - 1 - 0
Sebt 27	1 q: Thron	0 - 1 - 0
October 8	1 q: malassis	0 - 0 - 10
	1 b: W: Rom	0 - 0 - 9
	1 q: seiter	0 - 0 - 4
Novem 6	1 lb: Zucker	0 - 0 - 9
Decem 7	1/2 b: wein	0 - 0 - 7
22	1 q: Rom	0 - 1 - 0
1769		
January 21	1/4 Peffer 1/4 alspeis 1/2 Imber	0 - 2 - 1
Mertz 22	1 q: Rom	0 - 1 - 0
25	2 q: seiter	0 - 0 - 8
Aprill 20	1 q: W: Rom	0 - 1 - 6
Juny 20	1 q: Rom	0 - 1 - 0

No 307

1767	**Martin Bäÿer**	
October 25	2 w: schling 2 leb Kuchen	0 - 1 - 8
1768		
Aprill 2	1/2 b: wein	0 - 0 - 7
Augst 6	1 yd: floret un 1 w: schling	0 - 1 - 1
Sebt 3	1 hut	0 - 7 - 6
12	1 R: schling	0 - 0 - 6
	1 bol senckery	0 - 1 - 6
Octo 20	1 w: schling	0 - 0 - 9
29	1 w: schling	0 - 0 - 9
Nov. 6	1 w: schling	0 - 0 - 9
	2 q: seiter	0 - 0 - 6
Decem: 7	1 R: schling	0 - 0 - 6
27	1/2 lb: Pulver	0 - 1 - 6
1769		
January 2	1 q: Rom	0 - 1 - 0
	1 w: schling	0 - 0 - 9
	1 q: Rom	0 - 1 - 0
21	1/2 b wein 1/2 gill Rom	0 - 0 - 9
23	1 b: wein 1 yd: Band	0 - 1 - 11
febr: 14	1 b: wein	0 - 1 - 2
18	1 w: schling	0 - 0 - 9
Mertz 3	1/2 b: wein	0 - 0 - 7
13	1 b: wein	0 - 1 - 2
20	1 w: schling	0 - 0 - 9
26	1 w: schling	0 - 0 - 9
Aprill 3	1 b: wein 1 q: seiter	0 - 1 - 6
	1 gill Rom 1 b: wein	0 - 1 - 6
1770	**Martin Bayer**	
Sebtem	Bleibt schultig [Still owes]	[effaced]

[308, 309, 310, 311 missing leaves]

No 312

1768	**Nickolaus Cesinger**	
January 14	1 q: Bir	0 - 0 - 6
19	2 q: Bir	0 - 1 - 0
25	1 gill gatschall	0 - 0 - 5
	1 q: Bir	0 - 0 - 6
february 12	1 q: Bir	0 - 0 - 6
29	1 q: seiter	0 - 0 - 4
	1 gill Rom	0 - 0 - 4
Mertz 11	1 gill Rom 1 q: bir	0 - 0 - 10
14	1 gill Rom	0 - 0 - 4
	1/2 gill Rom	0 - 0 - 2
19	2 q: seiter	0 - 0 - 8
	1 R: schling	0 - 0 - 6
	1 q: seiter	0 - 0 - 4
Aprill 2	1 q: Rom	0 - 1 - 0
	1 q: seiter	0 - 0 - 4
	1 q: bir	0 - 0 - 6
May 1	1 q: bir 1 q: seiter	0 - 0 - 10
	Nickolaus Cesinger gerechnet d: 30ten Mertz 1769 bleibt schultig[Nickolaus Cesinger settled 30 March 1769. Still owes]	0 - 1 - 7

1769	**Nickolaus Cesinger**	
October 9	gerechnet Bleibt nichts [settled. Owes nothing]	
	3 q: seiter	0 - 1 - 0
28	2 q: seiter	0 - 0 - 8
Novem: 8	1 q: seiter	0 - 0 - 4

No 313		
1768	**Casper Iba**	
Aprill 20	1 q: Rom	0 - 1 - 0
23	1/2 gill Rom	0 - 0 - 2
May 1	1 hut	0 - 7 - 6
Augst 6	1 q: Rom	0 - 1 - 0
29	1/2 gill Rom	0 - 0 - 2
1769		
Janary 23	1 glas Verbrochen [1 glas broken]	0 - 0 - 8
Febr: 6	1 gill rom	0 - 0 - 4
18	Vor stroh	0 - 6 - 0
Aprill 3	1 q: Br: wein	0 - 0 - 9
Augst 5	3 Buschel Weitzen	0 -13- 6
Nove: 5	1 q: seiter	0 - 0 - 4
	1/2 gill gatchal	0 - 0 - 2
25	1 q: seiter	0 - 0 - 4
Decem 4	1 buschel saltz	0 - 3 - 6
20	3 Buschel Weitzen	0 -13- 6
1770		
febr: 12	1/2 b: wein 1/2 gill Baumöl	0 - 0 - 11
	2 q: Rom 1 b: wein	0 - 3 - 2
Mertz 14	1 q: Rom	0 - 1 - 0
	1 q: Rom	0 - 1 - 0
Aprill 18	1 Buschel Weitzen	0 - 9 - 0
May 12	1 q: Malassis	0 - 0 - 10
Juny 12	80 lb: Heu	0 - 1 - 11
	gelehnt	0 - 5 - 0
20	1 b: Rom	0 - 0 - 6
July 6	1 b: wein	0 - 1 - 4
Sebt 3	1 q: Rom	0 - 1 - 0
	1 Buschel Saltz	0 - 4 - 0
October 11	Vor Heuführen	0 - 6 - 0
Decem 8	1/2 gill Baumöl 1 Muscatennus	0 - 0 - 10
	1 b: wein	0 - 1 - 2
1771		
Janua: 12	1 b: wein	0 - 1 - 3
feb: 14	1 q: Rom	0 - 1 - 0
Mertz 16	1/2 b: wein	0 - 0 - 8
May 10	gelehnt	0 -15- 0
29	1/2 buschel Kalck	0 - 0 - 5
July 15	2 q: Mallassis	0 - 1 - 8
25	2 q: Dito	0 - 1 - 8
Augst 21	Vor Omet	2 - 0 - 0

No 314

1768	**Wilhelm Besh**	
October 29	1 q: seiter	0 - 0 - 4
Nov: 6	1 q: seiter 2 Peiffen	0 - 0 - 6
Decem: 22	1 q: seiter	0 - 0 - 4
1770	**Willem Besch**	
January 9	gerechnet Bleibt schultig [settled. Still owes]	0 - 1 - 10
	aufs Kiseckers Band Verechnet [on Kisecker's bond settled]	7 - 0 - 0
1770	**Willem Besch**	
Mertz 31	gerechnet Bleibt schultig [settled. Still owes]	3 - 7 - 1
	1 q: seiter	0 - 0 - 4
	Credit	1 - 0 - 0
	Credit	0 -15- 0
Aprill 6	9 lb: fleisch	0 - 2 - 3
	1 b: seiter 1 b: rom	0 - 0 - 8
May 5	1 q: Rom 1 q: seiter	0 - 1 - 4
7	2 q: seiter	0 - 0 - 8
24	2 q: seiter	0 - 0 - 8
	1 q: Rom 1 lb: Zucker 1 b: seiter	0 - 1 -11
	1 b: wein 1 q: seiter	0 - 1 - 6
	1 q: Rom 1 q: Thron	0 - 2 - 0
	2 1/2 q: Rom	0 - 2 - 6
Juny 12	1 q: seiter	0 - 0 - 4
	1 1/2 q: tram	0 - 1 - 2
20	1 q: Rom 2 q: seiter	0 - 1 - 8
July 6	1 q: Rom 1 q: Mallassis 1 q: seiter	0 - 2 - 2
Augst 9	1 q: seiter	0 - 0 - 4
18	1 q: Rom	0 - 1 - 0
20	1 q: seiter	0 - 0 - 4
	1 q: seiter	0 - 0 - 4
27	1 gill Rom	0 - 0 - 4
Sebtem: 3	1 R: schling	0 - 0 - 6
10	1 R: schling	0 - 0 - 6
19	1 1/2 b: Br: wein 1 q: seiter	0 - 1 - 0
Octob: 10	2 q: Br: wein	0 - 1 - 6
11	Credit	0 -10- 0
	---- seiter	0 - 0- 4

No 315

1769	**Henry Wm. Stigle**	
Mertz 23	muss zahlen vor Michael Kintzel [must pay for Michael Kintzel]	0 - 8 - 5
	vor Mahnes Miller [for Mahnes Miller]	0 - 2 - 8
	vor Caspar Oberman [for Caspar Oberman]	0 - 4 - 6
	vor John Geiger [for John Geiger]	0 -15- 5
	sein sohn [his son] d: gaul bey heu 6 q: haber	0 - 2 - 0
Octob: 17	Vor die Jury von Peffer un Stigel die Helft [For the Jury from Peffer and Stigel, half]	1 - 1 - 6
1770		
Octob: 28	1 bol mim	0 - 1 - 0
1771		
May 8	sein sohn verzehrt [his son ate]	0 - 5 - 4
		3 - 0 - 10

No 316

Casper Löb

	Bleibt schultig in der Rechnung [Still owes in the settlement]	0 - 5 - 0
	1 Par schuh 1 Par sollen	
	darauf Bezahlt [paid thereon]	0 - 5 - 0
	gerechnet mit Casper Löb d: 5 tn: November 1769 bleibt	0 -10- 0
	[Settled with Casper Löb 5 November 1769. Owes]	
	Casper Löb gerechnet d: 1: December 1770 Bleib ich ihm schuldig [Casper Löb settled 1 December 1770. I still owe him]	1 - 6 - 6
	noch Zwey Tag mist führen [two more days hauling manure]	0 - 4 - 0
	1 q: seiter	0 - 0 - 4
1771	Casper Löb gerechnet hat Credit	0 -17- 0
Aprill 4	[Casper Löb settled. Has credit]	

No 317

Carl Mickenfuss

22	1 q: seiter
1768	
January 23	1 q: seiter
Mertz 11	1 gill Baumöl
26	1 q: seiter
May 5	Vor Erdeden geschirr
Junly 24	1 b: Mallisses
	Vor erden geschirr
Decem 7	1 q: seiter 1 Peiff
	1 q: Malassis
1769	
febr: 9	1 q: seiter
1771	**Carl Muckenfuss**
January 7	gerechnet Bleibt nicht [settled. Owes nothing]

[This page is badly damaged]

No 318

1770	**Martin Heffelfinger**	
January 16	Bleibt Schultig in der abrechnung [Still owes in the settlement]	1 - 5 - 7

1768	**David Zöller**	
July 20	1 gaul bey heu	0 - 0 - 8
October 15	1/2 haut oberleder	0 - 7 -

[rear flyleaf]

die alt meyerin [old **Mrs. Meyer**] 1 lb: Zucker 10 p

Schwarz Schäfferin [The black Schäffer woman]

	Vor schab gut	0 - 7 - 0
Sebt: 20	1 q: Thron	0 - 1 - 0

Appendix I

Glossary of terms named in this record

A B C Buch	A B C book, the first schoolbook used to teach children to read; cf. Namenbuch, another name for it. cf. Walter Klinefelter, "The ABC Books of the Pennsylvania Germans," *Publications of the Pennsylvania German Society* (Breinigsville, 1973), VII, 1-104.
Affter Geschirr	quilor harness
Alspeis	allspice
ambel	?
annis	anise; the basic flavoring agent of licorice; also used in baking; the Pennsylvania Germans in the 18th century used oil of anise to flavor a distilled drink variously called *Gadsell* or *Gatschell.*
Apfel Bäum	apple trees, saplings
äffel, buschel	bushel of apples
auf blocken	to lay up the logs of a log building
auf schlagen	to put up the frame of a frame building
Backen Buch	pocket book, wallet
barget	fustian, a closely woven fabric used for bed ticks; cf. *bedzeig* and *bet barget*
baumöhl, bamöll, bamel=Baum öl,	"tree oil" = probably olive oil
Baumwolle	"tree wool" = cotton
Band	ribbon
Bar Geld	cash
bech; pech	shoemaker's wax, made from tar and beeswax.
beif	pipe (smoking); cf. *peif.*
bedzeig	bed case, i.e., for the feather bed under which people slept. A bedstead (*Bettlaad*) was the frame for roping. cf. *bet barget.*
beffer	pepper; cf. Peffer
bet barget	fustian (g. v.), ticking to contain the feathers for pillows, bolsters, and feather beds; of *bedzeig* and *barget.*
Bel Tag	= bell day, perhaps an otherwise unrecorded term for New Year's Day on which considerable noise was made. Lambert also reports *belle* meaning to serenade a recently married couple. The entry is dated January 1.
bendel	tape; heavier utilitarian fabric tapes made at home; cf. *band*, ribbon.
Bender	hinges made by a smith
Berl bier	a barrel of beer
Bett lad	the bedstead, in contrast to the bed itself; cf. *bedzeig*
bey und farb	to bleach and dye a piece of cloth
bitters	alcoholic beverage, probably imported, probably purchased for medicinal use for upset stomach. Bitters are produced from carefully kept secrets and result from infusion and distillation processes involving aromatic plants, seeds, herbs, barks, roots and fruits blended on a spirit base.
Bley	lead, used for casting bullets
bloss rohr	"blow pipe"
Borschet	fustian
Bort	boards
bottel	bottle
Zinner bottel	pewter bottle or flask
Br wein, Brandewein	brandy, a popular alcoholic drink among the Pennsylvania Germans prepared by distilling apple wine; i.e., apple jack
Brill	eyeglasses
Brodt	bread
leeb Brod	a loaf of bread

bsalder (psalter) — hymnal; the Reformed church initially used only metric psalm paraphrases in worship, hence the name. Eighteenth century German Reformed hymnals continued to contain Lobwasser's psalm paraphrases. May also be the book of Psalms used as a school reader.

buch — book

bunsch — punch;

  leims bunsch — lemon punch. A mixed drink whose precise recipe we lack.

Butter — butter

Caffe. — coffee, an expensive, imported beverage

Calendar — almanac, published annually by Christopher Sauer and others. Every family owned one, hanging from a string on a nail. The fact that some were purchased well after new year's day may reflect that these almanacs had their greatest use in agricultural activity which began in spring.

Calmick — English calimanco, probably a glazed linen fabric with a patter on one side only.

Camelgarn — mohair yarn

camlot — English camelot, cloth woven from mohair yarn

Catechismus — catechism. Lutheran youth preparing for confirmation used Luther's Small Catechism; Reformed youth used the Heidelberg Catechism. Both were printed in America at an early date to meet heavy demands for them.

  Spruch Catecismus — an extended version of the Lutheran catechism with additional texts; cf. Arthur C. Repp, *Luther's Catechism comes to America.*

Cattun, Cartun, Cardun — calico, printed cotton cloth

Corallen — beads; **fluss corellen**, Job's tears seeds, strung and used for decoration. They were also worn as a necklass by infants to cure the *schtick fluss.*

Cramben — ?

darr — tar

Deet — deed;

Deed zu Knaletschen — to acknowledge a deed, i.e., be a witness on it

Dick, Dück, halb — half thicks - a white fabric, not as thick or firm a cloth as duck, which is like canvas

dintenfass — inkwell

dinten pulver — ink powder, from which ink was made when a liquid agent was added to it

Drugget — druget; a coarse fabric, printed, used for floor coverings

Eimer — bucket

eissen — iron. All forms of iron had value, due to the laborious technology of extracting it from nature. Scrap iron frequently appears as *alt eisen,* old iron, on inventories.

Ertz — ore; in this instance iron ore, found in the Blue Mountains of Pennsylvania. The Stiegel iron works Elizabeth Furnace, south of Schaefferstown, met the area's needs for iron.

Essen — meal

  Mittagessen — noon meal

Hotels provided meals for transients. Generally hotel cooking in Pennsylvania was superior to home cooking both in quality and quantity. The day's chief meal was taken at noon.

farb — dyestuff

fass — barrel

  Fässgen — little barrel

feil — file

fensterglas — windowglass, panes; Stiegel's glass works, first at Elizabeth Furnace, later at Manheim, provided great quantities of utilitarian glass such as this.

feyerstein — flint

fisch	salted or dried fish (probably mackeral) in barrels, sold for consumption at home or as a snack at the bar.
fingerhut	thimble
fisch tron	lamp oil, sperm oil
flags samen	flax seed for planting. Quantities of flaxseed were also pressed for linseed oil; cf. *Leinsamen.*
fleisch	meat, pork. The chief meat of the Pennsylvania Germans was pork. Their documents specify *rindsfleisch* (beef) or *calbsfleisch* (veal). Fowl and mutton were rarely eaten, game when available.
flintenstein	flint
flenel	flannel
floret, flored, Foret	In Britain, a figured wood dress fabric.
floret bendel	ribbons made of floret
fuchs balg	fox skin
fuchs schwantz.	fox tail, perhaps for the bounty; cf. **fuchs balg**. The **schwantz** commanded 15 shillings, but the whole **balg** 0, 2, 6!
futtertuch	lining material
gading-mittel	?
gatsel, gadel	An alcoholic beverage made by adding anise and other elements to the distilling. An eighteenth century Pennsylvania German recipe is given in Larry M. Neff and Frederick S. Weiser, trans. and ed., *Friedrich Heinrich Gelwicks, Shoemaker and Distiller - Accounts, 1760-1783* (Breiningsville, Pa., 979), 92. A cordial.
Geil	horse
Geil bey Heu	horse at hay, a service provided by the hotel for customers' horses.
gelent	lent. Since there were no banks, persons with capital lent to others in need. The hotel sometimes provided customers with small change. Objects too were lent.
Genever	probably a corruption of Imber, etc., ginger
gerst	barley
gerüst	scaffolding used in masonry construction
Gesang Buch	hymnal; cf. *Bsalder*
geschirr	when this word appears alone in Pennsylvania German documents, it refers most often to dishes.
Zinern	pewter dishes
erden, Erdenen	earthenware dishes
Geschwey	perhaps brother-in-law
gewirtz	general term for spice. Allspice, anise, pepper, ginger, nutmeg, saffron, salt are the spices listed in this account. Surprisingly another favorite, cinnamon, is not.
gortel	belt ?
haber	oats
Erdenen Haffen	earthenware pot
Halb Leinen	linsey woolsey
Halls Duch, Seiden	
seiden hals diger	silk neckerchief(s)
Har	hair, gathered and used by plasterers
hasenbrick	A Pennsylvania Dutch corruption; the term also occurs here as *Ossnabrick* and is also given elsewhere as Hosenberg. Its correct English form is *Osnaburg*. It is a coarse, strong, plain weave cotton fabric coarser than sheeting. It could be printed with stripes or checks.
Haubengarn	yarn for kniting caps, *Hauben*. All women wore headcoverings in the eighteenth century.
haut	hide; skin
hem	shirt. The full entry in the one instance the word is used is "2 1/2 yards cloth and maker's fee for one shirt".
hirsch fell	deer skin
Hoi, Heu	hay

holtz	wood
roth holtz	a dying agent, an imported tropical wood which yielded its red color to wool.
Honig	honey, the commonest sweetening agent available in the eighteenth century.
hose	pants; breeches
ledner	leatherbreeches; one entry refers to a pair of old (i.e., used) *hosen.*
Hüt	hat, hats
stroh hut	straw hat. Men generally wore hats in summer or winter out-of-doors and, surprisingly perhaps, inside the church!
Hut Zucker	a peaked cone of sugar used for punches and pretentious occasions
Imber, Schimber, Schinwer, Genever	ginger. Probably the English word was making an impact on the distantly-related standard German **Ingver**. Used for flavoring in baking.
Indigo, Endego,	indigo, the blue dyestuff
Kalb fleisch	veal
Kalck	used with sand and water to form pointing mortar for stone and log construction, also for the white coat of plaster and for whitewash.
Kam, Enge	a small comb, probably for a lady's hair
Kap	cap, part of women's routine attire
Kelsch, Celsch	any kind of checked fabric
Kirschbäum	cherry trees, saplings
kist	chest, the lift-top box for storage prevalent in Pennsylvania German households gradually supplemented during the nineteenth century by chests of drawers.
kleien	bran
Kleser=Gläser	glasses for drinking
Knep	buttons
Knöp, seitenen	silk-covered buttons
hemderknöpff	shirt buttons, sold by the pair, for the cuffs
Kreb camelgarn	crape mohair
Kreben machen	grave digging ?
Kummet	horse collar
Kreiten	chalk
Lahn	English *lawn*, thin-weight cotton fabric
Lebkuchen	The spicier of the regularly baked cookies made by the Pennsylvania Dutch. Apparently sold at the bar for it appears in an entry "1 quart cider, 2 Lebkuchen".
Leder	leather
Leims	lime or lemon
Leimsbunsch	lime punch
leineohl	linseed oil
Leinsamen	(See also *Flagssamen*) linseed
Leinetuch	bedsheet
Lethig negel	small lath nails
licht, Ein licht	a light, lamp
Lichter	candles, sold by the pound
1 lot gezackert	1 lot plowed
lotten Zucker	a kind of sugar
Madery, Mathery wein	Madeira wine, produced on the Portugese island of Madira in the Atlantic at which British vessels frequently stopped en route to the New World, whence its great popularity in colonial America and among the Pennsylvania Dutch.
maltz	malt
mallasis	also: Molasses
Mantelbiss	mantelpiece
mehl	flour, meal
Merr	mare, female horse

Messer	knife
Mim or **Mimm**	an alcoholic beverage apparently drunk as a punch, sold by the bowl (*bole*, *boll*). Its contents have not been discovered.
mist-fahren	hauling manure
muscatnuss, muschcattenus,	
moskedetnoss	nutmeg
munstück	coins ?
Musteck	
Muslin	muslin
Namen Buch	the primer used in elementary schools. Since it contained a list of female and male given names it was frequently called a *Namenbuch*; cf. *ABC Buch.*
Nägel, negel	nails
clapport	clapboard nails
latignägel	lath nails
schintel	shingle nails
schunägel	shoenails
nagel bohrn	gimlet
nestel	?
Netz, neths	thread
Neths, Blauen	blue thread
Nickerfett	?
nodlen	needles
obenleder	upperleather, the more expensive shoeleather used for the top of the shoe and not the soles, *soleder.*
oehl	oil
Omet	the second cutting of meadow grasses and hay, the aftermath. The entry mentioning it is dated August 21.
ossnabrick	see Hasenbrick
oxenfuhrman	ox driver
papier bogen	sheet paper
bogen Buch	book paper, for binding
Peffer	peffer; cf. *Beffer*
Peif	pipe (smoking)
griene	probably refers to the color it was fired.
herhüter Peiffen	Moravian pipes, probably made in Bethlehem.
persig, bersig, tram	peach whiskey
Perssen	peaches ?
Pulwer, Bulfer	powder (for a gun or for explosives).
rahm	cream
Ram Haffen	cream pot, earthenware
Rattin, radien	?
reiss	rice, an imported food served for special occasions as an alternate to other starchy foods such as potatoes and noodles.
rend	rent
riegel	rails
riegel, machen	making (splitting) rails
Rindfleisch	beef
Rock	petticoat or men's coat
Rom	rum
westin, west indien Rom,	rum, along with Madeira wine, a popular alcoholic beverage. It was all made in the West Indies, but there were probably varying qualities available.
rom schlinck	Rum sling. A variety of "slings" were made in eighteenth century Pennsylvania German taverns. Perhaps combination of a sweet juice and the alcoholic beverage named or water, sugar, nutmeg with the rum.
Rossen Rein	a wine - Rhein
Rosenwein	Rosewine

Rothen Miny	a pigmentation element yielding red.
Rothen Zucker	a sugar colored red.
Rünnen geführt	hauling bark
saddle	saddle
Saffren	saffron, added to baked goods and dough products (noodles and pot pie) to yield color and taste.
saltz	salt
sand	sand
sattel Beck	saddle bags
Sau	sow
Schafhaut	sheepskin
schalun, schallun, shaloon,	shalloon, a mill woven wool cloth, probably imported from England
Schechter, Schechder	checked cloth
Scheiben glas	pane of glass
scher	scissors
schimber	See *Imber*
schissel, Zinnerne	bowl, pewter
Schling, schlinck	A beverage; see *rom schling*: punch.
Schlosch	lock ?
schnallen, hosen	breeches buckles. These were worn at the calf where the breeches and the stockings met.
Schnallen	buckles. Either for shoes or breeches.
Schnir	cord
schnub Tuch	handkerchief
schnuf toback	snuff
schap gut	shop goods
schap wahr	shop wares
schreiben	to write
band geschrieben	a bond written
schrot	lead shot, as in powder and shot, i. e., the pellets used in shooting.
schuh	shoe
Schulgeld.	school money, i. e., tuition. There were no public schools. The congregations maintained a school building and paid part of the schoolmaster's salary, but parents paid tuition which constituted the largest share of it.
schul Tisch	school table. In the Pennsylvania German schoolroom children sat on benches around a large table.
schuten metch	shooting match, a masculine entertainment on holidays and other occasions, still observed in some rural areas.
sagetgarn	saggathy yarn, a wool twill yarn
seiden, strang	silk thread, for embroidery, sold in a *strang* or *strengel*, a skein.
seider, seiter	cider, extremely popular apple juice beverage pressed all late summer, fall and winter as long as apples lasted; cf. *wasser seiter*.
seider oill, seiter eol, seol,	cider royal, a beverage made of apple cider and whiskey, still made by some Pennsylvania Germans.
Seifen	soap
Senckery	Sangria, a sweet wine drink made with sugar, fruit and wine.
sentz	scythe
Seuger	little pigs
sichel, sickel	sickle
gras sichel	grass sickle
soleder	sole leather; cf. *oberleder*
speck	bacon
spelle	pins
speltz	speltz, a grain
spielen	gambling
spinen	spinning
stein	stone, either foundation or masonry stones or limestone.
stiffel	boots

stober	cork, stopper
strimb	stockings, sold by the pair
strümb an zu stricken,	knitting new feet for stockings
strumpf bänder	garters
stroh	straw
Terbetinöl	terpentine
thee, deh, deeh	tea
Theelöffel	teaspoons
Thron	spermoil
Throt	wire (*Droht*)
tippig, deppich, Teppich	blanket, coverlet
tram, tran	whiskey or rum
Trincken	drinking
usually vor **trincken,**	for drinking. The account keeper sometimes specified what was consumed. When one person was charged for several persons' beverages, the broader term was more appropriate.
tubac, Dobach	tobacco, for smoking or chewing
Tuch	cloth, a general term for fabric
blau	blue
braun	brown
grin, krien	green
schwartz	black
weiss	white
wullen	woolen
Unschlit	tallow
Vendue	auction sale
Verzehrt	consumed, i.e., ate in the tavern
Vorhang Ring	rings for holding bed curtains
wachs	wax, beeswax
wagen leitern	wagon ladders, on a hay wagon
walnuss bort	walnut boards
Walzen	to roll plowed land to break up the clods
wasser seiter	a second pressing of apple pulp after cider had been pressed, usually used for vinegar, but perhaps sold as a drink as well.
weck	rolls, sold at the bar as a snack. Nineteenth century recipes survive.
wein	wine
warm wein	warmed wine
wein schling	wine sling; cf. Rom schling
weitzen	wheat
Wellen	?
werckentuch	tow cloth, made from the coarser flax fibers after the finer linen fibers were removed from the production.
wetzstein	whetstone
wipp	whip
zaum	bridle
Zehrung	nourishment, i. e., meals in the tavern
Zeig	cloth
Baumwollenzeug	cotton cloth
gestreefelt zeug	striped cloth
Zigel	tiles for roofing
Zollstab	measuring stick; ruler
Zucker	sugar
hut	cone sugar
Lof	loaf sugar
lotten	?
rothen	red sugar
weisen	white sugar
zwillig	twill

Measurements listed in this record

beint	pint	**gill, gil, gi, tschill, gill**	double shot
berl	barrel	**gallen**	gallon
bole, boll	bowl	**huxet**	hogshead
bol	bottle	**jert**	yard
buschell	bushel	**neb**	nip
centner	ton	**lb**	pound
dutzen, dutzet	dozen	**1/2 virtel**	=1/8 etc

Drinks named in this record

bitters
brandewein
bunsch, leimsbunsch
gatsel, gadel
madery, mathery wine
mim, mimm
persig, bersig tram
rom, westin, west indien rom
Rom schlinck; persig
seider
seider oill
senckery
tram, tran

Textiles named in this record

Band
Borschet
barget,
bet barget
calmick
cattun, cartun, cardun
Dick
Drugget, druget
flenel
floret
Foret
fettertuch
halb leinen
hasenbrick
haubengarn
kelsch
Lahn
muslin
schalun
segetgarn
seiden
zwillig

Appendix II

Heidelberg Township Tax List, 1771

(The only surviving list of taxation for Heidelberg township, then Lancaster, from 1787-1812 Dauphin, and since 1813 in Lebanon county, during the time the record of the King George Hotel was made is for the year 1771. A slight insight into many of the customers in the hotel is gained from this list.)

Key:

1. Clearland
2. Bushland
3. House & Lots
4. Interesse
5. Quit Rents
6. Mills
7. Horses & Mares
8. Cattle
9. Sheep
10. Servant
11. Negroes & Ages

	1	2	3	4	5	6	7	8	9	10	11
Albright Matthis	50	50	-	-	2	-	2	2	-	-	-
Basler Simon	70	90	-	-	-	-	3	6	6	-	-
Basler Thomas	15	40	-	-	-	Oil	2	2	2	-	-
Miller						Mill					
Bery. Peter	9	30	-	-	2	-	2	2	4	-	-
Benny Peter	20	30	-	-	2	-	2	1	-	-	-
Bucher Jacob	10	10	-	-	2	-	-	1	-	-	-
Backle [?] Ulrich	30	50	-	-	-	-	2	2	-	-	-
Batdorf Peter	40	30	-	-	-	-	3	2	-	-	-
Batdorf Martin	50	50	-	-	-	-	4	3	2	-	-
By seat: White George											
Brawn Widow [Wittow]	50	150	-	-	2	-	2	3	4	-	-
Brosman Frantz	-	-	1	3	-	-	-	-	-	-	-
By seat: Little Andrew											
Mebes George											
Braght, Michael	-	-	1	-	-	-	-	1	1	-	-
Brill, Henry	-	-	1	-	-	-	-	-	1	-	-
Taylor											
Batdorf, Peter Junior	30	50	-	-	2	-	2	1	-	-	-
By seat: Cashnitz, Christian											
Breidenbach, Philip	8	20	1	-	2	-	2	1	-	-	-
Saddler											
By seat: Bollinger, Michael											
Bayer, Martin	-	-	1	-	-	-	-	1	-	-	-
Innkeeper											
Burman, John	-	-	1	-	-	-	-	1	1	-	-
Bayer, John	50	40	-	-	2	-	2	1	-	-	-
Becker, George	80	60	-	-	2	-	4	4	2	-	-
Blaeger William	8	7	-	-	2	-	1	1	-	-	-
Bullman, Adam	40	35	-	-	2	-	2	2	3	-	-
freeman: Adam Bullman, Jr., by his father											
Brunner, Henry	40	130	-	-	2	-	2	-	2	-	-
Breght John	-	-	1	-	-	-	1	1	-	-	-
Innkeeper											
Barnd Jacob	-	-	-	-	-	-	1	-	-	-	-
Shopkeeper											
Bush, N:	-	-	1	-	-	-	-	1	-	-	-
Breght Jacob	-	-	1	-	-	-	-	1	-	-	-
Becker John	30	40	-	-	2	-	2	2	-	-	-
Conrad Peter	50	45	-	-	-	-	3	2	-	-	-

	1	2	3	4	5	6	7	8	9	10	11
Creitzer Andrew	60	50	-	-	2/50	-	4	4	6	-	-
Freeman: Creitzer Michael by his father											
Christ Adam	4	4	-	-	2	-	-	1	-	-	-
Chreebeel John	50	50	-	-	2	-	4	10	4	-	-
Chraal Theis	40	50	-	-	2	-	2	3	6	-	-
Conrad, Magnus	-	-	1	-	-	-	-	-	-	-	-
Deel Peter	10	40	-	-	2	-	2	2	-	-	-
Detzler Melchior	15	30	-	3	2	-	-	-	-	-	-
By seat: Wolf Jacob [crossed out]											
Deavenbach, Michael	40	40	-	-	2	-	2	2	2	-	-
Dinges Willm	50	60	-	-	2	-	2	2	3	-	-
Freemen: Dinnius John											
Dinges John	30	35	-	-	2	-	2	2	-	-	-
Day Jacob	40	50	-	-	2	-	2	2	2	-	-
Dinges, Nicholas	15	25	-	-	2	-	2	1	-	-	-
Deerwachter Erhard	30	70	-	-	2	-	2	2	-	-	-
Deerder Baltzer	25	30	-	-	2	-	2	1	-	-	-
By seat: Dinges Vallentine											
Dummy Durst	30	25	-	-	2	-	2	4	3	-	-
Dummy Durst Junior	40	50	-	-	2	-	2	1	1	-	-
Detweiler Jost	-	-	-	-	-	-	2	2	3	-	-
byseat: Danl Soleberger											
Dryon, Michael	3	-	1	-	-	-	1	1	-	-	-
Doctor											
Dubel Moretz	-	-	1	-	-	-	-	-	-	-	-
Drucken Miller Peter	-	-	1	-	-	-	1	-	-	-	-
Deel Christian	-	-	-	-	-	-	1	-	-	-	-
Debo Isaac	-	-	-	-	-	-	1	1	-	-	-
Innkeeper											
Etdiner, Bernhard	-	-	1	-	-	-	-	1	-	-	-
Taylor											
Eysenmener Henry	-	-	1	-	-	-	1	1	-	-	-
Butcher											
Earl Philip	-	20	1	-	2	-	1	1	-	-	-
Innkeeper											
Ehwey Nicholaus	-	-	1	-	-	-	-	1	-	-	-
Endes John	-	-	-	-	-	-	2	1	-	-	-
Foltz Joseph	40	40	-	-	2	-	4	2	3	-	-
Feehman Vallentin	80	150	–	-	2	-	2	1	-	-	-
House Seats: Feehman Caspar											
Feehman Adam											
Fritz Adam	25	75	-	-	2	-	4	2	4	-	-
freeman: Fritz Adam by his father											
Fehler Nicholaus	20	40	-	-	2	-	2	2	-	-	-
Fudler Jacob	-	-	1	-	-	-	-	-	-	-	-
Fogelgesong Jacob	-	-	-	-	-	-	-	1	-	-	-
freemann: Diesiner Henry by his father											
Focht Jacob	20	80	-	-	2	-	2	1	-	-	-
Grove Andrew	40	60	-	-	2	-	2	2	3	-	-
House Seat: Strickler George											
German Adam	15	50	-	-	2	-	1	1	-	-	-
Gosser Jacob	-	-	2	-	-	-	-	1	-	-	-
Mason											
House Seat: Buch Henry	-	-	1	-	-	-	-	1	-	-	-
Gast Christian	-	-	-	-	-	-	-	-	-	-	-
Mason											
Gast Nicholaus	-	-	1	-	-	-	-	-	-	-	-
Mason											

	1	2	3	4	5	6	7	8	9	10	11
Ginder Christian	-	-	1	-	-	-	-	-	-	-	-
Shoemacker											
Gonckel Leonhard	-	-	1	-	-	-	-	1	-	-	-
Potter											
Gemberling Jacob	-	-	1	-	-	-	1	1	-	-	-
Innkeeper											
Gramlick George	-	-	1	-	-	-	-	1	-	-	-
Hoster William	60	80	-	-	-	-	2	4	8	-	-
freeman: Hoster Christian by his father											
Haake Michael	70	100	-	-	-	-	3	4	5	-	-
Holstoner George	80	120	-	-	100?	-	4	4	6	-	1
House Seat: Endres John										age 15	
Hoofman Jost	120	160	-	-	-	-	-	-	-	-	-
Freeman: Hoofman George by his father											
House Seat: Smith John											
Heys Friederik	30	70	-	-	2	1	2	2	3	-	-
Miller											
House Seat: Bollender Adam											
Herchelrod Henry	40	60	-	-	2	-	2	2	-	-	-
Hoofman Adam	60	90	-	-	-	-	-	-	-	-	-
Hoofman Jost	60	80	-	-	2	-	2	1	-	-	-
Hafenfinger, Martin	40	50	-	-	2	-	2	2	3	-	-
Heigh Hold Martin	-	-	1	-	-	-	-	-	1	-	-
Taylor											
Immel John	50	50	-	-	-	-	4	6	4	-	-
Freeman: Immel Leonhard by his father											
Illig Leonhard	60	140	-	-	2	-	2	?	?	-	-
Iba Casper	-	-	1	-	-	-	-	-	-	-	-
Igolve Michael											
Koppenhefer Christoph	50	60	-	-	-	-	3	3	2	-	-
Koppenhefer Michael	40	60	-	-	50/2	-	3	3	1	-	-
House Seat: Dewald Shafer											
Koch Christian	40	100	-	-	2	-	2	2	2	-	-
Freeman: George Martin											
Kintzle Jacob	50	50	-	-	2	-	2	10	5	-	-
Kintzle John	4	50	-	-	2	-	1	1	-	-	-
Koppenhefer Simon	50	50	-	-	2	-	2	2	-	-	1
											age 40
Koppenhefer Henry	60	40		-	-	-	3	2	2	-	-
Kring Henry	50	100	-	-2	-	2	3	4	-	-	-
Kurtz Stoffle	50	50	-	-	-	-	3	4	5	-	-
House Seats: Smith Thomas											
Kuster John	50	50	-	-50/2	-	2	3	2	-	-	
House Seats: Beny Jacob											
Kurtz John	30	30	-	-	2	-	1	2	2	-	-
Kelleberger George	20	40	-	-	2	-	-	-	-	-	-
Freemen: Rab Frederick by Rab George											
Kochendarfer George	20	80	-	-	2	-	2	2	4	-	-
Klain George	50	50	-	-	2	-	2	2	2	-	-
Kappen Witten [Widow]	40	60	-	-	2	-	2	2	3	-	-
Keesecker Nicholaus	50	50	-	-	2	-	2	2	2	-	-
Kapp Martin	40	60	-	-	2	-	2	2	3	-	-
Kaffman Jacob	-	-	-	-	-	-	-	-	-	-	-
Kellern Wittow	50	70	-	-	2	-	2	3	-	-	-
King Daniel	-	-	1	-	-	-	-	1	-	-	-
Shoemaker											
Freeman: Shell Henry											

	1	2	3	4	5	6	7	8	9	10	11
Kapp Frederik	-	-	1	-	-	-	1	1	-	-	-
Smith											
Kiweller Wendel	-	-	1	-	-	-	-	1	-	-	-
Kreider Christian	-	-	1	-	-	-	-	1	-	-	-
Kratzer Joseph Junior	-	-	1	-	-	-	1	1	-	-	-
Tanner											
Krumbone Leonhard	-	-	1	-	-	-	-	1	-	-	-
Kratzer Joseph Senior	25	30	-	-	2	-	1	1	-	-	-
Klein Jacob	-	-	1	-	-	-	-	-	-	-	-
Kapp George	-	-	1	-	-	-	1	1	-	-	-
Kapp Andrew	-	-	-	-	-	-	-	1	-	-	-
Kitzmiller Jacob	-	-	1	-	-	-	-	1	-	-	-
Taylor											
Kurtz Leonhard	-	-	1	-	-	-	-	1	-	-	-
Lautermilk Melchior	25	25	-	-	2	-	2	3	2	-	-
Lautermilk George	15	40	-	-	2	-	1	1	3	-	-
Lautermilk John	50	50	-	-	2	-	3	3	2	-	-
Freeman: Lautermilk Adam											
Lehn John	25	50	-	-	-	-	2	2	2	-	-
Freeman: Lehn Peter by his father											
Loewenstone David	40	150	-	-	2	-	2	2	-	-	-
Lein Wittow	50	50	-	-	-	-	2	2	9	-	-
Lehman Christian	60	50	-	-	-	-	2	3	2	-	-
House Seats: Raub Adam, Zimmerman Christoph											
Lutz Christoph	24	20	-	-	2	-	1	1	-	-	-
Leitner Peter	40	60	-	-	2	-	2	1	-	-	-
Looser George	10	30	-	-	2	-	2	2	1	-	-
Leissner Conrad	18	30	-	-	2	-	2	2	-	-	-
Lentz Frederik	10	35	-	-	2	-	-	2	-	-	-
Louser John	-	-	1	-	-	-	-	1	-	-	-
weaver											
Ley Michael	60	100	-	-	-	-	4	4	3	-	-
Miller Peter	25	25	-	-	2	-	2	1	2	-	-
Moser Nicholaus	80	50	-	-	40/2	-	3	4	2	-	-
House Seats: Walk Teter and Henry Moser											
Miller Nicholas	50	50	-	-	-	-	2	2	-	-	-
House Seats: Miller Vallentin											
Myer Dewald	6	10	-	-	2	-	-	1	-	-	-
Myern Wittow	90	200	2	7	-	-	4	5	10	-	2
House seat: Armbruster Jacob										age 40, 30	
Meiser George	50	50	-	-	2	-	2	2	3	-	-
House Seat: Martersteck John											
Imhoof Benedict											
Miller Michael	100	50	-	-	-	1	3	2	3	-	-
Miller											
House Seat: Myer Michael											
Mook Henry	50	50	-	-	2	-	2	2	-	-	-
House Seat: Strickler Andrew											
Minnig Michael											
Mees Nicholas	40	30	-	-	2	-	2	2	2	-	-
House Seat: Reidennar George											
Menges Peter	40	60	-	-	-	-	2	3	2	-	-
Mosselman Jacob	20	40	-	-	2	-	2	1	-	-	-
Myer, Henry	40	60	-	-	2	-	3	2	3	-	-
House Seat: Minnig Henry											
Myer John	70	100	-	-	2	-	4	3	5	-	-
Freeman: Myer Henry by his father											
House Seat: Yunst William											

	1	2	3	4	5	6	7	8	9	10	11
Moore John	70	130	-	-	2	-	4	3	5	-	-
House Seat: Long Benedict											
Miller Nicholaus Junior	70	60	-	-	2	-	4	3	4	-	-
Meckbroad John											
Miller Jacob	-	-	1	-	-	-	-	1	-	-	-
Shoemacker											
Muckenfoot Carl	-	-	1	-	-	-	-	-	-	-	-
Noll Nicholaus	40	50	-	-	2	-	2	2	3	-	-
Neihty Peter	20	60	-	-	2	-	1	1	-	-	-
Noecker Christian	40	80	-	-	-	-	3	2	2	-	-
Freeman: Kintzler Rudy											
Noecker John											
Noll Matthis	30	40	-	-	2	-	2	2	-	-	-
Noll John	50	60	-	-	2	-	4	4	6	-	-
Freeman: Noll John by his father											
House Seat: Noll George											
Noeman Walther	40	60	-	10	2	-	2	2	-	-	-
Freeman: Noeman Henry by his father											
House Seat: Noeman David											
Noemenn Wittow	20	50	-	-	2	-	2	2	-	-	-
House Seat: Noeman Andrew											
Noeman Peter	20	50	-	-	2	-	2	2	-	-	-
Neeffe George	50	50	-	-	2	-	2	2	3	-	-
Neefe Jacob	50	50	-	-	2	-	3	4	3	-	-
Nathan Benjamin	-	-	1	-	-	-	-	-	-	-	-
Shopkeeper											
Overkers Michael	20	50	-	-	2	-	2	2	2	-	-
Oxenman John	-	-	1	-	-	-	-	-	-	-	-
weaver											
Philippy, Jacob	50	60	-	-	2	-	4	2	3	-	-
Philippy, Conrad	-	-	1	-	-	-	-	-	-	-	-
Peffer Henry Senior	-	-	-	-	-	-	-	-	-	-	-
Peffer Henry Junior	-	-	2	-	-	-	1	1	-	-	-
Brewer											
Ramler John	80	40	-	-	-	-	5	2	-	-	-
House Seat: Derther Jacob											
Ramler Jacob	80	100	-	-	-	-	3	4	-	-	-
Reeser Ulrig	40	50	-	-	2	-	2	2	3	-	-
Freeman: Reeser John by his father											
Reem Peter	40	60	-	-	2	-	2	2	3	-	-
Roth John	30	30	-	-	2	-	2	1	-	-	-
Ruhty Abraham	6	10	-	-	2	-	-	-	-	-	-
Ruthdolf Steffle	-	-	1	-	-	-	-	1	-	-	-
Roth Michael	-	-	-	-	-	-	-	1	-	-	-
Reed Peter	-	-	-	-	-	-	-	1	-	-	-
Reele Andrew	-	-	-	-	-	-	-	-	-	-	-
Schwengel Nicholaus	100	100	-	-	-	-	4	4	5	-	1
										age	36
Shell Peter	30	60	-	-	-	-	2	2	3	-	-
Shell, Martin	50	60	-	-	-	-	3	2	4	-	-
House seat: Lenenweaver Henry											
Sharff John	60	40	-	-	2	-	2	1	-	-	-
Spengler Michael	50	50	-	-	-	-	2	3	-	-	-
Freemen: Spengler Michael											
Spengler Peter by his father											
Stone Peter	40	60	-	-	2	-	2	2	3	-	-

	1	2	3	4	5	6	7	8	9	10	11
Syferth Christian	60	60	-	-	2	-	4	2	4	-	-
Saltzgiver John	20	30	-	-	2	-	1	1	-	-	-
House Seat: Saltzgiver Andrew											
Saltzgiver Henry	20	30	-	-	2	-	2	1	-	-	-
House Seat: Hudson George											
Shanck, Wendel	-	-	1	-	-	-	-	1	-	-	-
Weaver											
Strickler Andrew	50	60	-	-	2	-	2	2	3	-	-
Stump Christopher	50	100	-	-	-	-	2	3	10	-	1
House Seat: Arnold Lorence										age	20
Sholl Andrew	50	50	-	-	1 shilling- 100	2	2	3	-	-	
Shitz Peter	100	100	-	-	2	-	2	2	3	-	1
House seat: Syferth Frantz										age	18
Stohler George	50	60	-	-	2	-	2	2	-	-	-
Smith George	50	50	-	-	2	-	2	3	-	-	-
Freemen: Conrad											
(Kyler Jacob crossed out)											
Shefer Alexander	25	25	-	18	2	-	2	3	-	-	-
Innkeeper											
Shenck Michael	-	-	-	-	-	-	1	1	-	-	-
Shenck John	100	200	-	-	2	-	3	2	-	-	-
Stohler John	90	115	-	-	2	-	4	2	6	-	-
Stahner Frederik	15	60	-	-	-	-	2	1	-	-	-
Strack Henry	50	80	-	-	2	-	2	2	3	-	-
Stump Abraham	50	50	-	-	2	-	2	2	-	-	-
House Seat: Bish Andrew											
Spengler Jacob	50	60	-	-	2	-	2	2	3	-	-
Strickler Leonhard	25	40	-	-	2	-	2	1	-	-	-
Shenckel Carle	20	30	-	-	2	-	2	1	-	-	-
Shnelbecher, Jacob	25	40	-	-	2	-	2	2	5	-	-
Freeman: Shnelbecher George by his father											
Smith Jacob	30	60	-	-	2	-	2	3	3	-	-
Weaver											
Shefer John	30	30	-	-	2	-	-	2	-	-	-
Smith											
Shaller George	-	-	1	-	-	-	-	1	-	-	-
Shwitzer John	-	-	2	-	-	-	-	2	-	-	-
Shnider Abraham	-	-	1	-	-	-	-	-	-	-	-
Sharch Andrew	-	-	-	-	-	-	-	-	-	-	-
Saler Christoph	-	-	-	-	-	-	-	-	-	-	-
Shwitzer Casper	-	-	-	-	-	-	-	-	-	-	-
Speck Adam	-	-	-	-	-	-	-	-	-	-	-
Smith Frantz	-	-	1	-	-	-	-	-	-	-	-
Salenty Frederick	-	-	1	-	-	-	-	-	-	-	-
Smith Christian	-	-	1	-	-	-	-	-	-	-	-
Shram Henry	-	-	-	-	-	-	-	-	-	-	-
Theis John	25	50	-	-	2	-	2	2	4	-	-
Trautman George	50	50	-	-	2	-	2	2	-	-	-
Urrig Christian	30	50	-	-	2	-	2	2	2	-	-
Urrig Vallentin	50	90	-	-	2	-	3	3	3	-	-
House Seat: Urrig John											
Ulrig Paul	10	40	-	-	2	-	2	1	-	-	-
Walborn Herman	10	50	-	-	2	-	2	2	-	-	-
Wolfe Jacob	15	30	-	-	2	-	2	2	-	-	-
Weaver John	100	100	-	-	-	-	2	3	5	-	-
House Seat: Neyman William											

	1	2	3	4	5	6	7	8	9	10	11
Walborn Martin	60	50	-	-	-	-	2	2	5	-	-
Freemen: Balsle John											
Roll John											
Wisser John	50	50	-	-	50/2	-	4	2	2	-	-
Wolf Jacob	-	-	-	-	-	-	-	-	-	-	-
Weik Gerhard	15	40	-	-	2	-	1	1	-	-	-
Wittenmyer Lodowik	6	15	-	-	2	-	1	1	-	-	-
Weis Henry	40	40	-	-	2	-	2	2	-	-	-
Weis Christian	40	40	-	-	2	-	2	2	4	-	-
Freeman: Wicker Bardel											
Wolfersberger Philip	40	60	-	-	2	-	3	3	-	-	1
Freeman: Shanck Christoph											age 23
Wolfersberger Peter	50	100	-	-	2	-	2	3	4	-	-
Freeman: Wolfersberger Frederick											
Wolfersberger Michael											
Waagner Jacob	60	120	-	-	2	-	3	2	3	-	-
Winter Michael	-	-	-	-	-	-	-	-	-	-	-
House Seat: Wolfe Christian											
Wohlfarth Leonhard	6	20	-	-	2	-	1	1	-	-	-
Zeller David	60	60		-	-	2	-	3	2	3	-
House Seat: Schwanger Paul											
Zeller Henry	40	60	-	-	2	-	2	3	4	-	-
Hous Seat: Alberth Peter											
Zeller Peter	40	60	-	-	Rosen Land	-	2	2	2	-	-
Zenth Jacob	50	50	-	-	2	-	3	2	7	-	-
Zollinger Nicholaus	80	120	-	-	2	-	3	3	4	-	-

A just and true return of the Township
of Heidelberg made By me

s/ Michael Leÿ

Index